The Economics and Financing
of Media Companies

Business, Economics, and Legal Studies Series
Albert N. Greco, series editor

The Economics and Financing of Media Companies

ROBERT G. PICARD

FORDHAM UNIVERSITY PRESS
New York • 2002

For Phyllis Bryan Paytee, a wonderful teacher, who long ago taught me how to put thoughts on paper

Business, Economics, and Legal Studies Series, No. 1

Library of Congress Cataloging-in-Publication Data
is available
ISBN: 978-0-8232-2175-2

Printed in the United States of America
07 08 09   5 4 3
First Edition

CONTENTS

PREFACE

This book is intended to help the reader to develop a better understanding of how economic and financial forces influence the operations and developments of media and communications firms. It is designed to improve the knowledge of those who presently work or will work in such firms so that they can better cope with the increasing complexity of the environment in which their firms operate.

The book is designed to make managers and future managers more effective in confronting the demands of the increasingly competitive communications industries by improving their abilities to respond to the ever-changing problems and issues that arise in the course of managing such firms. It is also intended to give those who observe media a broader context in which to consider the operations and decisions made by media managers.

This book strives to provide concepts for understanding and analyzing communications companies and their environments, to increase readers' abilities to identify and evaluate alternative strategies and courses of action, and to allow them to work more effectively with specialists with deeper expertise in finance and economics.

The approach employed by this book is not theoretical. It uses a managerial economics approach that involves the use of economic theories and various tools to help managers make knowledgeable decisions and to help others understand why managers make those choices. The approach to financing is also practical and is based on the practices of contemporary capital sources and media firms.

The economics and financing of media companies are the foundations upon which all media activity takes place. Regardless of cultural, political, and social roles and expectations for media, media must cover their costs and create returns, just as any other business, or they will wither and disappear. The forces that require effective operation are the same for both private commercial media and noncommercial media such as public service broadcasting.

Since the beginning of the study of communications, attention has primarily been focused upon the roles, functions, and effects of communications. When media and other communications enterprises were studied, they were explored as social institutions, and much of the focus was on the social, political, legal, and technological influences on the enterprises and their operations. Scholars ignored, or only lightly attended to, the effects of economic forces. This should not come as a surprise to anyone familiar with the history of communications inquiry, because communications scholars initially came from the disciplines of sociology, psychology, political science, history, and literary criticism and then passed on their approaches to studying media to new generations of communications scholars who were produced during the second half of the twentieth century.

In the 1970s an increasing number of economics and business scholars began exploring media, especially as the result of changes leading to the development of cable television and problematic trends appearing in the newspaper industry. It was not until the 1980s, however, that communications scholars themselves began to accord economic and financial forces and issues the significant attention they were due. Since that time, a coherent and growing body of knowledge about economic issues and problems and the financial strategies and behavior of communications enterprises has developed. That literature has developed to help explain how economic and financial forces and strategies affect media developments and operations.

Several significant economic texts have emerged in the field, revealing how basic economic laws and principles can be applied to the study and operation of media,[1] exploring the economic structure and organization of various communication industries,[2] and

[1] Robert G. Picard, *Media Economics: Concepts and Issues* (Newbury Park, Calif.: Sage Publications, 1989).

[2] Alison Alexander, James Owers, and Rod Carveth, eds., *Media Economics: Theory and Practice* (Hillsdale, N.J.: Lawrence Erlbaum Associates, 1993); Nadine Toussaint Desmoulins, *L'Economie des medias*, 4th ed. (Paris: Press Universitaires de France, 1996).

focusing on economic issues in specific communication industries.[3] Excellent analyses have considered the political economy of communications enterprises and its effects on society and vice versa.[4]

This book seeks to expand upon those works concerned with how economic and financial pressures affect a variety of communications activities, systems, organizations, and enterprises across all media sectors and telecommunications. It builds upon those works and then introduces business concepts and their application in media firms to reveal how these factors influence choices and how they can be used to improve and understand industry decisions and practices.

[3] Bruce M. Owens and Stephen S. Wildman, *Video Economics* (Cambridge, Mass.: Harvard University Press, 1992); Robert G. Picard et al., *Press Concentration and Monopoly: New Perspectives on Newspaper Ownership and Operation* (Norwood, N.J.: Ablex Publishing, 1988); Richard Collins, Nicholas Garnham, and Gareth Locksley, *The Economics of Television: The UK Case* (London: Sage, 1989); Peter Dunnett, *The World Television Industry: An Economic Analysis* (New York: Routledge, 1990); Stuart McFadyen, Colin Hoskins, and David Gillen, *Canadian Broadcasting: Market Structure and Economic Performance* (Montreal: Institute for Research on Public Policy, 1980); Eli Noam, *Video Media Competition: Regulation, Economics, and Technology* (New York: Columbia University Press, 1985); R. Schmalensee, *Economics of Advertising* (Amsterdam: North-Holland, 1981); Centro Vejanouski and W. D. Bishop, *Choice by Cable: The Economics of a New Area in Television* (Lansing, U.K.: Institute of Economic Affairs, 1983); G. Kent Webb, *The Economics of Cable Television* (Lexington, Mass.: Lexington Books, 1983); Stephen Lacy and Todd F. Simon, *The Economics and Regulation of United States Newspapers* (Norwood, N.J.: Ablex Publishing, 1988).

[4] Kenneth Dyson and Peter Humphreys, eds., *The Political Economy of Information: International and European Dimensions* (London: Routledge, 1990); Nicholas Garnham, *Capitalism and Communication: Global Culture and Information Economics* (London: Sage, 1990); Vincent Mosco and Janet Wasko, eds., *The Political Economy of Information* (Madison: University of Wisconsin Press, 1988).

The Economics and Financing
of Media Companies

1

Media Firms as Economic and Business Entities

WHETHER a media company is a commercial or noncommercial operation, it faces a variety of economic and financial forces and must be operated as a business entity in order to effectively respond to and manage those forces.

The forms of media companies include the range of types of firms that exist in any industry. At the simplest level are sole proprietorships and partnerships. Sole proprietorships are firms owned and operated by one person. This form is found primarily among smaller newspapers and Internet design firms and small advertising firms. Partnerships are similar but involve ownership by more than one person. This business form is used when one person alone has insufficient capital or skills to operate independently; it is most often found in small publications, design firms, and advertising agencies.

More complex company forms involve incorporation, that is, the creation of a firm as a legal entity independent of its owners. This reduces the legal responsibility of individual owners for the performance or actions of the firm. Simple corporations can encompass sole proprietorships and partnerships of all size. Most media companies are incorporated as private corporations and tend to be small and midsized enterprises. Privately owned media firms include companies such as Bertelsmann and Hearst.

A number of larger firms have chosen to become public corporations—firms whose shares are publicly traded on stock markets—typically to gain additional capital. Examples of public media firms include News Corp., New York Times Co., Pearson, Tribune Co., and Viacom.

Another form of ownership found in media involves noncommercial firms that are typically created as not-for-profit corporations. These include public service broadcasters worldwide such as the British Broadcasting Corp. (BBC) and Australian Broadcasting Corp. (ABC), as well as publishers or media firms such as the *Christian Science Monitor* and *The Nation*.

All of these forms of media enterprises carry out the functions of acquiring and organizing resources to produce goods and services, just as other types of firms do. The organizational forms of businesses exist because they are an efficient means of carrying out the various steps in production and distribution of goods and services.

Companies have evolved into their current forms because they create organizations that can enter into structured relationships with owners of capital, workers, and suppliers and because the firm can provide the facilities, equipment, and management necessary to effectively produce and distribute the products.

In public service and other not-for-profit media, producing information and programming useful and interesting to audiences is the primary function. In commercial media, however, the primary function shifts to producing audiences for advertisers because of the necessity of obtaining financial revenue for continued operation.

The differences in primary functions do not mean that commercial media necessarily must produce poorer quality content, although that may be the case. The differences mean that managers of commercial media make content choices attending to the need to produce audiences desirable to specific advertisers or categories of advertisers and to maximize the profitability of the firm. Managers of public service and not-for-profit media, obviously, do not encounter these same pressures; however, they must make content choices attending to the need to provide optimal service based on the goals outlined for their operations and to maximize their service to different audience segments.

Social and cultural observers regularly argue about the desirability of commercial operations, particularly in broadcasting, because of their additional pressures and functions. This book will not debate the desirability of commercial media, recognizing that the decision of whether to have commercial operations—and the extent to which commercial operations are permitted—is primarily a question of domestic public policy and media regulation.

The requirements of the varying types of media operations affect the forms and structures of media firms, as do the scale and scope of those operations. Because the needs of media differ and because the organizational requirements to create media goods and services vary depending upon their markets, the sizes of media organizations cover the range from small to large.

These differences create separate problems and issues among media. There are, however, underlying economic and financial forces that affect all media and certain economic and financial factors that are unique to specific media. This book explores those factors and their implications in a way designed to provide information and understanding that can be used in making choices within media firms and in better analyzing media industries and companies.

COMMERCIAL MEDIA AND THE THEORY OF THE FIRM

The mere effective organization of resources and processes is not a sufficient reason for the creation of commercial business organizations. Underlying these structural elements is the fundamental goal of companies, which is explained by *the theory of the firm*. This theory asserts that the development and operations of firms is guided by the primary goal of maximizing profit and the value of the firm.

The purpose of the creation and operation of commercial media firms is thus to produce the most profit and highest value for the firm. The former tends to be a short-term annual goal, and the latter is a longer-term goal. If resources and the processes by which they are transformed into goods and services are efficiently and effectively organized and managed, the ability to achieve these goals becomes possible.

Some critics of this theory have argued that with the rise of modern corporations and the separation of management and ownership, the goal is sometimes maximization of sales rather than profit or firm value. Sales maximization proponents argue that once shareholders' basic needs for profit have been satisfied, the goal of some managers of modern corporations becomes maximization of sales to increase cash flow and that the measurement and ranking of firms by revenue has become a significant factor in executive compensation.

The questions of what factors promote and create above-average profitability are a concern of management and economic studies and theorists because profit is a primary goal of firms.

THE ROLES OF PROFIT AND RETURN

From the accounting perspective, profit is the money that remains after expenses are subtracted from income. From the managerial perspective, profit is a broader and essential element for the development of both commercial and noncommercial media. Profit is needed to provide opportunities to finance improvements in equipment and facilities, experiment with new methods, and develop new products and services that may or may not be successful.

For commercial firms, profit creates the money available to pay their owners or investors, make capital expenditures, and pay debts. For noncommercial media, owners/investors do not receive the profit, but it provides funds to improve the company through capital investments, make additional expenditures on content and other items, and pay debts.

Many business theorists and managers argue that profit should be considered a cost of operation, not the result of operations. In this view, the division of profits among company owners or investors and the internal reinvestment or uses of profit are expenses required to ensure the continued availability of capital and the viability of the firm.

Firms operating under this view construct budgets based on achieving a specific monetary or percentage return from their operations. They build into the budget profitability requirements or "costs" for their activities each year.

Monetary profit alone does not indicate the efficiency with which a firm produces the monetary result. To gain the broader picture one can use the concept of *return*, which indicates profitability of a firm in nonmonetary terms, to maximize the effectiveness of a firm's activities.

A manager who considers only a monetary figure only counts money that is left after expenses are paid. A manager who employs

Planning for Profit

Media and other companies can plan a specified level of profit in their budgeting process. Once a level of return is specified, it is essentially entered into financial calculations as a cost so that operating expenses, plus the desired return, are covered by operating income. In practice, this means that expenses are limited to a level at which the specified return can be achieved.

Knight Ridder, the second largest newspaper company in the United States, specifically used this process in developing its 1999 budget and planned cuts in payroll expenses, reductions in debt to save on interest expenses, and lower investments in equipment and facilities. The effort was part of a deliberate plan to increase their operating profit margin to 20 percent by 2000.

"We have very specific goals, disciplines in place for reaching them, and thresholds that will not be crossed as we review options for future allocations of cash," CEO Tony Ridder said when he revealed the plan to investment analysts.[1]

During a budget year in which profit levels have been planned, the desired return can be met only if projections of income and expenses are met or if expenses are reduced proportionally if income falls below projections.

This is especially important for publicly traded companies, because investors follow the performance of public companies in meeting profitability targets during the year by reviewing monthly and quarterly performance figures. Share prices and ratings typically rise or fall depending upon the extent to which a firm is meeting its projections or market expectations of profitability.

Worries about future profitability also affect share prices and trading. The day that the Walt Disney Co. reported its fourth quarter 2000 results, for example, its shares dropped about 15 percent, and recommendations about its shares were downgraded by analysts at Merrill Lynch, Salomon Smith Barney, and Deutsche Bank Alex Brown. Although analysts noted that the media company's income exceeded expectations for the quarter, they expressed concerns that the slowing economy would reducing advertising revenue and profitability in 2001.

the concept of return combines the ideas of overall revenue, the effort that took place to generate that revenue, and the profit produced.

The latter method produces an indicator of profitability that in-

---

[1] Robert Neuwirth, "Knight Ridder Squeezes Costs to Lift Profits," *Editor & Publisher*, Nov. 21, 1998, p. 16.

corporates efficiency of the internal operations, which is useful because profit creation is affected by the extent to which management is able to promote efficiency by holding down the costs of resources and increasing revenue from sales. When there is above-average performance in this regard, above-average profit or return can be achieved.

The achievement of above-average performance, or at least the avoidance of below-average performance, is necessary to achieve adequate returns, make the firm attractive when additional capital is required, or reduce significant fluctuations in the share prices of publicly traded firms.

The role of profit in capital investment decisions is explained by the *risk theory of profit*. This argues that the potential for high economic profits is necessary to induce investment, especially in industries with higher risk. As a result firms operating in these sectors or industries require above-average returns, or the capital will move to other more profitable investments.

Profit also arises as a premium paid by consumers for innovative products and services. Those returns tend to diminish rapidly, however, because other firms imitate successful goods and services. In order to promote innovation, governments provide incentives in the forms of limited monopolies on innovation provided by copyrights and patents. These extend the time in which better returns can be achieved by innovative firms and are justified on the basis that they promote research and development, investment, and other activities that promote social goals.

MEDIA FIRMS AND RISK

Because the future is unknown, media firms and their investors face risk when they make choices about current and future activities. Risk is a concept that results from uncertainty about the future and about the results of choices that must be made today.

All business decisions ultimately involve an estimation of their outcome and the risk that the outcome may vary from the expectation. There is obviously greater risk in any decision in which the probability of results cannot be estimated with reasonable certainty. This uncertainty is particularly important in communica-

The Importance of Profitability to Media Firms

Profitability is crucial to all media companies because it allows firms to produce their own financial resources and makes them more attractive to lenders and other capital sources when they require additional financing to support their strategies and activities.

Even noncommercial and not-for-profit media need to produce profit that can then be used to develop their content and organizations. If media firms are not able to operate profitably, they fall into a spiral of decline that makes it difficult to sustain their operations and to offer quality content. As illustrated in figure 1.1, a firm that does not operate profitably falls into a spiral of decreasing financial resources that continually reduces its ability to produce or acquire quality content, invest in personnel, upgrade equipment, or engage in marketing to attract audiences and advertisers.

Conversely, profitable media firms are able to reinvest in their operations to improve their content, making them more attractive to audiences and advertisers, ultimately making themselves more profitable.

If allowed to continue, the spiral makes it impossible for the firm to continue operating because it can no longer meet its expenses, much less invest internally to improve its operations. This spiral of decline combines with the increasing strength of profitable competitors to heavily disadvantage the less profitable or unprofitable firm. It ultimately leads to the death of weak commercial firms or dooms unprofitable noncommercial and not-for-profit media to precarious existences dependent upon outside funding.

tions industries today because managers are making decisions on how they will respond to changing technologies, changing audience use of communication products and services, and changing patterns of advertising expenditures.

Even on a daily basis certain media firms face greater risks than others do. Newspapers, magazines, and broadcasters face relatively less risk because reading, viewing, and listening patterns tend to be relatively stable in the near term and serve the same functions day to day. The risks of these firms are even lower if their revenues have been stabilized by audience subscriptions.

Book publishers, audio recording companies, multimedia producers, and motion picture producers, however, have higher risks each time they introduce a new book, recording, production, or film. This occurs because the content is not stable from product to product, consumer consumption patterns vary, and it is difficult to

Figure 1.1. Spiral of Decline Created by Lack of Profitability

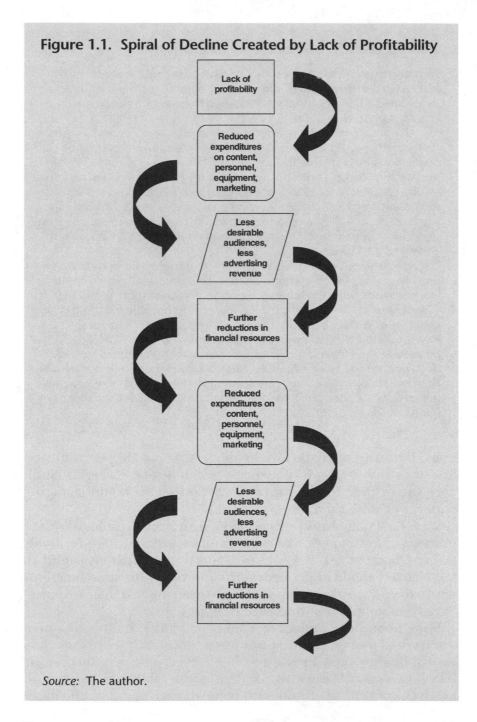

Source: The author.

determine how audiences will receive the combination of elements in each new product.

Managers usually try to diminish risk by spreading it across income-generating activities to reduce the effect of negative outcomes from some choices but to still allow firms to take advantage of potentially rewarding opportunities. This is sought by firms through ownership of multiple magazines, newspapers, or broadcasting outlets, and through the production of multiple books, recordings, TV programs, films, or Internet sites.

Although risks can be ameliorated, avoiding risk is dangerous to firms. Managers who try to avoid all additional risk place their firms in jeopardy by allowing other firms to achieve the rewards from those risks and gain competitive advantages that reduce the competitiveness of the risk-avoiding firm.

MARKET, FINANCIAL, AND OPERATIONAL CHARACTERISTICS OF MEDIA

The nature of media products and services, production and distribution necessities, and economic forces affect media and influence decisions of media managers. The effects of these factors are not common across all media but produce significant differences in the characteristics of media products and services. The differences affect the environments in which firms operate, force managers to respond differently to market and cost forces, and significantly affect market structures and operating choices.

The characteristics of major media products and services are shown in table 1.1. Although there are commonalities among the characteristics, such as the intensity of labor required, the products and services are most notable for wide differences in capital requirements, fixed costs, barriers to entry, levels of competition, complexity of logistics, and product and market strategies that can be employed. In the following chapters, the nature and importance of these factors will be explored.

Awareness of the limitations and opportunities afforded by the characteristics of the media products and services that a firm offers, as well as those offered by other firms, helps managers better understand their business environment in developing effective company and competitive strategies. The contexts or environ-

How Media Companies Spread Their Risk

The risk of failure of media products is high where individual titles or productions are involved because their producers make production decisions based on their estimates and beliefs about market demand.

It is difficult, however, for producers to anticipate changes in audience tastes and expectations and the extent to which their interest in specific genres will continue. Predicting the continuing success of currently popular performers, directors, or writers is also problematic. There is also an inability to foretell the success of marketing efforts or what competing products may be offered by competitors. These factors make it difficult for producers to estimate with any certainty demand for specific films, books, and audio recordings. The result is that there are few very successful titles each year and many more unsuccessful or less profitable media products.

In responding to the risks created by this uncertainty, media firms attempt to spread the risk among different titles. A recording company may produce fifty recordings with different artists recorded in several genres, or a motion picture company may finance ten widely different motion pictures. In 2001, for example, EMI Group issued Idlewild's *100 Broken Windows* through Capitol Records for rock music fans, the dance tune *One Last Time* by Quivver through its Virgin Record subsidiary, a recording of Holst's *The Planets* by the Los Angeles Philharmonic Orchestra through its EMI Classics label, and jazz saxophonist Cannonball Adderley in *Jazz Workshop Revisited* by its Blue Note Records label. That same year, Universal Pictures distributed the live action motion picture *Josie and the Pussycats* (based on the comic book and 1970s television cartoon), the action film *The Fast and the Furious,* the artsy *Captain Correlli's Mandolin,* and the romantic comedy *Head over Heels* in an efforts to attract a range of audiences and thus reduce its vulnerability to a flop in any one genre.

Some firms will attempt to spread their risk by operating in different media industries in hopes that lower performance of, say, its magazines during an unsuccessful year in the magazine industry will be offset by better performance of its television programming subsidiary.

Companies also seek to reduce the risks of rapid price increases and problems in the availability of necessary resources by entering into long-term contracts, becoming shareholders in suppliers' firms, or entering into joint ventures to own resource firms with competitors that also face similar risk.

10

ments in which firms in different media industries and sectors operate vary significantly. These contexts are important in understanding the contemporary situations of various types of media.

Publishing industries (book, magazines, and newspapers) are well-developed and mature industries throughout the developed world. They have traditionally been locally and nationally based but are increasingly operating at regional and global levels. Publishing industries have the potential for moderate growth in both the short and midterms. The ability to significantly increase revenue from advertising or circulation is generally limited, as is the ability to achieve significant growth through market expansion. Opportunities for electronic publishing are starting to be utilized in all three sectors, which are producing products and services based on the Internet and multimedia. The growth of revenue from these initiatives is slow, but the potential for growth is strong.

The broadcasting industries exist at different levels of development in developed nations, depending upon when privatization and commercial operations were authorized. In the United States both commercial and noncommercial radio and television are well developed and mature. In most other developed nations, noncommercial/public broadcasting is mature and well developed, but private broadcasting is still maturing because it developed only in the last quarter of the twentieth century. In markets in which commercial broadcasting is well established, the ability to increase advertising revenue is limited. In markets where commercial broadcasting is still developing, advertising expenditures can be expected to grow only to that approximating the average share of advertising expenditures for television in those nations with mature broadcasting industries. Increasing opportunities for analog and digital

Characteristics of Media

A variety of characteristics affect the operations, business models, and environments in which media and communications industries operate. Although there are some similarities among media, each has unique aspects that compel and constrain actions and affect their market structures, opportunities, and further development. Some of the more important aspects of these characteristics can be seen in table 1.1.

TABLE 1.1
Characteristics of Selected Media

Market Characteristics	Financial/Cost Characteristics	Operational Characteristics
Newspapers		
Strong link to specific geographic market	High capital requirements	Most firms are SMEs, a few large firms
Mature markets with limited growth potential	High fixed costs	Labor- and equipment-intensive
Short product lifespan	High production costs	Complex logistics
High barriers to entry	High distribution costs	Most costs are not related to core business
Relatively low level of direct competition in most markets	Low marketing costs	High dependence on advertising revenue
Stable circulation	High first-copy costs	Advertising purchases stabilized with long-term contracts
Declining market penetration	Moderate variable costs	Circulation purchases stabilized with subscriptions
Direct consumer sales through subscription and single copies through retailers and company sales	Rapidly declining average total costs	High cyclical financial performance
Low/no elasticity of demand for circulation		Product and market strategies limited
Advertiser preference for largest circulation paper		High paper waste creation, moderate chemical waste creation, high vehicle emission creation
Moderate/low elasticity of demand for advertising		
Low public-sector involvement (in developed nations)		
Threats from new technologies are high		

Books

Language-based market
Long product lifespan
Low barriers to entry
High level of direct competition
Most sales through retailers
Low public-sector involvement
Low threats from new technologies

Low capital requirements
Low fixed costs
High production costs
High distribution costs
Moderate marketing costs
High first-copy costs
Moderate variable costs
Rapidly declining average total costs

Most firms are SMEs, a few large multinational firms
Labor-intensive
Reliance on contract labor
Most content is acquired
External production is typical
Moderately complex logistics
Most costs are not related to core business
Moderate to high cyclical financial performance
Many product strategies possible
High paper waste creation, moderate chemical waste creation

Magazines

Strong link to special interest or topic
Mature markets with limited growth potential
Relatively short product lifespan
Low barriers to entry
Moderate level of direct competition
Increasing number of titles
Declining average circulation per title

Low capital requirements
Low fixed costs
Moderate production costs
High distribution costs
Moderate marketing costs
High first-copy costs
Moderate variable costs
Rapidly declining average total costs

Low labor intensity
Complex logistics
Most costs are not related to core business
Moderate dependence on advertising revenue
Advertising purchases stabilized with long-term contracts
Circulation purchases stabilized with subscriptions

(continues)

TABLE 1.1 (Continued)

Market Characteristics	Financial/Cost Characteristics	Operational Characteristics
Moderate to high elasticity of demand for circulation		High cyclical financial performance
Direct consumer sales through subscriptions and single-copy sales through retailers		Wide range of product and market strategies
Moderate elasticity of demand for circulation		High paper waste creation, moderate chemical waste creation
Moderate elasticity of demand for advertising		
Low public-sector involvement		
Threats from new technologies are moderately high		

Radio Stations

Market Characteristics	Financial/Cost Characteristics	Operational Characteristics
Strong format and geographic market link	Low capital requirements	Most firms are SMEs, a few large firms
No product lifespan	Low fixed costs	Labor and moderately equipment-intensive
Regulatory barriers to entry	Low production costs	Most costs are for core business
High level of direct competition	Low distribution costs	Most content is acquired
Unstable audience	Moderate marketing costs	High dependence on advertising revenue
High elasticity of demand for advertising		Advertising purchases stabilized with long-term contracts
High public-sector involvement		Moderate cyclical financial performance

Many product and
market strategies
possible
Low waste creation

Television Stations

Geographic market link	Moderate capital requirements	Most firms are medium to large sized
No product lifespan except through taping	Moderate fixed costs	Most costs are for core business
Regulatory barriers to entry	High production costs	Most content is acquired
Other entry barriers moderately high	Low distribution costs	High dependence on advertising revenue
Moderate level of direct competition	Moderate marketing costs	Advertising purchases stabilized with long-term contracts
Unstable audience	No variable costs	Low cyclical financial performance
High elasticity of demand for advertising		Product and market strategies limited
High public-sector involvement		Low waste creation
Moderate to high threats from new technologies		

Cable Systems

Geographic market link	High capital requirements	Most firms are medium to large sized
No product lifespan	High fixed costs	Most costs are for core business
Regulatory barriers to entry	High distribution costs	Most content is acquired
Other entry barriers high	Moderate marketing costs	High dependence on consumer revenue
Low direct competition		Consumer sales stabilized with subscriptions
Direct sales to consumers through subscription		Moderate cyclical financial performance
Moderate elasticity of consumer demand		

(continues)

TABLE 1.1 (Continued)

Market Characteristics	Financial/Cost Characteristics	Operational Characteristics
High threats from new technologies		A number of product strategies possible Low waste creation

Motion Pictures

Market Characteristics	Financial/Cost Characteristics	Operational Characteristics
National and global markets Strong secondary markets (cable-video-TV) Moderate entry barriers High level of direct competition Much substitution possible Genres and performers influence demand	High capital requirements Low fixed costs High production costs Low distribution costs High marketing costs High first-copy cost Low variable costs	Labor-intensive Most costs are for core business Moderate cyclical financial performance Market strategies are limited Dependence on limited number of theatrical distribution channels

Multimedia

Market Characteristics	Financial/Cost Characteristics	Operational Characteristics
Young market Low barriers to entry Moderate to long product lifespan High level of direct competition Sales through retailers High elasticity of consumer demand Low threats from new technologies	Low capital requirements Low fixed costs High creation costs Low manufacturing costs High distribution costs Moderate marketing costs High first-copy costs Rapidly declining average total costs	Most firms are SMEs, some large multinational firms Labor-intensive Reliance on contract labor Moderately complex logistics Access to distribution systems moderately difficult Many product strategies possible Low waste creation

Online Media

Low entry barriers	Low capital require-	Labor-intensive
High level of direct	ments	Most costs are for core
competition	Low fixed costs	business
Growing market	Low production costs	Dependence on adver-
Short- to long-term	Low distribution costs	tising revenue and
product lifespan	High marketing costs	e-commerce
Unstable audience	No variable costs	Many product and
Free and direct sales to	Rapid decline in aver-	market strategies
consumers	age total cost	possible
High elasticity of de-		Low waste creation
mand for adver-		
tising		
Low public-sector		
involvement		
Low threats from new		
technologies		

channels, as well as for market expansion via cable and satellite, are presenting significant new possibilities for growth of well-established broadcasters with regionally and globally recognized broadcasting brands.

The prospects for online and other digital media are clouded by a good deal of uncertainty because they are in early stages of development. Nevertheless, they have strong potential for growth. This potential is dependent upon the willingness of audiences to acquire necessary equipment, hardware, and software to access and use content. It is also dependent upon the development of methods of financing that are broadly acceptable to audiences, advertisers, or both. Despite the uncertainty, there is high interest in online and digital media activities among media and communication firms, capital sources, advertisers, and audiences. That interest is spurring a great deal of activity by media firms and some capital sources, but the movement of audiences and advertisers varies widely by nation and location.

Because the publishing industries are mature industries, and the same applies for broadcasting industries that have reached maturity, they do not face developmental and resource problems on the scale of those encountered by communications firms in industries such as audiovisual production, multimedia, information technologies, and telecommunications.

SUMMARY

Media companies are affected by their ownership structures, their needs to produce adequate returns, the risks they encounter, and the overall contexts in which they operate, as is illustrated by "The Context of Publishing Industries" on pages 19 and 20. The extent to which these economic and financial forces affect individual firms and firms within different media industries determines the constraints and requirements that managers encounter and the choices that are available to them.

The following chapters will explore these economic and financial forces in greater depth. They will focus on the nature and creation of media products and services, the market, cost, and regulatory milieus that affect operations, and the effects of business cycles, inflation, interest rates, and exchange rates on performance. Attention will be directed to the needs and choices of audiences and advertisers, and to how different levels of competition affect media, finance requirements, and sources of capital, including venture capital, equity markets, and debt.

The development of large media firms and the economic and financial pressures that play significant roles in the strategies and initiatives of their managers will be considered, as well as issues of how global trade in media products and services affects operations and choices. Ultimately the focus will turn to questions of how to understand and monitor the economic and financial health of media firms.

The Context of Publishing Industries

A number of specific aspects of the publishing industries are important in understanding their contexts and the contemporary issues they face:

- Most publishing firms fall into the small and medium enterprise (SME) category. Only a few truly large publishers exist, and these typically operate both regionally and globally.
- Barriers to entry are relatively low in the magazine, directory, and book publishing industries but higher in the newspaper industry.
- Most published products, with the exception of books, have relatively short life spans. Some of the content and data generated through these products, however, have residual value for additional uses.
- Economic fluctuations influence the amount of advertising support available.
- Economic fluctuations influence consumers' decisions to purchase publications.
- Consumption patterns for published materials and for advertising in published materials vary widely among nations.
- Wide differences in the patterns of subscription versus single-copy sales create varying marketing strategies and financial dependency of newspapers and magazines on these sources.
- Publishing is highly labor intensive, requiring highly skilled content creators and processors, information processing specialists, skilled printing craft workers, and distribution workers.
- Sophisticated logistics and transportation systems specifically designed for the publishing industry play important roles in the distribution of products to customers.
- Large amounts of material waste are created by the disposable nature of many published products. The primary waste results from newspapers and magazines that are thrown away after use. Recycling programs and use of recycled paper in production are being undertaken to address this issue.
- Production processes produce a variety of environmentally damaging solvents, wash residues, and other chemicals. Governments are addressing this issue by requiring investments in new equipment and developing processes for recovery and safe disposition of this waste.
- Traditional publishers are facing increasing threats and opportunities from the development of electronic publishing. The threats result mainly from not responding to the opportunities.
- Trade in published products has tended to face minimal levels of regulation.

- Publishing industries are not research-intensive industries by comparison to pharmaceutical, high technology, and consumer goods industries.
- Basic intellectual property protections are in place and generally protect published works in printed form within developed countries, but problems with property rights protections still exist in some other regions and nations.
- Protection of intellectual property and rights collection in the areas of electronic data, information, and knowledge production and distribution are not as well developed and impede growth of the electronic publishing sector.

2

Business Models, Workflows, and Value Chains in Media Firms

MEDIA COMPANIES are producers in that they acquire and combine resources to create a product or service that is purchased by others. The characteristics of media products and services, the ways they are intended to be provided in the marketplace, the methods by which they are produced and distributed, and the value created by these processes are central concerns in understanding commercial and competitive issues.

This chapter focuses on the work of media firms by exploring the nature of media products and services, the business models upon which different media are based, the type of work that takes place in media firms, and the value chains of media firms.

MEDIA PRODUCTS AND SERVICES

Although one often hears about media products and services and their industries, particular attributes of the products and services are typically assumed or ignored. This presents problems in discussions of industry issues and trends because it permits broad sweeping generalizations to be made about media that ignore important elements that distinguish the abilities of media and communication firms to serve the wants and needs of audiences and advertisers.

There are significant differences among media in terms of the ways they convey content that are dependent upon the human senses by which the content is perceived. These differences affect the context in which messages are received and the attention given to content. For example, print media rely upon the sense of sight, radio and recordings upon the sense of hearing, and television and motion pictures on both of those senses.

Most of us have had the experience of viewing a motion picture in a theater and on television. Although both communicate using audio and visual stimuli, the experience of viewing is different. This occurs because televisions have traditionally been unable to present the film in wide-screen format, because one does not typically view television in a darkened quiet environment that reduces distracting stimuli, and because the audio systems of televisions tend not to surround the viewer with sound and vibration as is found in motion picture theaters.

Print media tend to be used in different contexts as well. Persons reading books tend to seek solitude or focus their senses more heavily on the activity than do magazine readers. Newspaper readers focus more directly on its content than do readers of outdoor advertising.

The differences in formats and use produce significant differences in the ability of media to convey different types of content most effectively. Print media tend to be better for carrying significant amounts of information and sparking the imagination. Audio and audiovisual media tend to be best at providing diversion and work most effectively when they carry only basic levels of information.

These differences in the ability to better serve different needs make specific types of media products and services better at responding to the needs of audiences and advertisers. Although all media serve the needs of general or specialized audiences, only some media products and services serve the needs of advertisers, as shown in table 2.1.

Because the capabilities of certain media products and services can better provide diversion, general information, and specific information, and because they serve audience and advertiser needs differently, media products and services do not serve the same purposes and are used in varying ways by audiences and advertisers.

Although similarities may make some media interchangeable in limited ways for limited purposes, the differences are significant and do not permit complete substitution for all situations and uses. This is why newer media have not had a history of destroying more

TABLE 2.1
MEDIA SERVING DIVERSION, GENERAL INFORMATION, AND INFORMATION FUNCTIONS AND THEIR FOCUSES OF ACTIVITY

Diversion	General Information	Topic or Search-Specific Information	Focus
Audio Recordings			Audience needs
Books		Books	Audience needs
Film			Audience needs
Video		Video	Audience needs
Public-Service Broadcasting	Public-service Broadcasting		Audience needs
Commercial Radio			Audience and advertiser needs
Commercial TV			Audience and advertiser needs
Consumer Magazines	General magazines	Specialty magazines	Audience and advertiser needs
	Newspapers	Specialty newspapers	Audience and advertiser needs
Online Data and Services	Online data and services	Online data and services	Audience and advertiser needs

established media. They have altered industry structures, content, and use patterns of existing media, but their primary impact has been to bring new methods for communication as additional types of media rather than replacement media. Radio, for example, did not bring an end to print media or audio recordings. Television did not destroy the motion picture industry. Cable did not end local television broadcasting. Although it is still to early too determine their effects, multimedia and online media seem to be seeking to serve functions that parallel or complement existing media.

Studies of the introduction of additional media have produced little evidence of reductions in nonmedia time use or changes in consumer expenditures for existing media. Instead it appears that additional media produce specialization and permit greater choice by individual consumers rather than wholesale changes.

LIFE CYCLES OF MEDIA

Industries, as well as specific products and services associated with industries, have their own life cycles that progress through stages of introduction, growth, maturity, and decline. As the industry progresses through the life periods, changes in sales, costs per customer, profits, customers, and competitors occur that are common across industries.

As shown in table 2.2, sales rise in the introductory and growth periods and peak during the maturation period before entering the decline period. The costs of the industry relative to the customer begin high and decline until the maturation period. Profits begin to appear in the growth period and rise to a high level during the maturation period before dropping in the decline period. The types of customers across the periods are represented by the

TABLE 2.2
BUSINESS DEVELOPMENTS IN DIFFERENT PERIODS OF INDUSTRY LIFE CYCLES

	Period			
	Introductory	Growth	Maturation	Decline
Sales	Low	Rapidly rising	Peak	Declining
Costs/Customer	High	Medium	Low	Low
Profits	Negative	Rising	High	Declining
Customers	Innovators	Early adopters	Majority	Laggards
Competitors	Few	Growing	Stable	Declining

different types of individuals who adopt products and services at different rates. In the initial stages competition is low, but as an industry becomes profitable, more firms enter the market. By the maturation period, the number stabilizes before declining.

Media exist at different stages of industry life cycles, as shown in table 2.3. All the major traditional media industries are in the maturation period in developed countries. Print media (books, magazines, and newspapers) are in the late stages of maturity, close to the edge of the decline period because audiences and advertisers are becoming increasing familiar and comfortable with newer information and communications technology. The print media have enjoyed one of the longest known cycles of any manufacturing industry.

Business Models in Media

Business models provide an understanding of how a firm conducts commerce. The term "business model" is often confused with that of strategy, such as company strategies, product strategies, marketing strategies, or pricing strategies. These strategies are the means employed by firms to guide activities toward goals, but they are not models of the business.

A business model is much more fundamental. Business models

TABLE 2.3
Location of Media Industries in Periods of Industry Life Cycles

Period		
Introductory	*Growth*	*Maturation*
"Streaming" or online video	Satellite Television Online Media Multimedia	Audio Recordings Books Magazines Motion Pictures Newspapers Radio Recorded Video Television Cable television

are created and understood by stepping back from the business activity itself to look at its bases and the underlying characteristics that make commerce in the product or service possible. A business model involves the conception of how the business operates, its underlying foundations, and the exchange activities and financial flows upon which it can be successful.

Business models can be described as the architecture for product, service, and information flows, including a description of various business activities and their roles. They include a description of the potential benefits for the various business actors and the sources of revenues.

In terms of modern communications, business models need to account for the vital resources of production and distribution technologies, content creation or acquisition, and recovery of costs for creating, assembling, and presenting the content.

Understanding the business model under which a firm or product operates or will operate is especially important when new products or services are developed or when the industry in which one operates is in a state of significant change.

As the environment in which a firm or industry changes, the factors that support a business model change simultaneously. As a result, business models that were once successful may become less successful and be abandoned. Business models that seem appropriate for new products or services may not produce the support and structures necessary as the business milieu changes and may then be altered or abandoned in favor of other models.

Some individuals make the mistake of assuming that failed or abandoned business models can never again be successful. This is not always the case if the conditions under which they failed are no longer present or if resistance to some elements disappears. A situation may then arise in which such a model may be reintroduced successfully for the same or a different product or service.

WORKFLOWS IN MEDIA FIRMS

To understand the economics of a media firm, one needs to have a clear understanding of the work that takes place and the resources that are required to complete each stage. This can be aided

The Changing Business Models of Online Content Services

The business models of online content service providers have changed rapidly as firms have attempted to find a model that can support their operations. These firms, such as AOL.com (America Online), Yahoo!, MSN, Netscape Netcenter, Excite.com, CompuServe.com, digitalcity.-com, organize and provide users access to content of interest including news, information and entertainment, leisure activity, and other materials.

These companies are broad service portals that now also provide e-mail, messaging services, voice mail, user customization, online shopping, notification services, software downloads, chat rooms, and access to a wide variety of online communities and content.

The history of online content service providers includes four abandoned business models, a model in current use, and an emerging model evolving from the existing model. Each was made possible by particular developments in technology, had different financial bases, and produced different results.

The Videotext Model

This model was used in initial attempts to use television screens to convey text-based content. Efforts to create videotext as a commercially viable activity were led primarily by newspaper companies in the 1970s. The impetus for this new content service was the change to information and computer technology for phototypesetting, which allowed newspapers to reuse or easily alter content prepared for the newspaper in a videotext operation. The concept was particularly attractive because it allowed publishers to update materials and convey breaking news between printed newspaper editions.

Because most of the infrastructure and content creation and formatting costs were already covered by revenue from the newspaper operations, the financial costs of this secondary use and distribution of the content were relatively low. This permitted publishers to offer videotext at a low price or to provide it free as promotional costs for the newspaper itself.

Although the producers of videotext had strong cost advantages in producing and distributing the material, the consumers—either as audiences receiving it free or purchasers of the service—were generally uninterested. As a result, most content providers abandoned the videotext model.

The Paid Internet Model

When videotext did not produce results desirable to content providers, they began to seek other methods through which costs could be recovered from individual users. The preexisting infrastructure of the Internet became an attractive alternative for distribution.

The Internet and the software required for its operation had been originally funded by the U.S. government to support military research communications. Wider access to the system created the potential for commercial use, and in the 1980s content producers discovered that they could make their materials accessible through the Internet and charge a fee for access to the content.

The market, however, did not look kindly on the development. General audiences did not embrace the payment idea, and complicated processes were required to gain access to information. As a result, general content providers soon abandoned the model based on providing content through the Internet and recovering costs from audiences.

The Free Web Model

The World Wide Web and associated software and browsers made access to Internet materials easier. The development costs for these improvements were paid from efforts of the European nuclear science community to improve its ability to convey data, graphic displays, and other materials to researchers. The widespread distribution of browsers in standard software packages for new computers rapidly made the Web the primary online use of general consumers.

Many new types of content providers began moving rapidly onto the Web and generally provided materials free of charge as promotional materials for commercial firms or as special interest materials provided by individuals or organizations. Traditional media content providers grasped the utility of the Web and began operations to reuse existing materials again—as they had under the videotext model—but this time with the advantages of true graphic capabilities. Other firms developed means to organize materials in a way that reduced the frustrations of users seeking content.

Content users found this arrangement quite workable, and the lack of cost for use made it the equivalent of obtaining material from free television or radio. The model, however, did not provide means for commercial firms to recover costs for providing or organizing content from the users, and they soon rejected the model.

The Internet/Web Ad Push Model

In an effort to create a nonuser revenue stream, some content providers, Internet service providers, and content organizers attempted to use lists of subscribers and users, combined with demographic, lifestyle, and other profile information obtained through registration, as a means of attracting advertising. In other cases they attempted to find advertisers for products and services related to Web pages on which particular content was organized. In both cases, the firms "pushed" advertising toward audiences that would be most interested in the products or services offered.

The process based on user information was an advertising system based on direct mail models. Although the model created a revenue stream, audiences often were unhappy with intrusiveness of the content or the number of advertisements on Web sites. Many Internet service providers and content organizers did not want advertisers not associated with them to use their systems. Additionally, many advertisers saw negatives in the intrusiveness and effectiveness of the model. These problems led many online content providers to seek another model.

The Portal and Personal Portal Model

Content organizers that wanted an advertising revenue stream and control of advertising exposure moved to the current business model based on portals. In this system, users of Web browsers are brought to an organizing interface and advertisements. As users move to information of interest, additional or related advertising appears. The current revenue model is based on newspaper- and magazine-style advertising in which readers are brought into contact with advertisers' messages while making other use of the pages.

In most portals only a single ad appears on each page, and it is designed to "pull" or attract users to "click through" the ad to gain additional information from the advertiser.

The current model is attractive because user resistance is not strong and a regular advertising stream is being produced. In this model, portals create value by organizing access to content created by others in a way that creates a brand for the portal that attracts returning users. Despite its improvement over other business models, however, the current model is still not producing profits for most portal operators.

The Digital Portal Model

The current hope for portal providers, backed by significant investments and new competition from telecommunication firms, is the development of multipurpose digital portals. As bandwidth and compression technologies are improved and increasingly become available, the model will allow the combination of current content portals with streaming video and audio.

A user of this system will be able to view broadcast channels worldwide, obtain pay-per-view services, view potential nonbroadcast channels, search video clip archives, use a variety of multimedia materials, seek additional information about the content, chat with others while viewing a program, and determine the language in which the content is received.

Costs will be recouped by revenue from an advertising stream and from users through pay-for-view and premium services subscriptions such as those currently existing in cable and satellite services. Major content organizers in operation today are hoping to use this new environment and business model to capitalize on strong online portal brands created during operations under the current model.

by considering the workflow in a firm and the steps taken in the creation and distribution of the final product or service.

Differences in workflows and in the resources required for each media mean that managers need to be familiar with the entire process if they are to effectively manage the entire operation or even parts of the process. Differences between broad workflows in media can be illustrated by considering the workflow for a motion picture (fig. 2.1, p. 32) and the workflow for a magazine (fig. 2.2, p. 32).

In reviewing the broad workflows one can immediately see that magazine publishing involves more physical and mechanical processes than motion picture production. These workflow charts outline the major workflow steps, but each step can include dozens and even hundreds of activities that must take place in order to create and distribute media products and services.

Understanding the workflow characteristics of media is important because they result in significant differences in the structures and complexity of operations, investments required, and costs.

Media Value Chains

Creating value is the central activity of successful companies. For any business to survive it must create value for customers by providing products or services that fulfill their wants and needs, and the company must do so more effectively than its competitors. The process through which this value creation takes place involves the entire range of activities within firms and is conceptualized as value chains.

The value chains show the value that is added to a product or service at each step of its acquisition, transformation, management, marketing and sales, and distribution. The value chain concept for products and services is now well established in business literature.

The Changing Newspaper Business Model

The contemporary newspaper business model developed in the mid- to late nineteenth century, replacing a very different model that was based on a specialized audience rather than a mass audience.

During their first 100 to 150 years of publication, U.S. newspapers served a relatively small audience—about 15 to 25 percent of the population depending upon location, literacy, degree of economic development, and other social factors. The audience represented the politically, socially, and economically active members of the community. Papers were highly dependent upon circulation sales for their income, and the price of papers and subscriptions was very high. The business model was dependent upon circulation sales to this group, and the little advertising that existed was primarily for raw materials and imports available to merchants and manufacturers rather than retail advertising.

In the last half of the nineteenth century the market began to change as urbanization, the Industrial Revolution, wage earning, and literacy created social changes that resulted in discretionary income and leisure time among an increasing number of the population. Newspapers began changing to serve this larger and soon mass audience. New sections to serve diversionary interests and attract more readers were added to newspapers (entertainment, sports, comics, etc.). Papers were sold at a very low price. This altered the business model to put more emphasis on advertising revenue and produce a large mass audience of interest to retail advertisers.

The magnitude of this change in the business model can be seen in the fact that advertising provided one-half of the revenue of newspapers in the United States by 1880. That amount rose to two-thirds by 1910 and to about 80 percent in the year 2000.

The growth of readership and advertising support continued rather steadily until the years after World War II. When television appeared, it began to provide diversion and other information in forms increasingly attractive to those parts of the mass audience who were not part of the politically, socially, and economically active members of their communities. As a result, a portion of the reading audience began leaving newspapers behind, and many readers began spending less time with newspapers. That problem has been exacerbated with the rise of multiple networks and stations, cable, and other electronic information and diversion opportunities that have developed in recent years.

As the changes continue in the twenty-first century, changing audience and use patterns for newspapers will continue. One can expect that there will come a time when newspaper readership will look much more like its initial position rather than the position at its mid-twentieth-century height. Given the facts of greater income, literacy, and world outlook, it will probably not decline to the 15 percent level of the early nineteenth century. However, somewhere in the range of one-quarter to one-third of the population seems realistic.

As this change takes place, a new business model will evolve. It may look less like the current model and more like the model of the early history of the industry. Or it may take on a whole new rationale with additional factors involving new communications technologies.

Figure 2.1. Motion Picture Production and Distribution Flow Chart

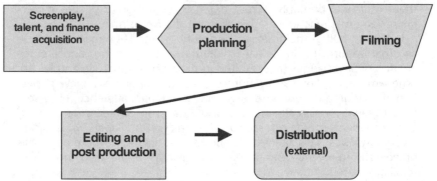

Figure 2.2. Magazine Publishing Flow Chart

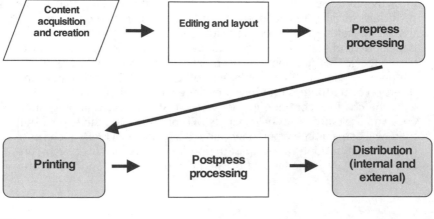

MEDIA COMPANIES

This value chain concept is particularly important in understanding market behavior because it places the emphasis on the value created for the *customer,* who ultimately makes consumption decisions. The concept is useful in considering those activities that are most central to the core activities of a firm and those that make the business operational. Although there are differences in the activities, creating the highest possible value in each activity is sought through the development of efficiency, quality, and service.

Several value chains are involved in any single firm's or industry's activities (fig. 2.3). These include the value chain of resources purchased from suppliers to make production possible. In media firms these include materials such as paper, videotape, editing stations, printing presses, and computer software.

The value chain of the producing firm involves the creation of value by using resources and processing them to create a product or service. A product or service is not worthwhile unless it is made available to purchasers, so another value chain involving distribution comes into play. Finally, there is a value chain created by use of the product or services by the purchaser.

The value in each of these chains is generated by the components purchased, the use of human resources and technology, the organizational structure, and the flow of information within the organization. In the end, however, it is the overall value of the activities that is valued by the customer.

If one focuses on the activities of media firms, one mostly considers the activities in the value chains of the producer and distribution (fig. 2.4). Although there are slight differences among media industries and firms, the basic value chain involves content—that is, selecting, organizing, packaging, and processing content—followed by activities preparing it for distribution, and then distribution and related marketing activities for the product or service.

Figure 2.3. Value Chains

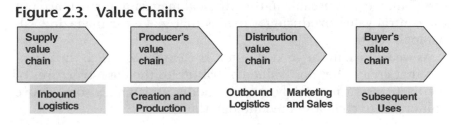

Figure 2.4. Media Firm Value Chains

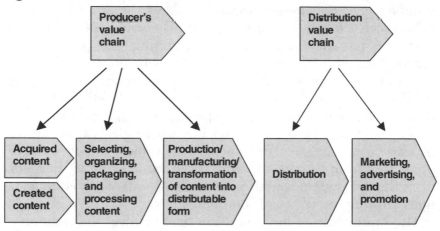

Magazine companies, for example, purchase and create text, photographs, and artwork that are to be the basis for a publication. The staff then selects, organizes, and packages this material in a way that gives the magazine its focus and personality. The processed materials are sent for prepress preparation, printing, and binding and other postpress activities. The printed copies are then distributed to subscribers, wholesalers, and retailers for single-copy sales. The distribution system is supported by marketing, advertising, and promotional activities.

If this process is considered in terms of the real value of media activities to customers, two links in the chain are especially important: the creation of content and the selection, organization, packaging, and processing of that content. These are important because the creation of content produces original material not available elsewhere, and the selecting, organizing, and packaging of it are tasks that make the content easier to find, use, and digest. The other activities, although important to making the product distributable and useable in the physical magazine format, are not the central value-producing activities that make the magazine valuable to readers.

As we will see in the next chapter, the extent to which the activities that create the most value contribute to the cost structures of media firms varies widely among media and makes some more vulnerable to changes in technology than others.

Are New Media New Products and Services?

The language surrounding industry and governmental discussion and decisions regarding new media tends to cast these technologies in terms of transforming lives and providing products and services previously unavailable. But are the changes really producing new communications products or services? Let's consider some examples.

First, consider digital television. The change from analog broadcasting to transmitting and receiving digital signals is underway worldwide and is increasing the number of channels available, improving reception quality, and increasing the width of television screens. Digital television is being implemented in many countries providing high definition television, increased number of channels, and datacasting in which text, images, sound, and video can provide a variety of interactive content.

Television digitalization is making many more hours of television programming available from more sources. And, in its integrated form, it permits viewers such options as viewing a newscast at any time of the day or selecting a single story for viewing. It provides opportunities to view and print a recipe at the same time it is being illustrated on a cooking show and to purchase and order ingredients.

But does digital television really produce a new product or service? The answer is no. It still transmits broadcast programming but does so with better reception and more choices. It uses the convergence possible through digitalization to view television and simultaneously access materials that would previously be available through or used in the forms of print media, the telephone, video players, the Internet, and other communications. So digital TV really cannot be considered to produce new products or services but rather just new ways of accessing, receiving, and using existing products or services. The supply and demand for the new possibilities created by digital television, then, will be interrelated to the supply and demand of existing products and services.

A second example can be seen in advances in mobile telephone capabilities. Mobile communications, which existed in radiotelephone form for many years and in mobile telephone form for about two decades, has already been transformed into a platform that allows users to use the phone to send and receive faxes, text messages, and e-mail. It is now allowing access to the Internet, global positioning, advertising reception, and other functions.

These functions, however, are not new. They represent convergence of products and services provided by mail, telephone, the Internet, positioning and mapping, printed schedules and brochures, radio, and narrowcasting. There are advantages in being able to access and use these in a mobile environment, but the ideas and concepts of the services are not new. As with digital television, the supply and demand for these services will be interrelated to their supply and demand in their original forms.

The reason such new technologies are not truly producing new products and services is because they provide no real new communications capabilities. They are not affecting communications in such fundamental ways as did the arrival of the printing press, telegraph and telephone, photography and motion pictures, and broadcasting, which provided the abilities to move text, sound, and images with or without terrestrial lines.

Their primary effects are increasing the speed and flexibility of communications, producing economies of scope and integration that change the economics of content production and distribution, and permitting the combination and integration of existing means of communications to allow readers/viewers/listeners more control and choice.

These are important improvements to existing media products and services, but they are not truly new products and services. The combination of existing content modes, the flexibility of use, and the shift of control provide significant advantages to users. And where there are advantages, there are consumers willing to spend time and money.

However, the demand for the "new" products and services providing these advantages must be understood as a part of, and an extension of, demand for existing content products and services. That demand comes from those who communicate and receive communications using existing means. To be commercially successful, new methods of accessing, using, and combining products and services must increase value to their users and help simplify their search for and access to the content and communication ability.

New media are increasingly being thought of as means for increasing the utility of traditional media use, not supplanting it. Digitalization of television and its linkage to the Internet may allow viewers to select television programming or motion pictures with video on demand, but its primary use will be to increase the number of programmed channels or to add new features to that programming. A viewer of a televised automotive program, for example, will be able to use the digital features of interactive television to receive written directions on how to carry out a repair being shown or to order the parts needed to do it.

Core Business

Part of the examination of the value chain of a media business is based on establishing the nature of the firm's core business.

Many managers mistakenly define their core business as the activities generating the highest turnover, necessitating the highest capital investment, or requiring the largest number of employees.

The core business, however, is better thought of as the central common activity of the firm. It is the fundamental activity of the firm that is supported by investment, company structure, personnel, and processes.

Those who adopt this view in media firms quickly come to the conclusion that content is the core business, central activity, and competency of their firms. The development of information and entertainment and its packaging and programming for use are the essential activities that take place in the value chain and the activities that provide the highest true value added in the process.

The Value of Content Organization

Technological and policy changes have increased the ability of individuals to select single motion pictures, television programs, recordings, and other materials for their personal use. Some observers argue that choice in acquiring such materials will render traditional television, cable, radio, and Internet content providers unnecessary and result in their demise.

These arguments are based on the view that the emerging free and pay choices offered through cable, satellite, and the Internet provide value to audiences. It is believed that the new offerings will supplant existing providers of services because audiences will find them more attractive. This is a tacit argument that there is less value in the current methods of presentation of that content.

This view, however, ignores the fact that the value created by the core business of television, cable, satellite, radio, newspapers, magazines, and Internet content providers is not distribution of that material but the selection, organization, and contextualization of that content.

The value is created for audiences because content organizers expend the time to consider the enormous amount of available or potentially available materials and make hundreds and even thousands of decisions about its quality, usefulness, importance, and entertainment value. Although individuals could make these choices for themselves and are sometimes willing to make the choices, they are not willing and do not have the time to do so on a daily basis.

This occurs because, although making individual choices is valuable to persons, it is not perceived as having the same value all the time. As the amount of available information and content increases, the value of that additional communication to individuals is diminished, and they seek to avoid content and the necessity of making decisions regarding it. As a result, there is a growing demand for blocking, avoidance, and filtering systems and the services of content-organizing media.

The production and distribution methods employed, and the business models utilized to gain compensation for the firm's activities, are structural necessities for the development and continuation of the core activity. Media managers differentiate their core activity by creating particular methods and types of presentation that create a personality for their publications or programs that becomes the brand of that product. These kinds of activities make *Elle* different from *Vogue*, *The Times of London* different from *The Daily Mirror*, yahoo.com different from digitalcity.com, and the Discovery Channel different from the Disney Channel. The core activity of these media, however, is the creation, acquisition, and packaging that transfers information and creates individual brands that serve consumer needs.

Value Chains and Convergence in Publishing Industries

Publishing industries today tend to be led by large national and international publishing firms that engage in information service strategies in which printed products are a base used for expansion into a wide range of information products and services. They are able to do this because the value produced in the creation, gathering, and presentation of content can be separated from the value of the production and distribution systems.

Many of the new products and services based on content creation, gathering, and presentation are electronic and Internet-based. It is clear that publishing in the twenty-first century will be increasingly an information-gathering, creating, packaging, and storage activity rather than a production or distribution activity based on a specific physical printed form. In adjusting to this new environment, publishing is moving farther away from its traditional position within the printing and paper industries to one under an emerging and not yet fully defined information and knowledge content industries umbrella.

Central to understanding the developments that are driving change is the distinction that must be drawn between publishing and printing. The difference involves the essential value-producing elements of the two activities. Publishing is the act of producing and issuing informative, educational, leisure, and cultural material. Printing is the act of placing that material on paper that can then be distributed.

Printing has always been important as a cost factor in publishing, but it is not synonymous with publishing. Even in past decades, many publishers did not print the titles they published, especially publishers in the magazine, book, and directory publishing industries. Today this distinction is becoming even clearer as publishers who traditionally used printing as the medium for distribution are increasingly using electronic means for an expanding variety of published materials.

The development of information and communications technology is leading publishers to transform themselves into broader content creators rather than thinking of themselves as merely paper-based publishers. The basic processes of information gathering, journalistic and literary writing, editing, design, and dissemination have value in forms other than traditional publishing.

Content generated through traditional publishing can be reorganized, repackaged, and used in many different forms. In order to remain competitive in the long run, innovative publishers are exploring and exploiting opportunities presented by these technologies for electronic publishing, multimedia products, and other information and communication technology products that enhance and operate parallel to the traditional publishing base that has made firms successful.

These changes are producing a new type of workflow in publishing and in turn its use by audiences. In the new flow, not only the publisher gains flexibility, but audiences too can become actively involved by using electronic information and reconstructing it in forms to their individual liking, and by responding to that information and becoming part of the creation process as well (fig. 2.5).

Although many firms are increasingly outsourcing portions of their activities, the opportunities for publishers and other media firms to use material in a number of ways is leading most firms in communications content to eschew large-scale outsourcing. Although outsourcing some functions can save costs, there is a loss of control over the form and quality of materials if it involves content. Many media, particularly those with time sensitivities, are also reticent to outsource distribution functions upon which they depend.

The concepts of value chains and how and where in the chains

Figure 2.5. Electronic Publishing Flow Chart

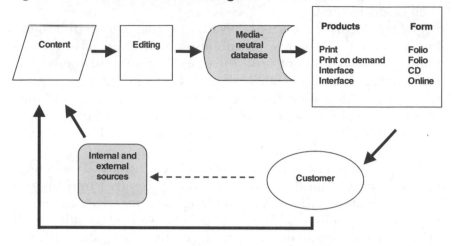

media firms produce value make it difficult to continue considering publishing within traditional industry definitions. Publishing has traditionally been thought of as the activity of separate industries: for example, newspaper publishing, magazine publishing, book publishing, and directory publishing. However, it is becoming less relevant to use such definitions to describe the actual activities and modes of operations of many publishing companies today.

Publishing firms of all sizes that were traditionally based in only one of the publishing industries now engage in activities in other publishing industries. Operations are increasingly intertwined and dependent upon each other to the extent that their revenues and costs cannot be easily segmented. The changes in the operations of industries and the convergence of operations are creating a cluster of industries that are increasingly interrelated. Firms now simultaneously operate in different industries in the cluster by creating content that can be used by a variety of means and in a variety of physical and digital formats. The nature of the cluster and its relationship to the printing industry and information technology industries are shown in figure 2.6 on page 43.

Perhaps the clearest example of problems with traditional definitions of publishing industries occurs in firms in the business information cluster because they are not specifically part of any one of the publishing industries. The firms in this cluster produce and

40   MEDIA COMPANIES

The Rise of the Concept

Media firms traditionally have produced discrete products or services that have dictated decision making about how choices of content should be made.

In media with continuing focused operations, such as newspapers or magazines, content has followed current events, persons, trends, and developments within the editorial scope of the publications. In radio broadcasting, content choices typically have been made within a format or content profile. In television and motion pictures, content choices have been made to provide a variety of types of programming.

Choices among content are typically made by considering the proposal of materials for use, with decisions on what stories to include being made by editors and decisions on what music, programs, or films to produce or broadcast being made by production companies and programmers. These decisions are typically made at the media unit level.

In making these choices, managers typically attempt to maximize their audiences or—in the case of public service or not-for-profit media—to maximize their service to audiences. In commercial media the choice to maximize audience also tends to maximize advertising, although specialized programming that maximizes a specific audience segment is also desirable to some advertisers. Although these choice patterns continue today, the rise of media conglomerates operating a number of media has also led to content choice patterns that attempt to maximize performance across media.

Two patterns exist for this concept approach. In the first pattern a successful product such as a book may become transformed into a concept for a motion picture or television program within the media conglomerate. Another example is a magazine that may be used as the basis for television programming. These activities thus extend and maximize the return from the concept of a media product or service already offered by the media conglomerate. In this pattern profitability is typically sought from all uses of the concept.

Thus, the magazine *Better Homes & Gardens* has used its success in the magazine industry to extend that well-recognized and respected brand by creating B&G TV (Better Homes & Garden Television), providing a platform for similar types of content but with the advantages of audio and visual communications. Both media outlets support each other with content and cross-marketing activities. Although the uses of this type of cross-media content and activity are increasing, they do not produce economies of scale in production or distribution that significantly reduce the costs of operations of either firm.

In the second pattern, a content concept or story is selected with the intent that it is simultaneously or progressively released in different forms by media within a conglomerate. Thus, a concept may produce a book, motion picture, television program, electronic game, and Web site. The result is that the marketing of each product or service supports the marketing and brand of the concept as a whole and vice versa. In this type of cross-media activity pattern, a company will wish to make a profit on each media use of the concept, but it may sometimes cross-subsidize the activities so that the overall use and profitability is maximized. When it is not advantageous or possible to follow this pattern within a conglomerate, outside firms may be used for some portions through joint ventures or licensing arrangements.

When DreamWorks released the animated motion picture *Chicken Run* in 2000, for example, it also published a number of *Chicken Run* books for children of different ages, approved the production of a *Chicken Run* game for PlayStation and Game Boy, and licensed additional products such as soft toys of the film's main characters. When it had maximized use in theaters and pay cable, it released the movie on videocassette and DVD.

Despite the contentions in the 1980s and 1990s that large media firms with holdings in different media would find ways to leverage that ownership into regular transformation of successful books into films, television programs, videos, and other products, that pattern has not successfully developed. Similarly, predictions that corporations owning motion picture and television programming firms along with television channels would work closely together on a regular basis have not been regularly borne out.

Although there are advantages in the development of concept media products, separate division management and independent corporate evaluations of divisions have kept incentives from developing for cooperating fully with other divisions, internally selling products at a lower price than to other companies, and sharing revenue across divisions. As a result, the development and exploitation of many concept products has involved firms from media companies that are otherwise competitors rather than corporate sisters or cousins.

distribute information that helps businesses understand and adjust to changing market conditions, follow trends in products and services, and locate potential new customers.

These firms are based less and less on single distribution channels, such as magazines or online services, but incorporate many methods of distribution, including periodicals, online services, radio and television broadcasts, books, and directories. Major firms in this cluster join multiple publishing associations and federations because their activities cross industries, and many company execu-

Figure 2.6. The Emerging Information and Knowledge Content Industries Cluster and Its Relation to the Printing Industry and Information Technology Industries

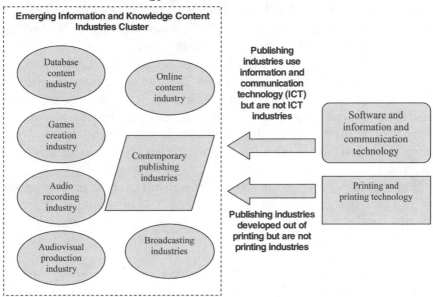

tives are frustrated by the narrowness of the perspectives of individual organizations.

The changes occurring around and throughout publishing force managers to reconsider their strategies and operations or risk being left behind. The necessity to innovate, question, and alter past strategies is more critical in the publishing industries today than ever before. This is occurring because the new environment is making it possible for firms from other industries and new firms to enter publishing. Many are doing so without having existing print-based traditions or having to face the difficult choices of what to do with existing operations, personnel, and facilities. These firms are able to change the foundations of the industry and become major companies through dramatic operational changes because that change does not threaten their existing operations.

Managers of publishing firms today face the prospect of letting new firms take away their business or beginning the process of internal innovation to remake their firms and industry. Otherwise they will face the certainty of steady decline for their business if they do not innovate to counteract the pressures of the new firms.

One factor in the ability of media firms to successfully carry out their roles as creators of value for audiences and advertisers is the extent to which they evidence competitiveness.

There is a tendency to think that just because a firm competes it is competitive. But the concept of competitiveness runs much deeper. *Competitiveness* is a term that indicates the degree to which a firm or industry can survive, sustain itself, and remain a viable economic contributor. It also involves the degree to which a firm or national industry can respond to market opportunities or threats.

The degree of competitiveness is the result of a variety of factors within the firm or national industry, and in their general environments, that support the ability to grow, expand markets, and respond to increased competition from other firms or national industries.

Some firms and national industries have competitive advantages that make it easier for them to challenge other firms in competitive situations. Competitive advantages arise from constant efforts to improve firms' performance and upgrade products and services. They result from internal atmospheres that support change and innovation. The kinds of competitive advantages occurring from these factors include

- Lower costs
- Differentiated products commanding a high price
- Proprietary assets
- Higher quality products and services
- Efficient production
- Rapid product development
- Advanced features
- Innovation.

Publishers of multiple magazines, for example, have advantages in production and distribution that reduce the cost per copy and create efficiencies in production compared to companies that publish few titles. Online media companies have tended to have advantages over traditional media companies because they have business cultures and company structures that allow them to rapidly alter existing products and change directions quickly to respond to new market opportunities. This has been a particular advantage over traditional media companies whose cultures and structures have tended to create barriers to rapid change.

It must be recognized that advantages to some firms and consequent disadvantages to other firms can also result from

- Protectionist government policies
- Subsidies
- Monopolies
- Actions designed to harm competition.

For example, postal rates can create cost advantages for different classes of media and communications services. These might favor direct mail firms over newspapers or magazines. Similarly the provision of monopolies or preferences in cable services in a market through franchising can advantage and disadvantage firms.

Some firms and industries also have advantages because they operate in nations that have advantages such as strategic location, better infrastructures, financial stability, higher levels of economic development, policies supportive of business and economic development, and beneficial developments from the clustering of specific industrial sectors. Competitiveness, then, represents the degree to which a firm uses advantages and managerial competence to proportionally generate more wealth than its competitors.

At the national level, for example, the outdoor advertising industry in Germany operates in a country with significant advantages owing to its high level of economic development, advertisers with significant advertising budgets, and a well-established outdoor advertising industry. These provide firms in the German industry significant competitive advantages when compared to outdoor advertising firms operating in a country such as Algeria.

The degree of company and industry competitiveness is typically evidenced by factors such as turnover, productivity, lower cost and efficiency, profitability, investments, research and development expenditures, personnel skills levels, and trade balances. It is desirable for a magazine company or a national cable television industry, as examples, to perform above average on such measures—or at least in the average range—when compared to other magazine companies or to the cable television industry in another nation.

Managers struggle between the need for short-term financial performance and the need for long-term sustainability of the firm. The goals of these choices are not contradictory, but they compete at the managerial level for attention, resources, and behavior. Attention to the issue of sustainability is critical to maintaining competitiveness because a firm that is competitive today can lose that competitiveness in future years.

Managers with a narrow view of their responsibilities focus primarily on short-term financial performance, seeking higher annual returns for owners, sometimes at the cost of reinvestment, by reducing resources for content quality or expenditures for labor.

Managers pursuing the longer-term goal of sustainability focus on broader issues that will affect the future development and value of the firm. Sustainability represents the viability of an industry or firm, its ability to maintain effectiveness and operations. Sustainability is affected by a variety of production, market, technological, social, and managerial forces (see fig. 2.7).

Managers thus seek to balance the needs of the short-term goal of financial performance with the longer-term goal of sustainability that requires attention and response to the variety of forces that affect firms or industries.

SUGGESTED READINGS

Becker, Lee B., and Klaus Schoenbach, eds. *Audience Responses to Media Diversification: Coping with Plenty.* Hillsdale, N.J.: Lawrence Erlbaum Associates, 1989.

Grieve Smith, John. *Business Strategy.* Cambridge, Mass.: Blackwell, 1990.

IMD. *World Competitiveness Yearbook 2000.* Lausanne: International Institute for Management Development, 2000.

Karlöf, Bengt. *Business Strategy: A Guide to Concepts and Models.* London: Macmillan, 1989.

Porter, Michael E. *Competitive Advantage: Creating and Sustaining Superior Performance.* New York: Free Press, 1985.

Porter, Michael E. *Competitive Advantage of Nations.* New York: Free Press, 1990.

Figure 2.7. Factors Affecting the Sustainability of Media Companies

Production Forces
Availability of raw materials
Capital costs
Labor costs
Energy costs
Taxes
Transportation/distribution costs

Sustainability

Market Forces
Consumer demand
Advertiser demand
Total revenue available
Demographic and Psychographic changes
Competition

Technological Forces
Availability of technology
User adoption of technology

Social Forces
Environmental demands
Political/legal demands
Cultural/social demands

Managerial Forces
Organizational effectiveness
Productivity
Financial control
Innovation
Responsiveness to change

3

Economic Forces Affecting Media

FOUR MAJOR CATEGORIES of economic forces affect operations and choices of managers in media firms: (1) market forces, (2) cost forces, (3) regulatory forces, and (4) barriers to entry and mobility.

Market forces are external forces based on structures and choices in the marketplace. Cost forces are internal pressures based on the operating expenses of firms. Regulatory forces represent the legal, political, and self-regulatory forces that constrain and direct operations of media firms. Barriers represent factors that make it difficult for new firms to enter and successfully compete in a market.

MARKET FORCES

The ability of a media firm to be established, prosper, and grow is affected by a variety of external pressures that affect its ability to gain the financing and revenue it needs and to effectively compete in the marketplace. These market forces include the availability and terms for obtaining capital, demand for the products and services offered, and the competitive situation.

Capital Availability and Rent

The availability of funds for the establishment and development of firms is a crucial element that determines whether and how many companies can exist. Without reasonable availability of funds, the number of media firms that will exist and the activities they can carry out will be limited. When capital is readily available at reasonable cost, existing firms can use those funds to further develop their activities and operations, and new persons or firms may be able to enter the media marketplace.

48   MEDIA COMPANIES

The problem of capital has been a factor in developing nations that tend to have less stable currencies and fewer mechanisms and institutions for capital accumulation, lending, and investment. This hampers the abilities of individuals and companies to acquire capital to establish private, commercial media. Even in developed nations, economic changes and political choices reduce or increase the availability of capital and the terms for its rent at different times, affecting the ability of individuals and firms to acquire and use capital.

Audience/Consumer Demand

The willingness and ability of audiences to use media or to acquire media products and services is another significant economic force that determines the success of media firms and the materials that they produce and disseminate.

The acquisition and use of media products and services requires individuals to expend time, money, or both on media. Because time and money are scarce resources, the decision to expend them for media is subject to the economic force of audience/consumer demand.

Given a twenty-four-hour day, of which two-thirds is typically devoted to sleep, work, education, and household maintenance, individuals have roughly eight hours per day for leisure and other activities, including media use. If individuals use three hours watching television, they cannot use those three hours to attend a concert. If individuals use one hour for online activities, they cannot use that hour to read a book. If individuals use two hours playing football, they cannot use that time to view a film in a theater. The activity choices made individually and collectively thus affect the demand for media products and services even when price is not involved.

When a price for the media product or service is involved, consumer choices take place within the entire available income. If individuals spend 35 percent of their income on shelter, they cannot use that income for cable subscriptions. If 2 percent of their income is spent on telecommunications, they cannot use that income to purchase food. If individuals spend 20 percent of their income on automobiles, they cannot use that income to purchase books.

Similarly, if an individual spends 5 percent of his or her money purchasing a DVD player, he or she cannot spend that money on DVD recordings.

The amount of money available to consumers, and the choices made for the use of that money among a range of products and services, thus affects demand for media products and services that are available at a price. Audience/consumer demand is also affected by a variety of other factors including the size of the population, tastes and preferences of individuals, and consumer expectations in a given market.

Demand is also affected by the amount of media already available. Each additional unit of a medium and each additional medium available reduces demand for individual units of a medium. As the number of channels of communications increase, the number of choices rise and individuals' behaviors diverge, thus reducing demand for specific media units. This audience fragmentation is the inevitable and unstoppable consequence of the increase in channels available to audiences. It is true whether one is discussing publishing, broadcasting, the Internet, or other forms of communications involving multiple individuals.

The result of fragmentation can clearly be seen in the decline of average television audience share when the number of available channels increases (fig. 3.1). The average share of the total television audience drops dramatically with the addition of each new

Figure 3.1. Diminishing Demand for Each New Television Station as Seen in Average Audience Share

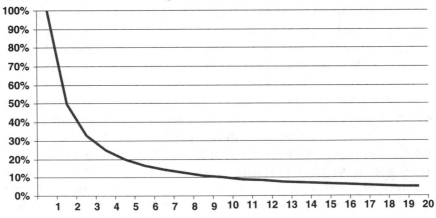

channel. Whereas the share of the total audience is 100 percent with one channel, it plummets to an average share of 20 percent of the total audience with only 5 channels and then to 5 percent at 20 channels.

When one looks beyond averages at actual television and cable markets, one finds that some channels must struggle to survive with only 1 or 2 percent shares after about a dozen channels are available, because they fall below the average share of the total television audience. This occurs because it is rare that audiences devote equal attention to each of the channels.

Advertiser Demand

Advertiser demand for media products and services is primarily dependent upon the needs of advertisers to reach audiences, the sizes and/or types of audiences produced by media, and prices for access to audiences.

Most media advertising is a part of the broader marketing efforts of manufacturers and retailers to draw attention to their products, increase sales, and build product loyalty. As a result, the extent to which advertisers require advertising to serve those needs may vary with the season, state of the economy, number of competitors they face, etc.

Demand for media advertising is also affected by the choices of advertisers among a range of marketing communications activities, including direct marketing (catalogs, advertising sheets, personalized mail) and sales promotion (point-of-sale displays, exhibitions, sponsorships). Different types of advertisers have different needs to communicate with audiences, and various types of advertising and marketing communications do not equally serve all needs.

Competition

The amount and degree of competition among media and media units are another economic factor that affects the development and success of media firms. When there are more competitors and the market is divided among them, no one firm will control the market, and each will take part in a continuing struggle to improve or maintain their market share.

Situations in which there are multiple media units help to produce benefits for audiences and advertisers. The competition process is one in which one competitor takes an action, and then other competitors in the market respond, inducing a reaction by the initial competitor, which results in responses by other competitors (fig. 3.2). It is this process that produces lower prices, innovations, new features, and other changes in products and services that benefit consumers.

The leadership in this process may be evident as price leadership (in which a firm provides goods or services at lower price), quality leadership, low-cost leadership (in which the firm finds ways to decrease its costs), technical leadership, or innovation.

However, there are winners and losers in this process. Firms cannot remain in a position in which they are always responding to the actions of a competitor. If they are to survive and develop, they must at some point break the cycle by taking some action

Figure 3.2. The Competition Process

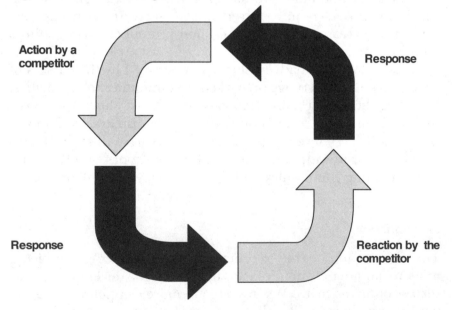

Action by a competitor

Response

Response

Reaction by the competitor

that cannot be copied by competitors or cannot be done as well by competitors. This makes one the leader rather than the follower.

This may be done by getting out of direct competition by changing the market though expansion or increased penetration, introducing new products or services, or reducing direct competition by operating in a desirable and specialized niche. Firms that set their own courses become market drivers that actively change the dynamics of the markets in which they operate. These firms are in more advantageous positions than companies whose strategies and activities are market driven and merely responses to changes induced by the actions of other firms.

This book will return to the issue of the nature and complexities of media competition in greater depth in chapter 7.

Substitutability

Substitutability refers to the degree to which competing products and services are equivalent and serve the same needs. The more substitutability between products and services, the greater the degree of competition between them.

Although the magazine industry is a competitive industry involving thousands of titles, most titles are not substitutes. *Vogue* does not provide similar content and does not attract a audience similar to that of *Car and Driver*. The content and audience of the *New Yorker* and *Penthouse* are sufficiently dissimilar to keep them from being interchangeable. Within niches of content there are substitutes, however. A subscriber to *Sailing*, for example, might be reasonably well served by *Cruising* should the former be unavailable or the subscriber decide for some reason to change to another magazine devoted to sailboats.

In the newspaper industry, where local competing daily newspapers are scarce, a national newspaper may provide international and national coverage just as a local newspaper, but the national paper is rarely a substitute for the local newspaper because it cannot provide local news and advertising. Similarly, the local paper is rarely a substitute for the national paper because of its more parochial focus and because it carries far less international and national coverage than the national paper.

Cost Forces

A variety of forces related to the costs of operations play important roles in the economics of media firms. These include economies and diseconomies of scale, scope and integration, and costs for content, production and distribution, and marketing.

Economies/Diseconomies of Scale

Costs for physical production activities in industries are typically affected by economies of scale and scope, and this is especially true of media firms that engage in physical production.

Economies of scale result from increasing production that reaches a cost-effective point. Because the basic costs of operations must be met regardless of the amount of goods produced, manufacturing and selling more of the product allows basic costs to be spread further across the goods produced. Thus, the basic operations of a newspaper may cost $25,000 per issue whether one copy or 25,000 copies are printed. If one copy is printed, the cost for that copy is $25,000, but if 25,000 copies are printed, the average copy cost is $1. Thus, there is an advantage, created by economies of scale, to those firms that are able to print and sell more copies than competitors.

Diseconomies of scale result from the problems of both small and large size. A firm with a small production run may operate less effectively than a firm whose production is sufficient to achieve economies of scale. Similarly, as production grows, additional investments in equipment, staff, and management may not be fully recovered by the greater production costs and may ultimately produce diseconomies of scale.

Economies/Diseconomies of Scope

These economies result through economies gained by joint activities—typically in manufacturing, distribution, and marketing—among separate products.

A recording and video distributor will have economies of scope over separate recording and video distributors because the distribution and retailing mechanisms for recordings and video are similar and overlapping. This permits the joint use of distribution systems and facilities in a cost-effective manner. Similarly, a magazine publisher will have advantages over independent publishers if it also produces a directory or yearbook. This occurs because of the advantages it has in terms of production, brand recognition, marketing, and distribution that make it less expensive to operate such secondary products.

Scope may also produce diseconomies if the operations are not, or cannot, be effectively integrated or if the scope produces administrative costs that are greater than any savings produced by expanding the firm's scope.

Economies/Diseconomies of Integration

These economies result from shared platforms for multiple services that allow more efficient introduction of new products and the packaging of services in a cost-advantageous manner. For media companies, economies of integration have especially been made accessible by the widespread adoption of information and communication technology (ICT). ICT makes it possible to share resources and increase the value of production, particularly because products based on digital technologies can share information, facilities, and equipment and can be coordinated to create new services.

Digital technologies have made it possible to complement or end physical production and distribution of products and to make profitable information operations possible even if the basic product is provided free of charge. Because computer power and the costs of processing data and information are decreasing, economies can be sought from integrating operations using ICT.

This development is primarily possible because marginal value rises while marginal cost declines as the audience size or number of users of ICT-based information products and services increase. As shown in figure 3.3, this produces a wide area in which companies can work out different successful strategies.

Just as with scale and scope, it is theoretically possible for diseconomies of integration to occur if the integration is not effective or produces costs beyond those of separate operations.

Figure 3.3. Economies of Integration

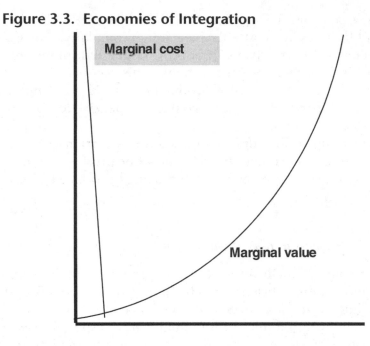

Fixed and Variable Costs

The structures of fixed and variable costs vary considerably among media and affect the operations and choices that can be made by media company managers.

Fixed costs represent those basic costs that must be incurred and met to make operation possible. They do not change in the short run based on amount of production. Television stations have basic expenses for facilities, studios, and transmitters that do not change significantly whether the stations broadcast sixteen hours per day or twenty-four hours per day.

Variable costs are those that vary depending upon the amount of production. A magazine that increases its press run from 100,000 to 125,000 will incur additional variable costs for paper, ink, production time, and distribution because of the added production. Conversely, if it reduces its press run, those costs will be reduced.

As media become increasingly digitalized, they simultaneously operate in less of a variable-cost environment, in which strategies of achieving lower unit costs by efficient production and pursuit of

MEDIA COMPANIES

Fixed Costs for a Book Publisher

When books are sold, the revenue received is used to pay a variety of costs, including author compensation, overhead, marketing, manufacturing, warehousing, distribution, retailer compensation, expenses for unsold copies, and profit.

Fixed costs do not change correspondingly with changes in the number of copies printed, so fixed costs in this environment include only marketing and overhead, which average about $3.50 on a hardback book priced at $25. All the remaining costs, except profit and unsold copies, can be classified as variable costs and account for $20 of the book price.

This means that only about 14 percent of the income received from a sale is used to pay fixed costs (fig. 3.4).

Figure 3.4. Distribution of Revenue from an Average-Priced Hardback Book

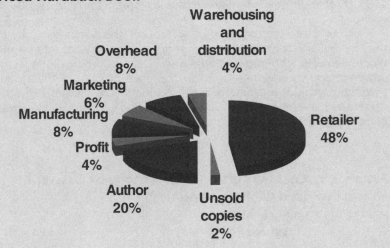

economies of scale, scope, and integration are critical to successful cost and price competition. This move into the fixed-cost realm has significant strategic and operational implications. In the fixed-cost environment, competitors soon operate with similar fixed costs because they use similar equipment and production techniques. As a result, they cannot compete effectively on the basis of prices for their media goods and services and must focus their activities to compete on the bases of quality, service, and brands.

Variable Costs as an Incentive to Online Music Sales

Variable costs are those expenses for factors of production and distribution that are related to the amount of goods produced. In the recording industry these include costs for manufacturing recordings, distribution, and retail expenses.

These types of expenses make up the bulk of the price of a CD sold to consumers, accounting for more than half of the costs (fig. 3.5). For every CD sold through the traditional manufacturing, distribution, and retail mechanism, 55 percent of the income from sales never reaches the recording companies, artists, and music publishers that create the underlying value of the product.

As a result, developments that can reduce the variable costs of operations are intriguing to recording firms, as they are for all physical goods producers. Assuming that the record company loses no benefits from economies of scale or scope, a recording firm using digital distribution, for example, would save approximately $7.15 in variable costs for each $13 CD sold outside the traditional physical production and distribution chain.

Thus, when a recording company reduces the amount of physical sales by digitally delivering some recordings via downloads sold through e-commerce, the firm can lower the price of the recording. If the recording company chooses not to lower the price of CDs by the amount saved, the amount retained from those variable costs savings could be used to increase return on sales for the recording company or to increase compensation for the artist, composer, or music publisher.

Figure 3.5. Cost Centers and Percentage of Costs for Normally Priced CD Recording

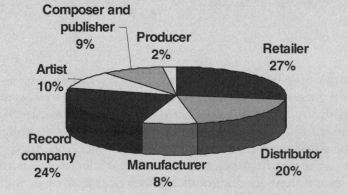

The cost structures of firms differ significantly among media, reflecting differences in operating processes and necessities and levels of competition experienced by the firms. These differences are seen in number of employees, fixed assets required, distribution systems, and other factors required for operation.

If one considers cost structures in relative terms, comparing contributions of important and common elements of media, the most important differences occur in content, production/distribution, and marketing/advertising costs.

Content Costs

Major differences can clearly be seen in the contributions of content and production/distribution costs to overall costs (fig. 3.6).

Content, which is the primary value-producing element in media value chains, is a higher contributor to overall costs for electronic media. It accounts for more than half of overall costs for average cable systems and one-quarter to one-third of all costs of

Figure 3.6. Differences in Content Costs among Selected Media

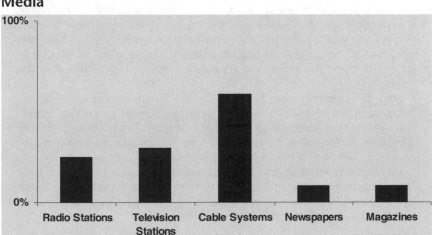

radio and television stations. For print media, such as newspaper and magazines, content typically accounts for 10 percent or less of total costs.

Production/Distribution Costs

The contributions of costs for preparation of materials for distribution (production) and distribution itself are reversed when com-

---

The Winner's Curse: The Problem of International and Major National Sports Rights

The rights to broadcast major international sporting events are an important programming resource for television, cable, and satellite channels.

There is little risk that major events such as the Olympic Games, World Cup, National Football League (U.S. football), and Premiere League Football (soccer) matches, Formula 1 racing, and others will not produce large and attractive audiences.

Because of the size of those audiences, and because managers of many television channels wish to use such broadcasts to create or maintain their brand images, the rights to such events are hotly contested, and significant bidding wars often ensue. Because of the high prices of acquiring rights, many program managers encounter what has been called "the winner's curse."

Although a channel may make the winning bid in the auction of the programming rights, it also wins the ability to lose a great deal of money. If advertisers are unwilling to pay the high prices upon which the managers predicated the bid, if the sporting events are not as interesting or prolonged (in the case of multiple final matches, for example) as expected, or if the audience produced is not as large and stable as expected, the channel may not be able to recoup its investment in the rights.

NBC, for example, paid $700 million for the television rights to the 2000 Summer Olympics Games in Sydney. Viewers, however, apparently found the coverage unattractive because of tape delays, format, and other factors, and the ratings for the broadcasts reached a thirty-year low. The network sold advertising based on a minimum average rating of 16.1, but the broadcasts achieved an average rating of only 14.1. The poorer performance in the ratings meant that the network had to provide compensation with seventy-two half-minute prime-time advertisements to its advertisers.

---

60   MEDIA COMPANIES

pared to content costs (fig. 3.7). Print media devote a far greater percentage of overall costs to these items, typically between 40 and 60 percent. This occurs, of course, because of the need for physical production and distribution of printed material.

Distribution costs represent the expenses for transferring the product or service from the producer to the consumer. In the cases of tangible products such as CD-ROMs, books, and videotapes, these include the costs of transportation and costs associated with making materials available through retailers.

Materials distributed through broadcasting, cablecasting, or satellite transmission incur distribution costs including transmitters, cable system infrastructure, uplinks, satellites, and any uses of telecommunications services necessary to link those systems to the station or channel.

In online media the actual distribution costs are typically borne not by the media firm but by the customer who pays for telecommunications use and access to online services.

The costs of distribution are particularly problematic for tangible media and communication products, because costs rise as the distance to customers increases (fig. 3.8). This occurs because it takes more time and effort to reach customers, and the costs for

Figure 3.7. Differences in Production/Distribution Costs among Selected Media

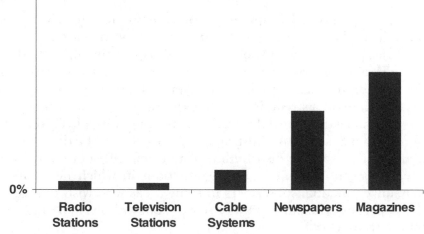

Figure 3.8. Distribution Costs Rise as Delivery Distance Increases

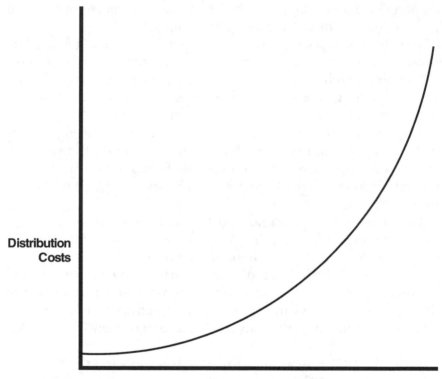

Distribution Costs

Distance to Delivery

transportation vehicles, operating costs, personnel, etc., rise as distance from the production to the delivery point increases.

This is particularly a problem for newspapers that operate their own distribution systems, because not only is distance a factor, but distribution density as well. If a carrier is delivering a newspaper to one home on a street, it is more expensive in terms of time and effort to make that one delivery than if the paper is delivered to ten homes on that street. As illustrated in figure 3.9, as the distribution density increases, the distribution cost declines. Distance and density issues can combine to create situations in which newspapers may have potential subscribers in some areas who wish to receive the paper, but the paper cannot serve them without making a loss on the transactions.

MEDIA COMPANIES

Figure 3.9. Distribution Costs Decline as Distribution Density Increases

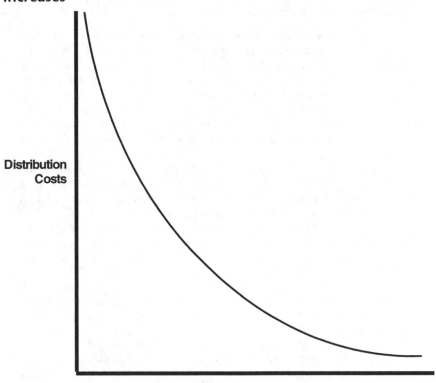

Distribution Costs

Distribution Density

Marketing and Advertising Costs

Differences in marketing and advertising costs that must be borne to effectively operate a media firm are another economic factor affecting media companies. When competition is low and only a few media exist in a market, the costs that media firms must bear to gain the attention of audiences, consumers, and advertisers are lower than when there are many outlets of the same medium and many media present in a market.

Because of the growing number of magazine and book titles, motion picture titles, television/cable channels, and other media and communication products and services, media and communication firms are now joining the list of the largest advertisers as they compete for attention and use.

Savings from Moving a Newspaper Online to End Physical Production and Distribution Costs

For several decades futurists have predicted the demise of printed newspapers, arguing that the costs of physical production and distribution and the increased speed of communications will induce publishers to give up traditional newspaper operations in favor of digital publication.

Setting aside issues of contemporary audience and advertiser acceptance, the potential of electronic operations is now nearly a reality. The compelling argument for online newspapers is the cost savings that would result from switching from printing and delivery of a physical product.

If one considers the financial operations of a model 38,000-circulation paper, typical of the average midsized newspaper market in the United States today, it has revenues of about $12.4 million, expenses of $8.4 million, and a return on sales of 32.4 percent.

Moving such a paper from physical to online production and distribution would reduce expenses in production costs by $3 million and in distribution by $1.1 million, a total savings of $4.1 million and nearly doubling the profit as indicated by return on sales (table 3.1).

Although moving to online delivery would eliminate the costs associated with the current physical delivery system, new expenses related to online delivery would replace some of those costs, which are estimated here at $450,000 annually.

Thus, the total cost savings from moving online would be $3.65 million, with online distribution reducing total costs by 44 percent. This would make the move to online newspapers a very attractive alternative from a cost perspective.

The problem with this scenario, however, is that it assumes there would be no effects on circulation and advertising revenue if the paper moved online—hardly an assumption that anyone who seriously considers the business model of the newspaper could accept. This example, however, reveals the extent to which noncore business aspects of production and distribution affect the operations of newspapers.

In 1998, for example, Sony, Time Warner, and Walt Disney were among the top twenty advertisers worldwide (see table 3.2, p. 66). Sony ranked above the other two because it manufactures and markets equipment as well as content to consumers. These three firms alone incurred expenses of $3.5 billion to advertise their services.

The importance of such expenditures differs among media

64

TABLE 3.1
OPERATING STATEMENT FOR THE MODEL NEWSPAPER

	Printed Newspaper	Online Newspaper
Revenue		
Circulation	$ 2,280,000	$ 2,280,000
Advertising		
Classified	3,500,000	3,500,000
National	150,000	150,000
Retail/Display	4,600,000	4,600,000
Preprint	1,900,000	1,900,000
Total Revenue	**$12,430,000**	**$12,430,000**
Expenses		
Advertising	$ 1,200,000	$ 1,200,000
Circulation/Distribution	1,100,000	450,000
News-Editorial	1,200,000	1,200,000
Production (Incl. Newsprint and Ink)	3,000,000	0
General/Administration (Incl. Building)	1,900,000	1,900,000
Total Expenses	**$ 8,400,000**	**$ 4,750,000**
Operating Profit/Loss	$ 4,030,000	$ 7,680,000
Return on Sales	32.4%	61.8%

products and services, as indicated in figure 3.10 on page 67, which shows the relative contributions of marketing costs to overall expenses. Because the expenditures are designed to capture attention, develop interest, and change or maintain use and purchasing behavior by audiences and advertisers, the amounts spent reflect the levels of competition encountered.

Because of their market structures and the amount of market power exercised, higher levels of competition occur on the Internet and in motion pictures and electronic media industries, and lower levels in print media, such as magazines and newspapers. These levels of competition are mirrored in the percentage of total company expenditures devoted to marketing for these media.

In a broader context, advertising costs affect not only media firms but all firms that engage in advertising.

Advertising initially increases the costs of goods and services, as

TABLE 3.2
WORLDWIDE ADVERTISING EXPENDITURES ON TOP 20 ADVERTISERS, 1998

	Billion U.S.$
Procter & Gamble	4.8
Unilever	3.4
General Motors	3.2
Ford	2.2
Philip Morris	2
DaimlerChrysler	1.9
Nestlé	1.8
Toyota	1.7
Volkswagen	1.3
Coca-Cola	1.3
Sony	**1.3**
L'Oréal	1.2
McDonald's	1.2
Nissan	1.1
Johnson & Johnson	1.1
Walt Disney	**1.1**
Time Warner	**1.1**
Honda	1.1
Mars	1.1
Diageo	0.9

shown in figure 3.11 on page 68. Costs for products both with and without advertising decline as the amount of products or services sold increases. Because advertising is intended to increase sales, its costs may be covered by the additional sales generated as a result of the advertising, and the increased sales of the product may keep prices from raising or lowering the overall price to consumers.

Transaction Costs

An important economic factor in the operation of companies involves the need to rationalize the process and costs associated with each transaction that a firm makes. This approach to costs, articulated by Williamson (1985), examines the needs of firms to focus on the costs and efficiency of the transactions they make in order to create efficiency. This idea drew upon earlier work by R. H.

Figure 3.10. Average Marketing Costs as a Percentage of Total Costs of Media Operations

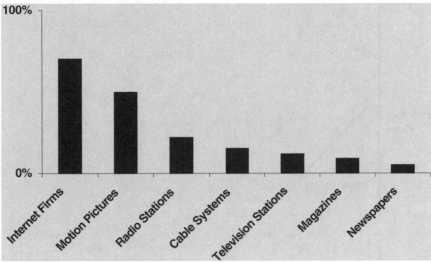

Coase (1937), who argued that relational contracting, in which stabilized relations are created with suppliers, is useful in reducing activity and costs for firms.

Examination of transaction costs requires firms to seek economies in the transactions they make not only with suppliers but also with their own customers. They need to rationalize contracts and transactions to simplify and stabilize the information needed about products and services and behavior in the market.

The result of the need to reduce transaction costs is seen in media firms in subscriptions for magazines, newspapers, and cable, satellite, and online services. On the supply side, contracts are made for important resources such as news and feature services provided by firms such as Associated Press and Universal Syndicate. In television programming, broadcasters typically buy the rights to a number of episodes of series simultaneously, and successful television, motion picture, and audio stars and directors often enter into contracts with producers and studios for additional programs, films, or recordings that will be made in future years—a process that reduces the transaction costs for each of them.

Figure 3.11. Cost of a Good or Service with and without Advertising

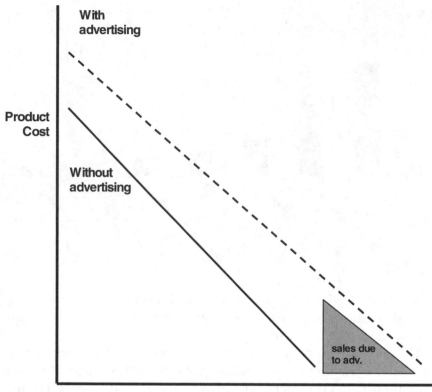

Nonmonetary Costs

Firms incur monetary costs, that is, expenses requiring direct payment, for labor, supplies, materials, rents, equipment, etc., as they produce goods and services for audiences and consumers. But it must also be recognized that they incur nonmonetary costs such as opportunity costs and costs for uncompensated use of labor and equipment and the like as well.

These latter factors become significant when firms produce multiple media products. A magazine firm, for example, may choose to close or sell one of its magazines because it believes the financial investment and time spent by staff may produce better returns if another type of magazine is produced. This is because it incurs opportunity costs, that is, the cost of lower returns vis-à-vis the potential for higher returns elsewhere, if it continues operation of the poorly performing publication.

Uncompensated costs are expenses that are incurred but are not fully compensated by the product or service for which the expenses are incurred. These types of expenses are often found when a media company operates a secondary product.

A newspaper, for example, may choose to reuse portions of its current contents and archives, as well as the firm's information technology infrastructure, to produce an online newspaper site. By using these resources at no cost or below real cost, the firm does not require that the online operation actually pays true costs for the resources. Even if full costs are paid, the firm may nonetheless incur nonmonetary costs because of the additional supervision that top managers must give the operation, the additional workload the operation requires for the information technology managers, etc.

Regulatory Forces and Intervention

Regulatory forces involve approvals for media operations or requirements placed on media to avoid or to behave in certain ways. Despite rhetoric to the contrary, Western governments—even in nations practicing the highest degrees of laissez-faire capitalism such as the United States—have regularly intervened in markets. The roles that governments play in economic affairs are necessary to create and perpetuate markets.

At the broadest level, actions by governments make economic markets possible. Economies are not self-generating and perpetuating. They require coordination for production and distribution and for exchange to take place. Governments play significant political and legal roles in creating the framework in which enterprises can operate by creating and enforcing property, contract, corporate, and other rights necessary for markets to function. In addition governments create currency, implement tax activities, and affect and intervene in economies through various fiscal and monetary policies.

Governments also intervene at the level of specific industries.

The rationales have typically been to promote activities or results beneficial to the public good, to limit or halt activities or results harmful to the public good, and to fulfill needs that markets cannot efficiently serve.

Although media tend to be given more latitude in liberal democratic states because of concerns over freedom of expression, governments regularly intervene in communications markets. The primary rationales for intervention in communications are that government intervention serves important social, political, and economic needs in democratic, capitalist societies and that governments need to promote and increase communications opportunities. Additional rationales promote intervention to control behaviors of communications firms that harm social, political, and economic interests and to permit government to provide basic services or supplement services of commercial firms when they do not serve important social, political, and economic needs of society.

Regulations exist to facilitate communications as well as to promote or constrain certain types of communications activities.

Technical/Structural Regulations

Technical regulations exist when governments or nongovernmental organizations set and maintain standards or control technology to make some communications possible. For example, the International Telecommunications Union through the World Administrative Radio Conference assigns frequencies for use by different nations so that users of radio waves for terrestrial and satellite broadcasting, mobile communications, and other communications using radio waves do not interfere with each other and make radio communications impossible. At the national level, government organizations such as the Federal Communications Commission then assign frequencies to users for operating radio stations, mobile telephones, radio-controlled toys, etc.

Regulations also exist to standardize communications, creating the ability to link telephone systems worldwide and to ensure that television set manufacturers and television broadcasters are using similar standards so that reception is possible. Without such regulation, systems and operations of both domestic and global media systems would be impossible.

Structural regulations also control the structure of media markets, such as limiting the number of radio stations to ensure profitable and stable operations or the establishment of limited monopolies in cable or television services. Controls also affect ownership structure. In the United States, for example, foreign owners may own no more than 25 percent of a radio or television broadcasting entity, and no single owner may have a penetration of more than 35 percent in their market with multiple stations. The United Kingdom prohibits foreign ownership of broadcasting, except for owners from other European Union nations.

Governments provide licenses, that is, the rights to operate, to media and communications systems. In democratic nations these tend in practice to be limited to licenses to use radio frequencies or rights to operate cable systems and telecommunications systems. In less democratic nations, licenses are sometimes required for print and other media as well.

Behavioral Regulation

Behavioral regulation either prohibits media firms from engaging in certain practices or requires them to engage in specified practices. These are economic factors when they affect market choices of media managers and require firms to forego certain revenue or to incur specific costs.

Proscriptive regulation regulates the carrying of pornography, offensive speech, violence and libelous expression, material damaging to national security, advertising for certain products, and other material deemed harmful to broad social interests. Proscriptive regulation is an economic force when it reduces the ability of a firm to benefit in the marketplace. This occurs, for example, if regulations prohibit the carrying of advertising for alcohol products and media firms are thus denied a source of income from sales to alcoholic beverage firms.

Prescriptive regulation requires behavior such as broadcasters carrying a certain amount of public affairs or children's programming, the production of television receivers capable of receiving captions for the hearing impaired, or the use of a specified percentage of independent producers as sources of programming.

Regulations requiring specified behavior are an economic force because they require certain expenditures and limit the choices of managers to carry materials that might cost less or be more profitable to provide.

BARRIERS TO ENTRY AND MOBILITY IN MEDIA MARKETS

Barriers to entry are economic factors that halt or make it difficult for new competitors to successfully enter a market in which they have not previously competed. These barriers typically result from the market, cost, and regulatory forces discussed above.

Two main types of entrants are affected by these barriers. First, there are firms entering the market for the first time, that is, establishing new businesses. An example of this type of firm is a newly established company that is beginning to publish a new magazine. The second type of entrants are preexisting firms entering the market by expanding their markets or moving into a new type of market. Examples of this type of firm are a magazine publisher that is internationalizing a title by establishing a subsidiary operation in another country, or a television network that is expanding its operations by beginning the operation of an online service.

New businesses encounter barriers to entry, and established businesses encounter what are called barriers to mobility. Some of the barriers are the same in both cases.

There are many factors that can act as barriers to entry and mobility. Among the major barriers are capital requirements, economies of scale, product differentiation, switching costs, limited access to distribution channels, government policies, and competitive advantages.

Capital Requirements

Capital requirements involve the financing needed to establish operations and pay start-up losses. Capital becomes a barrier when insufficient capital is available or when it is available only to certain firms or at preferential rates to certain firms. For example, a firm or entrepreneur may have the knowledge and desire to establish and operate a cable television distribution system but may not have the capital required to purchase the equipment and optical fiber lines necessary to construct and operate the system.

Economies of Scale

As previously noted, economies of scale are created when unit costs decline as the volume used or produced increases. Existing firms with high volumes will thus operate at a lower cost per unit than a new firm entering the market. Large established firms also experience economies of scale in the cost of purchasing supplies because of bulk purchase discounts. Other economies are found in production costs and distribution costs, such as the costs of servicing newsstands. A firm serving newsstands or kiosks with two hundred titles will most likely have economies of scale over a firm serving them with only twenty-five titles.

Firms with economics of scale can thus sell products and services at a lower price or retain greater profits than can firms with lower economies of scale or diseconomies of scale.

Product Differentiation

Differentiation creates consumer loyalties and identification with existing products. These loyalties are difficult for a new firm to overcome in order to induce customers to substitute the new product or service.

Product differentiation is a strategy used by firms to make their products unique and more desirable to a group of consumers than products of a similar type by other producers. Product differentiation in media occurs through a variety of techniques designed to vary the elements of media products and services, as shown in table 3.4 on page 78.

The more differentiation among units of a medium and among media, the more difficult it is for others to enter the market because they will need to differentiate their new product or service and make larger marketing expenditures to try to create a successful entry.

Switching Costs

Switching costs are consumer costs associated with changing from the use of one product to another. Consumers who switch from

The Problem of Newspaper Market Entry

The trend toward local markets with one daily newspaper has taken hold across the Western world since the middle of the twentieth century in response to advertiser preferences for the paper with the largest circulation and because of the cost structures inherent to newspaper operations.

Efforts to enter markets already served by a local daily have nearly always failed because of the barriers to entry created by capital requirements and high fixed costs, and because of competitive advantages such as market dominance and economies of scale held by existing newspapers.

High first-copy costs require a newspaper to achieve significant sales to spread the costs across an adequate amount of circulation. In addition, the fixed costs of newspaper publishing limit the ability of managers of startup papers to substantially lower their cost-per-thousand for advertising and maintain unprofitably low rates over a long period of time.

These factors make it improbable for a successful entry to occur. The financial problems faced in entering a market are illustrated in a model of the entry of a newspaper into an average market in the United States. Using the most optimistic scenarios possible, the model shows that the firm would not operate profitably at any point (see fig. 3.12). It would incur an operating loss of $286.1 million and net loss of $540.5 million over a ten-year startup period (see table 3.3, pp. 76–77).

The model assumes "success" in circulation (that is, parity with the preexisting newspaper) in the tenth year of the startup period. Even with that assumption the enterprise would still incur an operating loss of $11.2 million and a net loss of $26.7 million for that year. Operating losses of that magnitude would be expected to be incurred in subsequent years as well, but the net loss would be reduced, because the cost of capital would end unless additional capital was borrowed.

The model shows that entry into the market, even if a firm could operate at a loss for a long period of time, would not produce a commercially viable operation.

analogue TV receivers to digital receivers will have to make substantial investments. These costs make it more difficult for new communications and media technology that offers substantially the same benefits as an existing technology to enter a market. Switching costs can also be psychological as well as financial. There is some psychological discomfort when changing products with which one is familiar.

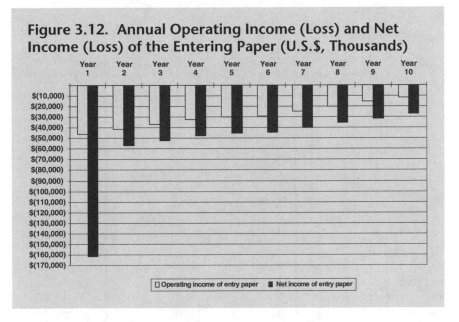

Figure 3.12. Annual Operating Income (Loss) and Net Income (Loss) of the Entering Paper (U.S.$, Thousands)

Limited Access to Distribution Channels

If access is limited because of exclusive contracts or because a new product is not seen as important enough, obtaining good distribution becomes a problem. Joint distribution systems may choose not to carry a new competitor, or it may be difficult for a new magazine to gain prominent display at newsstands and magazine racks. This access issue has been a particular problem for cable networks because cable channel capacity has not been high enough in many markets to make channels available to all companies wishing to have their networks carried.

Government Policies

Licensing and franchising regulations may provide barriers to new broadcasters and cablecasters. If the government agency in charge of such issues has only twelve available frequencies, a company that is not granted use of one of those frequencies will not be able to operate a radio station, no matter how much it wishes to do so.

Antitrust and other regulatory controls may limit some firms from entering specific markets in order to preserve competition or

TABLE 3.3
FINANCIAL AND PERFORMANCE PROJECTIONS FOR THE ENTERING PAPER

	Year										10-Year Total
	1	2	3	4	5	6	7	8	9	10	
Market Revenue											
Circulation Revenue	$ 18,000,000	$ 18,000,000	$ 18,000,000	$ 18,000,000	$ 18,000,000	$ 18,000,000	$ 18,000,000	$ 18,000,000	$ 18,000,000	$ 18,000,000	$ 180,000,000
Advertising Revenue	$ 74,400,000	$ 74,400,000	$ 74,400,000	$ 74,400,000	$ 74,400,000	$ 74,400,000	$ 74,400,000	$ 74,400,000	$ 74,400,000	$ 74,400,000	$ 744,000,000
Total Revenue	$ 92,400,000	$ 92,400,000	$ 92,400,000	$ 92,400,000	$ 92,400,000	$ 92,400,000	$ 92,400,000	$ 92,400,000	$ 92,400,000	$ 92,400,000	$ 924,000,000
Entry Paper's Revenue											
Circulation Share of Entry Paper	15%	20%	25%	30%	35%	38%	41%	44%	47%	50%	
Circulation Revenue of Entry Paper	$ 2,700,000	$ 3,600,000	$ 4,500,000	$ 5,400,000	$ 6,300,000	$ 6,840,000	$ 7,380,000	$ 7,920,000	$ 8,460,000	$ 9,000,000	$ 62,100,000
Advertising Share of Entry Paper	10%	15%	20%	25%	27%	30%	35%	40%	45%	50%	
Advertising Revenue of Entry Paper	$ 7,440,000	$ 11,160,000	$ 14,880,000	$ 18,600,000	$ 20,088,000	$ 22,320,000	$ 26,040,000	$ 29,760,000	$ 33,480,000	$ 37,200,000	$ 220,968,000
Circulation and Ad Revenue of Entry Paper	$ 10,140,000	$ 14,760,000	$ 19,380,000	$ 24,000,000	$ 26,388,000	$ 29,160,000	$ 33,420,000	$ 37,680,000	$ 41,940,000	$ 46,200,000	$ 283,068,000
Competitive Increase (15%)[a]	$ 1,521,000	$ 2,214,000	$ 2,907,000	$ 3,600,000	$ 3,958,200	$ 4,374,000	$ 5,013,000	$ 5,652,000	$ 6,291,000	$ 6,930,000	$ 42,460,200
Operating Revenues of Entry Paper	$ 11,661,000	$ 16,974,000	$ 22,287,000	$ 27,600,000	$ 30,346,200	$ 33,534,000	$ 38,433,000	$ 43,332,000	$ 48,231,000	$ 53,130,000	$ 325,528,200
Operating Expenses											
Editorial	$ 9,282,000	$ 9,282,000	$ 9,282,000	$ 9,282,000	$ 9,282,000	$ 9,282,000	$ 9,282,000	$ 9,282,000	$ 9,282,000	$ 9,282,000	$ 92,820,000
Advertising	$ 6,188,000	$ 6,188,000	$ 6,188,000	$ 6,188,000	$ 6,188,000	$ 6,188,000	$ 6,188,000	$ 6,188,000	$ 6,188,000	$ 6,188,000	$ 61,880,000

	Year 1	Year 2	Year 3	Year 4	Year 5	Year 6	Year 7	Year 8	Year 9	Year 10	Total
Circulation	$ 9,282,000	$ 9,282,000	$ 9,282,000	$ 9,282,000	$ 9,282,000	$ 9,282,000	$ 9,282,000	$ 9,282,000	$ 9,282,000	$ 9,282,000	$ 92,820,000
Administration	$ 6,961,500	$ 6,961,500	$ 6,961,500	$ 6,961,500	$ 6,961,500	$ 6,961,500	$ 6,961,500	$ 6,961,500	$ 6,961,500	$ 6,961,500	$ 69,615,000
Marketing and Promotion[b]	$ 10,000,000	$ 10,000,000	$ 10,000,000	$ 10,000,000	$ 10,000,000	$ 10,000,000	$ 10,000,000	$ 10,000,000	$ 10,000,000	$ 10,000,000	$ 100,000,000
Capital Expenditures[c]	$ 2,000,000	$ 2,000,000	$ 2,000,000	$ 4,000,000	$ 4,000,000	$ 4,000,000	$ 4,000,000	$ 4,000,000	$ 4,000,000		$ 30,000,000
Production	$ 11,602,500	$ 11,602,500	$ 11,602,500	$ 11,602,500	$ 11,602,500	$ 11,602,500	$ 11,602,500	$ 11,602,500	$ 11,602,500	$ 11,602,500	$ 116,025,000
Newsprint and Ink[d]	$ 2,107,500	$ 2,810,000	$ 3,512,500	$ 4,215,000	$ 4,917,500	$ 5,339,000	$ 5,760,500	$ 6,182,000	$ 6,603,500	$ 7,025,000	$ 48,472,500
Operating Expense of Entry Paper	$ 57,423,500	$ 58,126,000	$ 58,828,500	$ 59,531,000	$ 60,233,500	$ 62,655,000	$ 63,076,500	$ 63,498,000	$ 63,919,500	$ 64,341,000	$ 611,632,500
Operating Income of Entry Paper	$ (45,769,500)	$ (41,152,000)	$ (36,541,500)	$ (31,931,000)	$ (29,887,300)	$ (29,121,000)	$ (24,643,500)	$ (20,166,000)	$ (15,688,500)	$ (12,211,000)	$ (286,104,300)
Nonoperating Expenses											
Capital Expenditures	$ 100,000,000										$ 100,000,000
Capital Costs[e]	$ 15,441,630	$ 15,441,630	$ 15,441,630	$ 15,441,630	$ 15,441,630	$ 15,441,630	$ 15,441,630	$ 15,441,630	$ 15,441,630	$ 15,441,630	$ 154,416,300
Nonoperating expenses	$ 115,441,630	$ 15,441,630	$ 15,441,630	$ 15,441,630	$ 15,441,630	$ 15,441,630	$ 15,441,630	$ 15,441,630	$ 15,441,630	$ 15,441,630	$ 254,416,300
Net Income of Entry Paper	$ (161,204,130)	$ (56,593,630)	$ (51,983,130)	$ (47,372,630)	$ (45,328,930)	$ (44,562,630)	$ (40,085,130)	$ (35,607,630)	$ (31,130,130)	$ (26,652,630)	$ (540,520,600)

[a] Primarily due to duplicative advertising and circulation.
[b] Estimate includes direct marketing expenditures and the effects of sampling and discounts.
[c] Used for expenditure for land, building, production equipment, vehicles, furnishings, etc., and first-year operating costs.
[d] Variable cost increases proportionately with circulation and advertising market share.
[e] Assuming 9%, 10-year loan.

TABLE 3.4

FACTORS USED TO DIFFERENTIATE SELECTED MEDIA PRODUCTS AND SERVICES AND THEIR COMMON MANIFESTATIONS

	Newspapers	Magazines	Radio Stations	Television Stations	General Online Portals
Time Offered	Morning Evening All Day		Time of specific programming Counterprogramming	Time of specific programming	
Frequency	Daily Weekly	Weekly Monthly Quarterly			Rapidity of content updates
Content Choices	Coverage emphasis News focus Presentation tone Readability level	General interest Specialized interest	Music format Specialized format Mixed format		
Production Choices	Tabloid or broadsheet Paper quality Paper color Ink colors Binding	Size Paper quality Ink colors Binding	Analog Digital Live or taped broadcast Amount of self-production	Analog Digital Live or taped broadcast Amount of self-production	Complexity of design Degree of interactivity Number of graphics Audio Video
Sales Method	Subscription Single-copy sales Free distribution	Subscription Single-copy sales Free/controlled circulation			Subscription Free
Target Audience	General Target	General Target	General Target Segmentation by program	General Target Segmentation by program	
Target Place of Use	Home Office Commuting	Home Office Other	Home Office Commuting	Home Office	Home Office

serve other social purposes. Thus, a newspaper firm may not be able to operate a television station in its hometown if regulations prohibit cross-ownership of media in the same locality.

Competitive Advantages

Certain firms have inherent advantages over other competitors. These arise from factors such as patents, trademarks, reputation, experience, preferred locations, better employees, and innovations. If two firms are considering entering a new market, the better known will be likely to have more success because it already has recognition when it enters the market. Thus, a programmer such as Canal + may be able to enter a new cable market more easily than a smaller, less internationalized firm with less experience in foreign markets.

Overcoming and Reducing Barriers

Barriers to entry and mobility can sometimes be overcome by the ability of existing firms to invest sufficient resources over a longer period of time. A well-funded firm may be able to bear negative or low returns in the short to midterm to achieve desirable long-term returns. Small and start-up firms rarely have sufficient funds on their own to pursue this option.

Firms introducing new techniques and methods of operations that avoid traditional cost structures can sometimes overcome barriers to entry. They can also be overcome by the introduction of products that are sufficiently innovative to surmount the traditional barriers.

Another method of overcoming barriers is to engage in joint ventures with existing firms in the market or in related markets or with firms that have resources needed to overcome the barriers. Such tactics allow one to lessen the risk borne by a single company and to pool competencies in various firms. For example, a magazine with no online experience, or with personnel unfamiliar with the tasks needed to start an online magazine, might enter into a joint venture with a firm that provides online design and management services and telecommunications access.

Government policies can help reduce barriers as a means of increasing competition and the number of firms in an industry. One mechanism is guaranteed and subsidized loan funds that provide venture capital or capital for technology acquisition. Operation subsidies that provide another source of revenue and reduce operating losses in start-up firms can also be provided in some settings. Preferential awarding of licenses and franchises so that small companies have advantages in entering broadcasting or telecommunications is another mechanism of overcoming barriers for new firms.

Suggested Readings

Albarran, Alan B. *Media Economics: Understanding Markets, Industries and Concepts*. Ames: Iowa State University Press, 1996.

Alexander, Alison, James Owers, and Rodney Carveth, eds. *Media Economics Theory and Practice*. Hillsdale, N.J.: Lawrence Erlbaum Associates, 1993.

Coase, R. H. "The Nature of the Firm." *Economica* 4 (1937): 386–405.

Picard, Robert G. *Media Economics: Concepts and Issues*. Thousand Oaks, Calif.: Sage Publications, 1989.

Williamson, O. E. *The Economic Institutions of Capitalism: Firms, Markets, Relational Contracting*. New York: Free Press, 1985.

4

The Influence of the General Economy on Media

GENERAL ECONOMIC AND FINANCIAL FORCES are important to media and communications firms because these business enterprises are simultaneously consumers and producers. Changes in the economy and economic activity affect the consumption of goods and services by media and communications firms as well as the production and sales of media and communications goods and services.

A number of influences by the general economy are significant to financial developments of media firms and have an impact on the well-being of companies and the choices available to managers. This chapter focuses on four economic factors that need to be well understood because of their effects on the operations and financial health of firms.

First, it considers the causes and effects of growth and contraction of the general economy and how these changes affect media and communication firms. Second, the chapter looks at the effect of inflation on these companies. Third, it reviews how interest rates constrain the choices of managers and affect budgets and operations. Finally, the chapter considers the issue of exchange rates and why these rates are important in the globalized and increasingly internationalized environment of media and communication firms.

GROWTH AND CONTRACTION OF THE ECONOMY

Perhaps the most noticeable external influence on short-term performance of media companies results from directional changes in the general economy itself.

Regular growth and contraction in the general economy is often called the "business cycle." These are significant to communications managers because business cycles affect revenue, cost and availability of supplies, profits, production, and employment.

Expansions and contractions of the economy have been recognized for three centuries. Adam Smith, David Ricardo, and John Stuart Mill explained them as the results of external disruptions to production or labor. In the early 1800s business cycles were asserted to result from the underconsumption of goods in the economy. In the early twentieth century, they were explained by investment, cost price, and long-wave theories and then by John Maynard Keynes's argument that investment volatility creates self-generating pressures that lead to recession and recovery.

Today many economists believe that business cycles are natural, self-perpetuating phenomena in which economic forces create prosperity and then other forces react to that prosperity in counteracting ways. The cycle works as illustrated in figure 4.1.

This occurs because prosperity increases the costs of doing business by leading to expansion and increased capacity, increases in wages and benefits, and increases in costs for items such as sup-

Figure 4.1. Economic Forces and Developments that Create and Perpetuate the Business Cycle

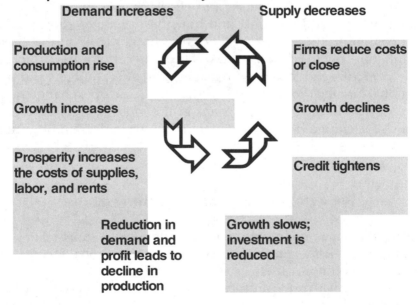

plies, rents, and interest rates on short-term loans. Ultimately, output increases and demand and investment decline, which are greeted by tighter credit, declining growth, and then company reductions in production, workforces, etc.

Although the processes of expansion and contraction are generally agreed upon, economists still debate whether there actually is a cycle per se because the periodicity and magnitude of vacillations are not always consistent. As a result, some economists prefer to use the phrase "fluctuations in the economy." Common language in business and economics still speaks of cycles, however, to indicate these upward and downward movements of the economy.

If a contraction of the business cycle is very strong it can result in a recession or a depression. A depression is a very deep and prolonged recession. Recessions and depressions can also result from other shocks to the economic system, such as a decline in key resources, monetary or fiscal policies, and problems with key customers or trading regions.

As a general rule, companies and investors in companies suffer during recessions because of a decline in income and usually in profit. Depressions and recessions result in fewer sales, less production, lower employment. When the economy improves, this process is reversed. As demand increases and companies experience improvements in their financial performance, they begin investing more money into advertising and other marketing activities.

Media, then, are particularly sensitive to such changes in the economy for two reasons. First, sales of communication products and services are affected by general economic conditions. Second, advertising sales are strongly affected by changes in the general economy.

Sales of communications products and services are affected by fluctuations in the economy because consumers' expenditures overall and expenditures on media are affected by perceptions of their current and future economic situations (see fig. 4.2).

During downturns in the economy, consumers tend to postpone purchases of expensive communications hardware such as television sets, computers, satellite receivers, and stereo systems. Purchases of media "software" such as CDs, videotapes, and DVDs also decline as consumers tighten their belts. The use of subscribed

Figure 4.2. Consumer Sales of Communication Products and Services and the General Economy

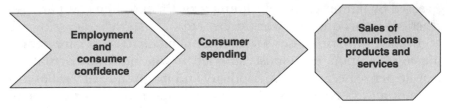

media and communications services declines somewhat as well. For example, premium services offered by cable and satellite television systems show a decline when a significant number of households is most affected by a downturn. In such cases, the group of subscribers most affected tends to reduce or drop premium services and retain only basic services. Except during the most severe downturns, only a small amount of households cut their subscriptions altogether.

Advertising sales are highly influenced by the business cycle and other factors that affect the businesses of major advertisers. The producers and retailers of automobiles, luxury goods, and major appliances are significantly affected because consumers tend to reduce purchases of such items during poor economic times. These companies respond by reducing their advertising budgets and buying fewer advertisements in magazines, newspapers, and on broadcasts, as well as reducing outdoor, cinema, and other types of advertising and promotion. Additionally, advertising for real estate sales, travel services, and employment are significantly reduced (see fig. 4.3).

The effects of recession vary depending upon the depth of the decline and the breadth of sectors of the economy involved. It is

Figure 4.3. Effects of Changes in the Economy on Advertising Sales

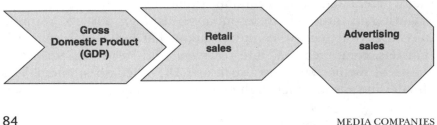

MEDIA COMPANIES

clear, however, that when the gross domestic product (GDP) declines into negative figures, it produces a significant downward movement in advertising expenditures. The rate of decline is highest with a small amount of decline in the GDP and then slows as the depth of decline in the GDP increases, as illustrated in figure 4.4.

The degree to which expenditures are affected is also related to the timing of when advertisers change their purchasing behavior. In most cases it appears that major advertisers reduce expenditures concurrently with changes in the economy that may be the result of their own tracking of sales and the economy.

There is evidence that reductions of advertising in developed nations more strongly affect print media advertising expenditures than expenditures for electronic media, especially television. This may result from differences in the types of advertisers most carried by those media and the uses of media by the advertisers. Newspapers, for example, are the primary advertising medium for retail establishments, especially local retailers. Magazines are widely used by manufacturers and large service providers to advertise a wide range of consumer goods and to support brand images. Specialty magazines also receive a good deal of advertising from retailers serving their fields. Manufacturers and large service firms and a few larger multilocation retailers primarily use television. Some

Figure 4.4. Change in Advertising Expenditures Is Greater than Change in GDP

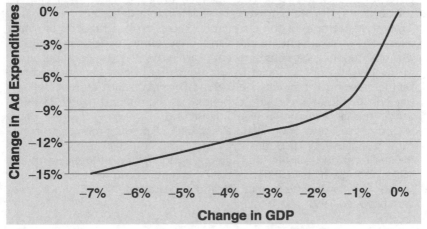

manufacturers, large service firms, and local retailers tend to use radio as a complement to their other advertising choices.

Because recessions affect retail sales, local and large multilocation retailers cut their expenditures, as do real estate firms and automobile dealers. Because such firms are prime advertisers for newspapers and radio, expenditures in these two media fall more noticeably. Television expenditures are apparently less affected because the manufacturers, large service providers, and larger multilocation retailers appear less willing to cut their expenditures in television than in other media.

INFLATION

Inflation is a sustained rise in the general price levels for goods and services that affects the buying power of producers and con-

---

Effects Of Recent Recessions on Media

Examples from several recessions during the 1990s clearly reveal the effects of economic downturns on media products and services.

In the United States during 1990 and 1991, for example, the newspaper industry experienced a serious recession because of a general economic decline in which retail sales in constant dollars declined from a growth rate of 2.7 percent in 1989 to 0.7 in 1990 and finally to −2.0 percent in 1991. Simultaneously bankruptcies and reorganizations of many large department stores and retailers reduced both retail and classified advertising. The newspaper industry suffered an overall decline in advertising revenue of 6 percent between 1990 and 1991 as a result of the downturn (fig. 4.5), its worst recession in four decades.

Another example of the effects of a recession can be seen in total expenditures for advertising in Finland. That country experienced one of the most serious recessions of recent years in the Western world because of the breakup of the Soviet Union, which had been a major trading partner. During the period 1990–93, GDP in constant currency fell 8 percent, but total advertising expenditures plummeted nearly 25 percent in the same period, as seen in figure 4.6.

Declines in the economy also affect sales of media products to consumers, as illustrated in figure 4.7, which shows the decline in consumer expenditures on books in the United Kingdom during the recession of 1993, during which GDP declined 9.8 percent. Consumer expenditures for books followed the general decline and dropped more than 8 percent between 1992 and 1993.

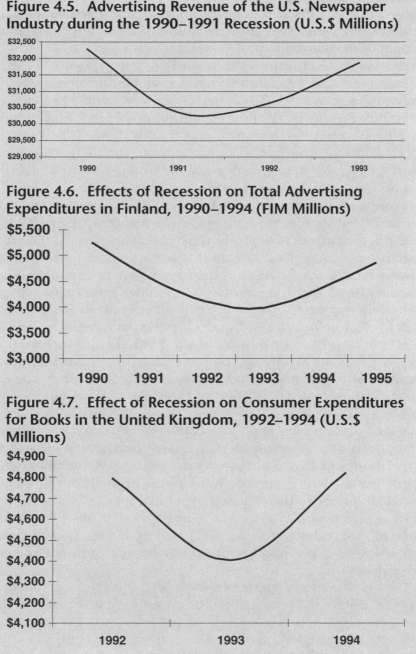

Figure 4.5. Advertising Revenue of the U.S. Newspaper Industry during the 1990–1991 Recession (U.S.$ Millions)

Figure 4.6. Effects of Recession on Total Advertising Expenditures in Finland, 1990–1994 (FIM Millions)

Figure 4.7. Effect of Recession on Consumer Expenditures for Books in the United Kingdom, 1992–1994 (U.S.$ Millions)

sumers by increasing the costs of goods and services. Inflation is caused by a number of factors, including rapid growth in the general economy, concerns over the value of a currency caused by economic turmoil, and war or other national crises.

A nominal level of inflation is normal and generally constant when the economy expands. It tends to diminish when the economy contracts. When inflation ranges between 1 and 3 percent per year, it does not typically pose significant problems for businesses. If inflation rates rise higher, however, it is difficult for firms to increase their turnover and return rates to the higher levels required to achieve real growth rates. This occurs because high inflation rates slow the growth rate of the economy as a whole.

Economists measure inflation by collecting the prices of a sample of goods and services at regular intervals and comparing changes in the aggregate prices to previous periods. The primary measures used are producer price indexes that measure prices paid by producers for necessary resources, and consumer price indexes that measure prices paid by consumers to purchase goods and services.

In the short term, inflation forces businesses to adjust their budgets to account for increased prices; most often it requires them to pass on the costs to consumers in the form of price increases. If the increases are significant, however, they may affect consumer demand adversely and reduce income for the firm, so managers must carefully monitor inflation and the firm's reaction to it.

The ability of media managers to respond to inflation is sometimes limited by sales strategies employed to stabilize audiences and advertising. A magazine that relies primarily on subscribed circulation is unable to increase its prices and revenue until existing subscriptions are fulfilled, thus limiting its ability to respond to increased prices for printing and paper that may result during the subscription period. Similarly, a newspaper that has annual rate contracts with advertisers who purchase large amounts of advertising is unable to respond to inflation by increasing prices for that advertising.

Because businesses operate on fiscal years, the effects of inflation over time are sometimes ignored or seen as unimportant by some managers. This is problematic, however, because in the long term inflation has the effects of decreasing the wealth of firms when the growth of the value of the firms or their assets does not equal or surpass the inflation rates. As a result, some responses must be made to inflation through growth and reinvestment.

When comparing financial data from different time periods (usually years but sometimes quarterly if inflation rates are high), adjustments for inflation need to be made if one is to gain an accurate understanding of trends and developments. To do so, data must be adjusted with a deflator that reduces successive values by the amount of inflation. When a deflator has been used, the data are reported as being in constant currencies (constant $, constant €, constant £, constant ¥, etc.).

A magazine that has been sold at a cover price of $2.50 for the past decade does not offset the costs of its production and distribution today at the same level as ten years ago. In the United States, for example, the purchasing power of that $2.50 in the year 2000 was about one-third lower than it was in 1990.

Adjusting for Inflation Alters Perception of Financial Performance

The usefulness of adjusting for inflation can be seen in the financial performance of a sample media company. If the financial performance of the firm is considered using annual data for operating and net income, the firm appears to be strong and healthy, with both measures increasing each year (table 4.1). Its operating income (revenue) increased from $1.2 billion to $3.5 billion during the ten-year period, experiencing an average annual growth rate of nearly 19 percent per year, and its net income or profit after taxes and adjustments grew an average of 16 percent annually.

If those figures are adjusted for inflation, one gets an additional perspective on the condition of the firm (table 4.2). Operating income increased from $1.2 billion to $2.1 billion, an average annual growth rate of 7 percent. Net income grew from $152 million to $233 million, an annual growth of 5 percent. These figures still indicate overall health, but a closer look reveals that in constant currency the net income figures twice declined, including the current year (Year 10) because inflation rates were stronger than the growth rate for income.

The effects of inflation are quite explicit when current and constant currency figures are displayed in graphic form. This is illustrated in figure 4.8 on page 91 using advertising expenditure data for France, which reveal that although expenditures in 1995 were higher than in 1990 in current currency, they were actually 11 percent lower when viewed in constant currency.

TABLE 4.1
FINANCIAL PERFORMANCE FOR A SAMPLE MEDIA COMPANY (U.S.$ THOUSANDS)

Year	Operating Income	Net Income
1	$1,214,983	$151,985
2	$1,356,171	$172,506
3	$1,519,514	$180,507
4	$1,703,646	$191,665
5	$1,960,421	$223,934
6	$2,209,421	$253,277
7	$2,801,497	$276,404
8	$3,079,447	$319,395
9	$3,314,485	$364,460
10	$3,518,189	$398,509

TABLE 4.2
FINANCIAL PERFORMANCE FOR A SAMPLE MEDIA COMPANY IN CONSTANT CURRENCY (U.S.$ THOUSANDS)

Year	Operating Income (Constant $)	Net Income (Constant $)
1	$1,214,983	$151,985
2	$1,250,961	$157,843
3	$1,320,458	$155,056
4	$1,410,619	$158,699
5	$1,538,755	$175,788
6	$1,652,647	$189,451
7	$2,039,490	$201,222
8	$2,118,660	$219,744
9	$2,124,585	$233,619
10	$2,054,622	$232,729

Some additional problems in analyzing data and correcting for inflation, particularly in cross-national settings, must be noted. This is important in comparing industries or the performance of divisions or subsidiaries operating in other nations. There are sometimes differences in measures used, so that the products and services that make up the national producer and consumer price indexes differ. If these differences are significant, or if costs for only certain resources are being reviewed, one may have to make

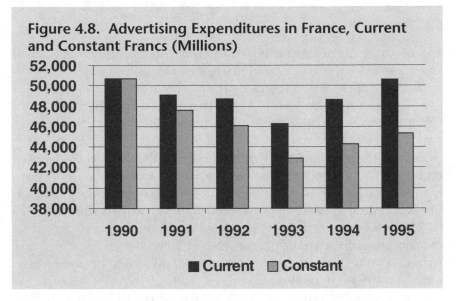

Figure 4.8. Advertising Expenditures in France, Current and Constant Francs (Millions)

specific adjustments or take these into consideration when making comparisons among national media industries and companies.

Additionally there are differences in national and regional inflation rates that may require examination when making comparisons between media firms and national media industries. This occurs because the inflation rate in New Mexico usually differs from that in Massachusetts, the inflation rate in the United Kingdom may differ from that in Germany, and the inflation rate in Japan may differ from that in South Africa.

It should also be noted that communication products and services are not equally affected because they depend on different resources. Broadcasting and telecommunication firms are not affected by increases in paper and ink and distribution costs to the extent that changes in costs for those resources affect print media. As a result, one may need to make distinctions about the effects of inflation rates when comparing the performance of media firms or industries.

When inflation rises to unhealthy levels, political pressures rise for governments to implement fiscal and monetary policies designed to slow or lower inflation rates. These general economic policies ultimately affect sales of media products and services and the short-term performance of media firms.

Intcrest rates represent the cost for borrowing capital. If interest rates increase, the cost of acquiring the capital increases. This affects the ability of managers to fund new initiatives, expand, or arrange cash flow financing. If the cost rises too high, many firms cannot borrow and use the capital in an effective way to produce profit.

For example, a cable television network that has plans to purchase shares in satellites that will allow it to expand its operations into Asia may have based the budget for the operation on obtaining the capital at an interest rate of 6.25 percent. If the rate rises to 7 or 7.5 percent, the management could be forced to postpone or abandon the expansion because it may not able to operate profitably or recoup the investment in an adequate period of time based on the higher rates.

Because higher interest rates reduce the growth and activities of firms, there is less investment and general economic activity tends to slow when interest rates increase. Conversely, when interest rates are lower, firms have a greater ability to use the capital effectively and tend to make investments and increase production in ways that help the general economy grow.

The link between interest rates and the general economy is used by central banks to help regulate the growth rate of the economy and inflation rates that move simultaneously with such growth. By deliberately increasing and decreasing interest rates, banks such as the Federal Reserve Bank and the European Central Bank can slow or spur economic activity and inflation.

When interest rates are increased, the result is typically a slowing of the economy, which lowers sales of goods and services, including media and communications goods and services. And, as noted previously, when retail sales decline, advertising expenditures by manufacturers, retailers, employers, and other advertisers also decline, reducing the revenue of media firms supported by advertising.

Interests rates are important to media and communications firms because nearly all firms are dependent upon loans to fund acquisitions, growth, and large capital expenditures. The largest media firms borrow billions of dollars of capital to carry out their

Effects of Interest Rates on Company Costs

The costs of borrowing capital are affected by interest rates and the length of loan terms. Even small changes in interest rates have significant effects on the costs of capital. For example, a one-half percent increase in the interest rate on a $1 million loan will cost a firm an additional $12,985 over a five-year period. Similarly, as the length of the loan term increases, it costs more to borrow the capital. But the rate of increase declines annually because each additional year the principal remaining on the loan declines. The effects of these interest rate and time factors can be seen in the following examples.

Example 1

A newspaper publisher is borrowing $15 million on a fifteen-year loan to help finance the purchase of a new printing press. If the company is able to obtain financing at a 6.5 percent interest rate instead of 8.5 percent, it will save $3.1 million in the cost of the capital (table 4.3).

Example 2

A television station needs an additional $5 million to acquire digital studio equipment and remodel its facilities so that it can produce news and local programming in full digital format to be broadcast on its new digital transmitter.

If the management is able to select a five-year loan instead of a ten-year loan term, it will save $3.3 million in the cost of capital (table 4.4). The table indicates that the cost of capital increases with the length of the loan because the capital is tied up longer. However, the rate of cost increase from each of the previous years diminishes annually.

TABLE 4.3

COST OF $15,000,000 CAPITAL FOR A 15-YEAR PRESS LOAN AT
THREE DIFFERENT INTEREST RATES

Interest Rate	Cost of Capital
6.5%	$ 8,519,898
7.5	10,029,334
8.5	11,587,968

TABLE 4.4

COST OF $15,000,000 CAPITAL FOR A FIVE-, SEVEN-, AND TEN-YEAR
LOAN FOR STUDIO DIGITALIZATION AT 7.5% INTEREST RATE

Loan Term (years)	Cost of Capital	Change
5	$3,034,154	—
6	3,673,321	$638,167 (21.2%)
7	4,326,074	652,753 (18.9)
8	4,992,772	666,698 (15.4)
9	5,672,846	680,074 (13.7)
10	6,366,518	694,672 (12.2)

strategies and operations, and even small media firms often have millions of dollars in such debt. The cost of this capital is thus significant to many managerial decisions about whether to reinvest in equipment, whether to acquire or establish new operations, what levels of return will be required from subsidiaries or divisions, and how various departments will be budgeted.

Over time interest rates force managers to make decisions about whether to borrow capital, how much to borrow, how long to borrow, whether to use additional financial resources to pay down debt more rapidly than planned, or whether to try to refinance existing borrowed capital.

EXCHANGE RATES

Exchange rates represent the value given to a currency when it is exchanged for another currency. These rates change not only daily but by the minute, and few companies are completely unaffected by these changes.

If a company's entire operations and exchange relations take place within one country, exchange rates are a relatively unimportant economic factor. If purchases are made outside of the country, or involve products made outside of the country, or if the company has sales outside of the country, exchange rates will affect its costs and revenues.

Media companies typically have a number of direct or indirect activities that involve the flow of goods and services and money across borders. For example, a magazine publisher in the Netherlands may purchase coated paper from a German paper manufacturer. A Hollywood film studio rents and sells motion pictures and videos worldwide. A newspaper publisher in Brazil may purchase a printing press from a Japanese manufacturer. A Web portal operating in Australia may purchase rights to carry information from a news service in the United Kingdom. A publisher in New York may have books printed in Hong Kong.

Because of these operations and relationships, exchange rates for currencies are important factors in the profitability of firms as the number of nondomestic activities increase. The effect of changes in exchange rates is to make imports and exports become more or less expensive. Ultimately, consumption and production will increase or decrease somewhat when significant changes in exchange rates occur.

Domestic accounting standards, such as Statement 52 of the Financial Accounting Standards Board in the United States, directs how the financial operations in foreign currencies should be converted and reported on income statements and balance sheets. Gains or losses in conversion are typically reported as adjustments after operating income on the operating statements and as adjustments to owner's equity on the balance sheet.

The importance of exchange rates on corporate performance was illustrated recently by their effects on CanWest Global Communications, the Canadian media conglomerate. The firm, which owns the TEN television group in Australia and Global Television in New Zealand, experienced a drop in corporate earnings (EBITDA—earnings before interest, taxes, depreciation, and amortization) of CAN$5 million because of foreign currency losses. The 16 percent decline in corporate earnings in the first quarter of 2001 resulted because the Australian dollar declined 14 percent

Effects of Exchange Rates on Company Operations

The effects of changes in exchange rates can either help or hurt the purchasing power and revenue of a firm, depending upon which of the two currencies involved is strengthened or diminished. This can be seen in the following examples.

Example 1: The Price of Imported Newsprint

A newspaper corporation in the United States agrees to purchase 50,000 metric tons of newsprint for its local newspapers from a Finnish newsprint company in the coming year at €400 per ton, at a total price of €20 million payable in Euros. At the time of the contract the exchange rate is such that the newsprint will cost the company 21 million U.S. dollars.

If the exchange rates change, however, the newspaper company will pay more or less than the $21 million. For example, if the exchange rate for the Euro rises just 5 percent in favor of the European currency, the newspaper company will lose more than $1 million because it will have to exchange 22,050,000 U.S. dollars for the Euros.

Example 2: The Price of CDs

A British record company sells compact discs featuring its recording artists worldwide. The firm sells approximately 10 million copies annually in India at an average annual price of 500 rupees, producing a turnover of 5 billion rupees. Past experience has shown that lowering the price by 50 rupees will result in an increase of sales of 500,000 copies, producing a turnover of 4.725 billion rupees but a decline of 275 million rupees in revenue.

If the pound diminishes against the rupee by 10 percent and the prices for the imported CDs are lowered, accordingly the company will increase sales by 500,000 CDs. The increased sales will provide additional income for the company's artists, but the company itself may be helped, hurt, or relatively unaffected by the change depending upon its costs structures. If the net profit from the increased sales is more than 275 million rupees, the company will benefit from the increased sales. If the net profit is less than 275 million rupees, the company will be harmed by the change in exchange rates, even though sales have increased.

Example 3: Selling Postproduction Services

The value of services received is also affected by exchange rates. For example, a production house in London that films and provides postproduction services for television advertisements can have its workload reduced by the effect of exchange rates on its prices.

If a Japanese advertising agency is considering the company for production of an advertisement, the choice between the British firm and an equally proficient production company in Los Angeles may be based on the value received for the cost.

If the Japanese yen is weaker against the British pound than the U.S. dollar, the agency may choose to use the U.S. firm. If the agency views the two firms' abilities, skills, technology, and creativity as equal, the decision may be primarily based on the amount of yen that must be exchanged for pounds or dollars to obtain the same services.

and the New Zealand dollar declined 18 percent against the Canadian dollar.

PREPARING FOR ECONOMIC CHANGES

Media and communications firm managers who wish to prepare for changes that will affect revenues and costs, and the concurrent problems these present for their companies' operations and performance, watch for changes in economic indicators that signal a downturn or upturn in the economy. Statistics on production and retail sales, inflation, interest rates, and exchange rates provide evidence of the changing state of the general economy and the situation of the firm.

Changes in the economy occur locally, nationally, regionally, and globally. Managers need to be aware of changes in all locations in which products and services are purchased and sold and locations from which advertising is obtained because the economies of different geographic areas change in different ways and at different times.

Managers should have a clear understanding of their priorities and contingency plans for what their firms or divisions will do when the general economy changes. Otherwise they are doomed to riding out economic turbulence and hoping they will not sink in the storm. If one monitors economic changes, however, one can prepare and implement strategies before the storm fully arrives to avoid or reduce its effects.

Preparing for Fluctuations in the Economy

Because the business cycle is created by a group of changing events over time, the factors that create changes in the general economy that will affect media companies can be monitored regularly using both general and sophisticated methods.

Most of the influencing forces that create changes are regularly reported upon by the business press in publications such as the *Wall Street Journal, Financial Times, Investor's Business Daily, Barron's,* and *Business Week.* These stories result from monthly and quarterly statistical reports from government agencies and central banks and sometimes include forecasts for future developments. A variety of other business and economic publications and newsletters track developments in the general economy in individual nations. By attending to such stories a manager can get a reasonable understanding of where the economy is in a business cycle and what the short- and midterm prospects are for the overall economy.

More sophisticated methods of tracking and forecasting are available by specific and regular tracking of the economy in the national and local markets in which firms operate. These can be conducted by corporate intelligence or research departments or by collecting and tracking available economic data at the company or unit level each quarter. Some firms, both large and small, keep economists on contract or in part- or full-time employment to track and forecast economic developments and how they will affect the firm's operations.

With a good understanding of economic trends and forecasts, the management of a magazine corporation can decide whether it is an auspicious time to expand or contract operations, introduce new magazines or online services, increase employment, acquire or reduce debt, or make other decisions affecting financial operations. If the economy is expanding and expected to continue growing in the coming quarters or year(s), increased costs can reasonably be expected to be offset by increased revenue as sales increase correspondingly. If the economy is contracting, that expectation is unrealistic, and the managers may even need to prepare contingency plans for reductions in expenditures if a decline in the economy is expected.

Preparing for Changes in Inflation

Inflation is rarely a sudden and unexpected development, absent extraordinary shocks to the economy such as war. In developed economies inflation tends to develop more slowly so that monthly and quarterly reports provide sufficient time to respond.

As previously discussed, inflation has the effect of reducing asset values and inducing economic choices that slow the general economy.

When inflation is high, the manager of a newspaper company will ensure that company reserve funds for future capital expenditures are held in investments that will not be adversely affected by inflation. If the inflation rates are rising significantly in a short period of time, managers will work to collect accounts payable more rapidly or shorten times for payment so that the values of the accounts are not diminished by the inflation.

Preparing for Changes in Interest Rates

Interest rates tend to change slowly, rising or falling monthly or quarterly. By following the prime rate or the basic business loan rates from a firm's primary bank, a manager can determine the direction of changes. By monitoring the general economy through general and specialized methods, a manager can see the trend of change over time.

Preparation for changes in interest rates is important if the firm is expecting to borrow capital or has adjustable rate debts.

If a cable system operator, for example, is planning to borrow capital to upgrade its system into a multiple-use fiber optic network, managers will find it prudent to base financial plans on several potential interest rates if changes are anticipated. If these different projections are used in making the decision of whether to go ahead with the project, the managers will not encounter great surprises in their financial performance based on the interest rate the loan ultimately requires.

Preparing for Changes in Exchange Rates

In order to minimize the financial effects of currency rate changes, managers of media firms operating internationally can use a variety of currency exposure management techniques, that is, strategies for reducing the risks of holding funds in currencies that are volatile and likely to fluctuate. They begin with regular, often daily, monitoring of currencies in countries in which they have subsidiaries, divisions, or significant sales. When currencies become unstable, they may engage in hedging practices to offset assets with equivalent liabilities in local currencies. Because both assets and liabilities in the local currency are affected equally, exchange issues do not become a financial factor in the health of the firm.

If managers fear that the value of the currency will decline, they can reduce cash that will be affected by the change in the worrisome currency through purchases of inventory or fixed assets. They can also reduce trade credit extended or terms of credit in nations with worrisome currencies so that the value of these current assets is not significantly affected.

Managers can also borrow in domestic currency to replace advances by the parent firm in a stronger currency or vary the currency in billing for international transfers of components, goods, or services. They can also engage in forward exchange rate activities (a form of buying and selling currency futures) or use swap arrangements in which it is agreed to exchange currency at a future date and specified rate. The latter strategies provide a form of insurance against significant changes in currency value.

Managers need to be aware of the influences of these economic factors on a company and its operations. By understanding their impact, following trends and forecasts, and preparing plans to respond to changes, managers of media firms prepare their firms for survival and the creation of greater stability in the financial performance of the firm over time.

SUGGESTED READINGS

Barro, Robert J. *Modern Business Cycle Theory*. Cambridge, Mass.: Harvard University Press, 1989.
Baye, Michael R. *Managerial Economics and Business Strategy*. New York: McGraw-Hill, 1999.

Cooley, Thomas F. *Frontiers of Business Cycle Research*. Princeton: Princeton University Press, 1995.

Corden, Warner Max. *Inflation, Exchange Rates, and the World Economy*. Chicago: University of Chicago Press, 1986.

Maurice, S. Charles, and Christopher R. Thomas. *Managerial Economics*. New York: McGraw-Hill, 1998.

Wessells, Walter J. *Economics*. Hauppauge, N.Y.: Barrons Educational Series, 2000.

5

Audiences and Consumers

THE CONCEPTS of consumers and audiences are not synonymous when dealing with media and communications industries. Despite the tendency to use the two interchangeably in common discussion, the differences between the two concepts are important and affect how their activities are measured and understood.

Consumers are individuals or firms who acquire and consume something, typically through a monetary exchange. Individuals purchasing subscriptions to satellite television systems or buying CD players are clearly consumers, as are online content providers purchasing the rights to material to place on their sites.

The term "audience," however, focuses not merely on acquisition but on actual use of the product or service by persons. Members of an audience may or may not fall into the category of consumers depending upon whether they pay for the media or communication product. This latter distinction is a fine point, however, because even if individuals don't make monetary payments for a product or service, they must exchange the very scarce resource of time when they use media or other communication products or services.

In the last two decades, as the number of television, cable, and satellite channels have risen dramatically across the developed world, the amount of time spent on television viewing has not risen proportionally because demand for more content has grown more slowly than the supply of programming. This is further constrained by the fact that the time available for viewing is limited by needs for sleep, work, and other daily activities.

The basic relationship requirements for use of media and communication products and services are given in table 5.1 and show that individuals who use them are variously consumers, audiences, or both.

This chapter will explore these audience and consumer relation-

TABLE 5.1
RELATIONSHIP REQUIREMENTS FOR USERS TO SELECTED MEDIA
AND COMMUNICATIONS

	Hardware	*Software/Content*	*Additional Consumption Required*
Newspapers		Consumer of copies Audience of copies	
Magazines		Consumer of copies Audience of copies	
Books		Consumer of copies Audience of copies	
Telephone	Consumer of telephone/line	Consumer of telephony services	
Radio	Consumer of radio receiver	Audience of programming	Electricity/batteries
Television	Consumer of television receiver	Audience of programming	Electricity
Cable Television	Consumer of television receiver	Consumer of service subscription and decoder Audience of programming	Electricity
Videocassette/DVD Player	Consumer of television receiver/screen Consumer of videocassette/DVD player	Consumer of recordings Audience of recordings	Electricity
Internet	Consumer of computer Consumer of modem Consumer of telephone line or mobile hardware	Consumer of telephony services Consumer of Internet access service Audience of Internet content	Electricity

ships with media and issues that influence how companies deal with the individuals with whom they interact.

We need to understand the idea of the audience as an abstract concept denoting those persons who attend to a communications channel. It is not the population. It is not those who have access to a medium or channel. It is those who actually select a channel for use. The audience is the whole of those persons that is measured as a collective. Nevertheless, it is made up of individuals, and the behavior of these individuals dictates the behavior of the audience.

These individuals are different persons who use communications to satisfy their different wants and needs for information, ideas, and diversion in different ways. They spend different amounts of time serving their different wants with different media and in doing so create multiple audiences, that is, multiple collections of individuals seeking to serve those needs simultaneously.

The audience for a particular media channel is never stable. It is a constantly changing collective. There is rarely a single audience for any media channel, but rather there are many audiences for most channels.

A central reality of audiences in a multiple-channel world is that they cannot be controlled but can merely be courted. In order to court audiences in a highly competitive environment, media managers in broadcasting, cable, and publishing—especially magazine publishers—tend to engage in audience segmentation. This means that they work to serve an audience with characteristics that differ from the general audience for their medium.

The forces promoting these segmentation efforts are made possible by advances in audience measurement that stem from the audience fragmentation created by multiple channels, audience polarization to specific content of their choice, and advertiser interests in reaching specialized audiences.

Media content providers tend to segment the audiences by their motives for using media, the dominant characteristics of these groups of persons, and their interests. In doing so they make efforts to appeal to different groups with different types of content and to offer a package of content that maximizes the audience that they have chosen to reach.

At the broad level, print media and newspapers in particular tend to emphasize serving the information-seeking motives of audiences, whereas electronic media typically emphasize serving entertainment issues. This does not mean there is not entertainment or diversionary material in print media or informational material in electronic media, only that the overall emphases differ in terms of motivations served.

Even within a media firm there are efforts to appeal to different audiences. Thus, a television channel may offer a variety of programming that caters to women staying in the home during the day, young persons home from school in the afternoon, workers arriving home in the early evening, and a broad general audience in the evening. Similarly, a sailing magazine may have material of general interest to all sailors, recipes and cooking tips for those who prepare food on board, technical materials for those who make repairs, and games for children who may be aboard.

In order to segment and target audiences effectively, media managers make significant efforts to understand the wants and needs of audiences.

Wants and Needs of Audiences

As noted above, media and communications users have individual purposes, desires, and use patterns. Collectively, however, these individuals constitute the audiences with collective wants and needs that are served and sought by content providers.

These wants and needs include information on events and public activities occurring at the local, national, and international levels, discussions of ideas and opinions, entertainment or diversion, and information on how to meet other wants and needs. This last category includes information in the form of advertising about the availability and pricing of goods individuals consume, information on employment offers, listings of community activities, etc.

Individuals and audiences want media that can be acquired or accessed with ease. This means that they do not wish to engage in complicated processes to receive media and that systems for delivery need to operated simply. These needs are served, for example, by publishers who made it easy for persons wanting to obtain subscriptions to magazines or newspapers to do so through simple postcards, phone calls, or Web sites. Similarly, manufacturers of hardware and software designed to make video recordings of television programs easier are serving the need for easy acquisition of the programs.

Media users also want the costs of acquisition to be low because, like all consumers, they have limited financial resources and use those resources for a variety of purposes. This is why free media such as free television have larger audiences than media for which payments must be made. And when payments are required, audiences want the payments to be low. This, of course, serves as a counteracting economic force to media and communications firms that want the payments to be as high as possible.

In addition to the desires for easy and inexpensive acquisition, audiences want to have high-quality media and communication products. This concept of high quality should not be confused with the concepts of high and popular culture. In this market sense, high quality refers to production qualities evidenced in writing and editing, acting or performance, direction, imagery, reproduction, etc.

The degree to which media and communication products serve these various needs affects their success in generating audiences. A significant limitation on the ability of managers to meet these wants and needs is that there are conflicts among the wants and needs and conflicts in patterns of how they are fulfilled. Audiences, for example, want high-quality television programs but are not willing to pay for everything they watch. Also, the amount of information and the pattern of information and entertainment content sought differ widely, and media try to find a balance of methods of serving these different wants and needs.

Audience Measures

Media managers spend a great deal of effort and money trying to understand audiences and their behavior so they can create strategies to optimally serve the conflicting wants and needs. The tools of audience research are used for these purposes, and they include business data analysis, market data analysis, survey and focus group methods, and use monitoring methods.

Three major types of audience measurements are employed. First, demographic measurement methods are used to help identify the basic characteristics of an audience and to identify dominant audience elements. This measurement is concerned with describing *who* the audience is. The primary characteristics studied elements such as age, gender, income, language, and race/ethnic group.

The second type of measure is psychographic measurement, which is concerned with the internal attributes of the audience. It focuses on *what* they are and *how* they think. Indicators used in this type of analysis focus on attitudes and opinions, values, needs, personality, preferences, and interests.

A third type of measure develops profiles of audience groupings by lifestyle. It is concerned with how audiences live and what they do with their time. To make these determinations, researchers study time expenditures, activities, social contexts, purchasing behavior, product uses, and media use patterns.

Audience measures are used to help position media products, to differentiate them from other media products, and to differentiate audiences that can then be made available to advertisers. The results are used to make market and product strategy choices that segment audiences by audience motives, type, usage, interest, and quality of use.

The audience measures and their usefulness are not universally lauded, although they are widely utilized by media and advertisers. A number of problems have led to criticisms of inaccuracies in measurement and different means of measurement. Advertisers are wary of data reported by media and have sought to have the data audited by independent organizations to ensure accurate and standardized reporting of media use and audience characteristics. These audits are typically done by organizations created jointly or supported by advertising and media companies. The earliest auditing organizations were created for newspapers, but organizations now provide similar auditing of audiences for magazines, freesheets/direct mail, radio, television, and Internet media.

Over the years there have been changes in the perception of what should actually be measured and debates over what is actually measured. Depending on the method employed, audience research measures availability, reception, penetration, and reach, or actual use of a medium.

In measuring audiences in the newspaper and magazine industries, for example, one can measure output by the number of copies produced in a press run, the number of copies delivered to homes and retailers, paid circulation, household penetration, readers per copy, or circulation within the population.

Cable television audience research can measure households passed by cable or homes with televisions as a measure of availability. But it can also measure reception by types of subscriptions, the penetration by number of homes with cable, and the reach of cable television by the number of persons in those homes. In addition, research can measure cable use by demographics, the amount of use, how it is used, under what conditions it is used, and for what purposes.

In studying television and cable television use, researchers use a variety of methods. Sometimes diaries are used and TV audiences record when they watch and what they view. The diary method is problematic, however, because it requires literacy and viewers must remember to complete the diaries daily. This method may also skew results because research has shown that diaries are more likely to be completed by women than men.

Another method is to employ a use recorder that electronically tracks usage. A problem with this method is that it merely records when a television is on and to which channel it is tuned. It does not record actual viewing or who is viewing. To overcome these problems researchers created technologies in which individual viewers sign in regularly to show who is actually watching. The reliability of results obtained by such methods has been criticized, however, because many viewers contacted by researchers refuse to use them, men are more likely to record their use than women, and younger, heavy television users are more likely to record use than are other persons.

As a result of such problems there are clearly difficulties with the accuracy, representativeness, and use of broadcast media ratings. Critics have also argued that there is an over-reliance on rating in programming and advertising decisions and that important statistical significance issues in the data are often ignored.

Advertisers and online media firms are currently wrestling with determining how to measure audience use of the Internet. Some have used measures of the number of computer users, but this is highly problematic because using computer penetration to measure Internet use is like using literacy to measure magazine readership. Others have argued that online service subscription is an appropriate measure, but the availability of the Internet is not synonymous with its use. Some advertisers and media prefer the number of hits on a particular site, but these may be the result of multiple hits by a few users and do not necessarily mean that a hit was effective use. Others have argued that the time connected or the time spent viewing a site are important because a longer connection presumably means more use and exposure to messages. Others argue that the proper measure should be interaction such as click-throughs, downloads, or orders.

The debates over measuring audiences will continue as technologies change and the ability to measure different audience aspects changes. Media managers need to be aware that the type of measures they are given result from the methods employed and that the methods used must be taken into consideration when making decisions about audiences and content.

Audience Fragmentation

The basic problems of audience creation, segmentation, and measurement are compounded as the number of channels of communications increase. As the number of choices rise and individuals' behaviors diverge, the mass audience fragments. *Audience fragmentation* is a term that describes this process and the result of demassification of the audience. It represents the breakdown of a mass audience into smaller audiences.

Audience fragmentation is the inevitable and unstoppable consequence of increasing the channels available to audiences. It is true whether one is discussing publishing, broadcasting, the Internet, or other forms of communications involving multiple content providers and individuals.

The result of fragmentation can be clearly seen in the decline of average television audience share when the number of available channels increases (fig. 5.1). The share of the total television audi-

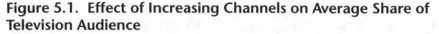
Figure 5.1. Effect of Increasing Channels on Average Share of Television Audience

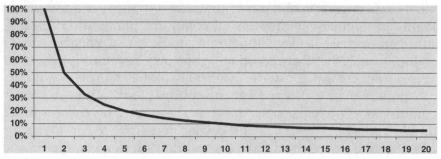

ence drops dramatically with the addition of each new channel. The share of the total audience is 100 percent with one channel, of course, but it plummets to an average share of 20 percent of the total audience with only five channels and then to 5 percent at twenty channels.

When one looks beyond averages at actual television and cable markets, one finds that some channels must struggle to survive with only 1 or 2 percent shares after about a dozen channels are available because they fall below the average share of the total television audience. This occurs because it is rare that audiences watch each of the channels equally, and the fragmentation pattern results from individual choices.

This, of course, raises the question of whether individuals view channels or programs. When the number of channels is low, viewers tend to watch channels. As the number of channels increases, however, particular programs become attractive regardless of channel. Nevertheless, there is a tendency for individuals to focus most viewing on a relatively few number of channels even in a multichannel environment.

There are also some national and industry structural factors that reduce the rapid decline of audiences in some markets. National language can be a significant protection, and channels that provide content in that language tend to have higher than average ratings when other channels provide content in other languages. Similarly, when domestic news, domestic cultural content, and domestic entertainment content are available from only a few channels, these tend to get higher than average ratings.

These fragmentation issues and patterns create an environment in which managers' choices are constrained, and many pursue similar types of strategies that limit innovation and diversity in content and approach.

Time and Media Use

Time is a scarce resource that is becoming increasingly significant to the media environment and media research. The temporal demands of modern society are placing increased pressure on individuals' leisure time and media use.

Time spent on media and communications is part of the overall time use patterns of individuals and audiences. Approximately one-third of a person's time is unavailable for media use in average lives because it is used for sleep. Another third is typically consumed by work, schooling, and other daily routines during which only limited media use can occur. The final third of the day is allocated to commuting, shopping, eating, and leisure.

The large portions of media use devoted to entertainment and diversion can be considered just one of the myriads of possible leisure time activities such as sports, performances, and hobbies. It is the time available for this type of activity that media companies seek as well as that time when limited use can occur as other activities take place.

Individuals make personal time decisions, but there are collective uses of time for overall activity and media use. Americans, for example, collectively spend about two-thirds of their media time use on electronic media and only about one-third on print media (see fig. 5.2). These use patterns reflect a difference in the ways and purposes for which audiences use different media.

Companies that are introducing new media or increasing the number of units of a medium must then try to induce audiences or consumers to alter their media time use patterns or to increase their overall media use time by taking time away from other activities.

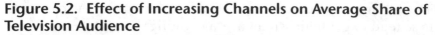

Figure 5.2. Effect of Increasing Channels on Average Share of Television Audience

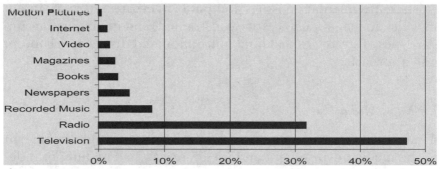

Source: Calculated from hours per person per year data reported by U.S. Census Bureau, *Statistical Abstract of the United States, 1999,* table 920.

CONSUMERS

As previously noted, consumers in a media and communication context are the individuals and companies who purchase media and the individuals and companies who purchase advertising.

Consumer spending data reveal how much revenue is available from consumers, how consumers are dividing their spending among media, and how demand is shifting over time. Spending is typically measured by tracking actual monetary expenditures and expenditures as a percentage of all spending.

Actual monetary spending focuses on the amount of money paid by consumers for something like mass media or all communications products and services. Such expenditures are typically reported as the total amount of money spent, the total amount of money spent per each household or individual, or the total amount of money spent on each type of media or communication product or service.

The actual amount of money spent, however, does not give us an understanding of the relative importance of the media expenditures in comparison to other spending. This is typically done by comparing media expenditures to total spending.

When dealing with individuals or households, the best figures are based on disposable personal income (DPI), because it is based on the actual money with which consumers make choices (i.e., money left after taxes). Media spending can thus be reported as a percentage of DPI.

It is often useful to compare spending patterns over time to gain an understanding of overall changes and trends. Such comparisons, however, face the two major problems of currency value differences and market size difference.

The first problem with comparisons results because currency value changes over time because of inflation and other factors. Thus, if consumers spent $500 million on audio recordings in 1940, the amount held more value than if they spent $500 million on audio recordings today.

The second problem with comparisons occurs because market size changes with time. The population is constantly changing and altering the potential for sales. For example, the world had only 2.5 billion people in 1950, whereas today it has 6 billion inhabitants. Thus, if 500 million people bought magazines in 1950, it was a greater portion of the population than if the same number bought magazines today.

The primary means for overcoming these difficulties is to use currency figures in constant currencies that adjust for changes in monetary value and to adjust market size by using figures based on expenditures per household or individual.

Another means of understanding collective consumer behavior related to the media and communication products and services is measurement of household penetration rates. This allows managers to follow the acquisition of new products and services and to observe media and communication use patterns when constructing business strategies and plans.

When one looks at such patterns, one immediately sees that there are significant differences in the penetration of various media and communications products and services in households, with the radio, television, and telephone being the most acquired products and services (see fig. 5.3).

Various types of penetration rates are also used to measure how rapidly different technologies have been adopted. One can, for example, study how rapidly telephones reached a certain number of households or a percentage of the population and compare the time to how rapidly mobile phones reached the same number of

Figure 5.3. Penetration of Selected Media and Communications in U.S. Households

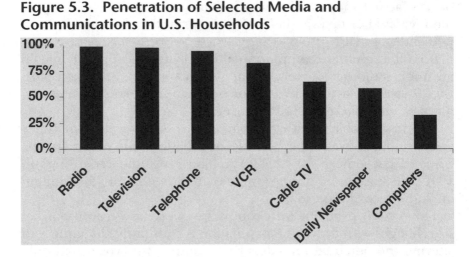

households or percentage of the population. This type of comparison must be made carefully, however, to ensure that the comparisons are appropriate, as shown in the box "Problems with Media Data Use."

Media companies are increasingly creating consumer relationships with those who read, listen to, or view their content. Much of this trend is related to financial demands created by increasing audience segmentation and fragmentation. The dominant business model of the twentieth century—particularly for commercial broadcasting—cannot produce sufficient revenue to cover operating costs as the audience shares decline because of segmentation and fragmentation. As a result, audiences are being increasingly asked to bear costs they had not previously borne, thus being transformed into consumers making monetary payments for cable television, satellite television, and premium services. Even in print media, where advertisers had previously borne large portions of the expenses, additional costs are beginning to be shifted to readers because advertisers are no longer willing to pay as much for de-massified audiences. Many online, multimedia, and mobile telephone content services operate with direct payments from users, but users are currently resisting making payments for content on most newspaper and magazine online operations.

In 2000 American consumers spent an average of $630 annually per person on media consumption, with the largest expenditures

Problems with Media Use Data: Did Consumers Really Jump to the Web Faster than Other Media?

In recent years it has been argued that the rapidity of expansion of the Internet is unusual and that consumers' acceptance shows it is an extremely desirable technology. A widely distributed group of statistics used to illustrate the point shows the number of years it took for the World Wide Web to reach 50 million users globally.

Telephone	74 years
Radio	38 years
Personal Computer	16 years
Television	13 years
World Wide Web	4 years

Setting aside issues of whether the numbers themselves are accurate, can one accept the figures as meaningful comparisons, as many observers have done? Unfortunately, the comparisons are highly problematic for a number of reasons.

The first reason is that the different media were introduced at times when the population differed greatly. Gaining 50 million users in the year 2000, when the global population was 6.1 billion, represents a different success rate than reaching 50 million users in 1900, when world population was estimated to be 1.65 billion.[1] As a result the consumption comparison of World Wide Web penetration is fallacious. To improve the calculation, one would at least need to adjust comparative data for the population at the time of the introduction of the technology and the date at which it reached the 50 million users mark.

The cost of acquisition of the technologies is hardly comparable as well. Even by today's standard, the cost of a television is far higher than the cost of acquiring World Wide Web access if one already has a computer. This doesn't even begin to account for the issues of the value of currency and the differences in disposable income available to consumers at the different points when the technologies were introduced. Even then, however, the comparison would be highly problematic for several reasons.

First, the existence of the telephone requires electricity and a telephone network. The telephone was introduced relatively concurrently with electrification in many parts of the United States before and at the

---

[1] United Nations, 1996, "World Population from Year 0 to Stabilization," gopher:// gopher.undp.org:70/00/ungophers/popin/wdtrends/histor, and U.S. Bureau of the Census, "World PopClock Projection," http://www.census.gov/cgi-bin/ipc/popclockw.

turn of the twentieth century, and the penetration of both technologies was related to population mobility, urbanization, and the development of large businesses. Because the availability of electricity and telephone networks was limited, much of the U.S. population and that of the rest of the world—even in relatively developed nations—could not have had a telephone even if they wanted one at that time.

Radio was similarly affected by the fact that electrification was needed and the ability to receive radio broadcasts was required. Because electrification of areas such as North America and Europe was still underway when radio was introduced, and because many persons with electricity could even then not receive signals because transmitters were not located within their reception area, they could not have made use of a radio receiver.

Television and the World Wide Web were introduced at much later states in development. Both are dependent upon electrification and telephone systems that were already in place throughout the developed world and to a less extent elsewhere.[2] And both were able to use the technologies and infrastructure developed by heavy investments in the creation and development of the Internet and World Wide Web by the U.S. military and the European nuclear science community. Thus, the comparison to the earlier technologies that did not have preexisting infrastructures upon which to build gives a false picture of consumption desires or abilities.

Those factors taken into consideration, it really is impossible to tell from available information whether the Internet attracted consumers more rapidly than other media. The example, however, illustrates that one must have a critical approach to consumption and audience data upon which one is basing business strategies and decisions in media firms. As with all statistics, one must consider how they were gathered, what they actually measure, and whether they are comparable to other data.

going for television and cable, video recordings, and books (fig. 5.4).

DEMAND AND PRICES OF MEDIA PRODUCTS AND SERVICES

The basic economic principle of demand indicates that the willingness of individuals to consume is related to price. When prices are

---

[2] Television is dependent upon telephone-based systems for sending signals to transmitters and for receiving programming via microwave and satellite distribution systems.

MEDIA COMPANIES

Figure 5.4. U.S. Consumer Spending on Media per Person, 2000

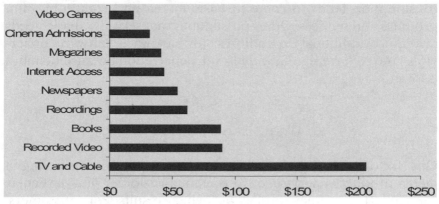

Source: U.S. Census Bureau, *Statistical Abstract of the United States, 1999,* table 920. Estimated expenditure for 2000.

high there will be less consumption, and when prices are low there will be more persons willing to consume.

In addition to price alone, the willingness of individuals to consume is affected by a variety of factors including consumers' perceptions of the state of the general economy, the stability of their employment or income sources, or whether the product requires additional purchases.

Individuals who are concerned that the economy is becoming unstable or that they may lose income, for example, tend to postpone additional consumption in order to pay debts or save some money for use if income is reduced. Companies, as well as individuals, tend to behave in this same way.

Consumers also consider whether their purchases require additional consumption for use. A consumer purchasing a DVD player, for example, cannot use the equipment without also making additional expenditures to purchase or rent DVD recordings. Similarly, persons can purchase an advanced mobile telephone but cannot use it to access the Internet, use interactive mobile telephone services, or make telephone calls unless they also purchase telecommunications service. As a result, one can make the general observation that the more additional items a consumer must purchase to use a medium, the lower the penetration of that medium.

If one considers the list of services by household penetration shown earlier in Figure 5-3, one immediately sees that the greatest consumption tends to come in basic media and communication products and services. Other possibilities that serve less basic needs or require additional expenditures for hardware, software, or services tend to have significantly lower penetration because demand is lower.

CUSTOMER SATISFACTION

One factor affecting the willingness to continue consuming a media product or service, or to remain a customer of a particular company, is customer satisfaction, which results from customers' perceptions and choices regarding issues of quality, price, and service.

From the business perspective, creating customer satisfaction is the driver of success for a company. If the product or service does not create customer satisfaction, there will be a constant turnover of customers, and the reputation of the company will decline. Thus, satisfaction is key to finding and keeping customers. For media companies, this issue applies to both audiences and consumers.

Producing satisfaction thus becomes a critical component of quality management, and managers need to understand the expectations and requirements of their customers and how well their company and competitors are meeting them. They then can use that information to develop strategies and standards for their operations and programs to improve their performance.

A newspaper, for example, may develop methods to track and improve delivery problems. A cable system may work to reduce the number of service calls it must handle by improving the quality of its equipment and installations. An Internet portal may work to increase the ease with which customers can use the site if the current site creates dissatisfaction.

A wide variety of product/service attributes, customer service attributes, purchase attributes, and billing issues affect the satisfaction of audiences and customers of all media and communication systems. By carefully considering these attributes and what customers want, one can make regular determinations of customer satisfaction and track performance over time.

A variety of methods and tools for measuring satisfaction exist and are being increasingly applied to media and communications as competition and audience and consumer choice increases.

AUDIENCE SUBSTITUTION OF MEDIA AND COMMUNICATIONS

The basic issues of demand and satisfaction, as well as the uses that audiences and consumers make of media and communications, affect their willingness to substitute the use of one medium for another.

Although it is tempting to think that all products and services are interchangeable, they are not. One needs to be aware of the difference between media and communication products and services and the inherent advantages and disadvantages in content and use. Further, the ability to substitute products and services is limited by the availability and penetration of the necessary communications technology in the market.

In determining the degree of substitution among media products and services one needs to ask fundamental questions about interactions that occur. First, does a price change in one product increase demand for the other? A change in price for cable television service, for example, will not have a significant effect on sales of books. A change in the price of CDs, however, may increase or decrease demand for MP3 recordings purchased over the Internet. Thus, price is sometimes, but not always, the determinant of substitution.

Second, do the media products and services actually serve the same customers? If one considers television and cable television audiences, one can reasonably say that cable audiences can substitute terrestrial television (traditional broadcast TV) for their viewing. This applies, of course, only if terrestrial channels are available, if the audience is willing to give up use of additional channels available on cable, or if they cannot find something desirable on cable. Terrestrial television viewers, however, typically find less ability to substitute cable because cable is not universally available and there are additional expenditure requirements associated with its acquisition and use.

Third, audiences and consumers tend to use a mix of media at different times, and these times limit substitution. For example, while some employees may listen to radio or recordings in the workplace, they typically don't have the choice of substituting television. Similarly, commuters driving to work tend not to read newspapers and magazines during that period, using audio media instead.

How audiences react to the increasing amount of media channels and the rising entertainment and information choices available is important. In television viewing, for example, the addition of more television, cable, and satellite channels, and the availability of videocassette recorders and players, has not produced a significant change in other media time use, except in places where very little television had previously been available. Both the time and money spent on print media, audio recordings, and radio listening have not been significantly reduced as video media availability and use has increased. A reason for this pattern seems to be that most of the newer media have tended to seek smaller niche audiences by specializing their content via focusing on specific interests.

Strengthening and Stabilizing Audience and Consumer Relationships

Because of the importance of creating audiences that advertisers want to reach and the necessity of income from consumer sales, media and communications firms use a variety of methods to strengthen their relationships with audiences.

Subscriptions, for example, are used by cable television services, newspapers, magazines, and online firms to create a stable consumption relationship that reduces the transaction costs associated with separate sales. A number of media and communication firms have audience clubs, publications, and Web sites that are designed to increase frequency of contact with customers and to build a closer, stronger relationship. Some media provide gifts, special offers, or special reports or books as premiums for good customers or those willing to enter into prolonged relationships.

The methods of strengthening relationships are supported by audience and consumer studies and by efforts to brand media products and services, develop and improve content and its relevance, and improve the quality. In most firms, individual departments are responsible for these audience and consumer activities, with separate efforts being made to strengthen relationships conducted by sales and circulation departments, marketing and promotion departments, and editorial and programming departments. Some media and communications firms are beginning to establish audience relationship teams comprised of staff from the various departments to help improve and coordinate efforts to strengthen the relationships with audiences and consumers.

Suggested Readings

Ball-Rokeach, S., and M. Cantor, eds. *Media, Audience and Social Structure*. Newbury Park, Calif.: Sage Publications, 1986.

Barwise, Patrick, and Andrew Ehrenberg. *Television and Its Audience*. Newbury Park, Calif.: Sage Publications, 1988.

Becker, Lee, and Klaus Schoenbach. *Audience Responses to Media Diversification*. Mahwah, N.J.: Lawrence Erlbaum Associates, 1989.

Ettema, J., and D. Whitney, eds. *Audiencemaking: How the Media Create the Audience*. Thousand Oaks, Calif.: Sage Publications, 1994.

Neuman, W. *The Future of Mass Audience*. Cambridge: Cambridge University Press, 1991.

Webster, J. G., and L. Lichty. *Ratings Analysis: The Theory and Practice of Audience Research*. 2nd ed. Hillsdale, N.J.: Lawrence Erlbaum Associates, 2000.

Webster, J., and P. Phalen. *The Mass Audience: Rediscovering the Dominant Model*. Mahwah, N.J.: Lawrence Erlbaum Associates, 1997.

6

Media, Advertisers, and Advertising

ADVERTISERS are critical to the success of commercial media because they provide the primary revenue stream that keeps most of them viable. Broadcasters, trade magazine publishers, and newspaper publishers exhibit the highest levels of dependence on advertising income among media firms (fig. 6.1). Advertisers, however, do not provide these financial resources in order to make media possible; they do so in order to pursue their own interests and purposes.

As a result, those working within and managing media enterprises need to understand the purposes and choices of advertisers

Figure 6.1. Relative Dependence of Selected Media on Advertising Income

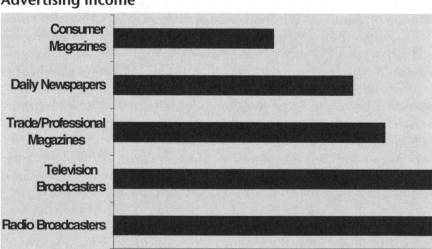

and the dynamics of the relationships between media and advertisers if their media enterprises are to be more successful.

WHY ADVERTISING EXISTS

Advertising is designed to spur consumption of specific goods and services. Consumer advertising began to appear when excess goods and services developed after the Industrial Revolution. Before that time most trade was in raw materials, and the number of sellers of the few finished goods and services available were relatively small and did not require significant advertising to gain the notice of potential customers.

Even as manufactured goods began to appear, advertising primarily promoted products to distributors and retailers. Because companies sold all the products and services they had available, there was no need to engage in heavy advertising to consumers. When the amount of goods increased and differences between products appeared, advertising began being directed toward consumers to attract their attention and influence their choices. Today the wide range of products and services with different attributes that are available requires companies in both the consumer and business markets to advertise their goods and activities.

Because advertisers must cover the expenses of planning, producing, and placing advertising through the purchase of advertising space and time, advertising adds monetary expenses to the costs of a good or service. These costs are spread across all sales, and, if consumption of the good or service increases sufficiently, the costs for the good will normally go down over time because the increased sales reduce unit costs.

Advertiser wants and needs are served by media that are designed to attract broad general audiences with a variety of informational and entertainment types as well as focused media that present information or entertainment with a narrow focus or that focus content and activities toward a particular group of persons or a geographic location.

In selecting among the many potential advertising opportunities, advertisers seek to gain access to specific target audiences made up of persons most likely to use their product or service. Although that access is a primary purpose of their activities, advertisers also seek a suitable message environment in which their advertising messages are not diluted by a clutter of advertising, not ignored by the audience, and not sullied by the media content.

In addition, advertisers want a high-quality media product, a low price for the space or time purchased, and high-quality service and billing from the media firm with which they do business.

Advertising, however, cannot be considered in isolation as *the* method in which advertisers pursue satisfaction of their wants and needs. It is only one part of the marketing mix through which companies manage brand images and promote sales. It is only one method used, and advertising is usually employed concurrently with a variety of advertiser marketing communications activities, including sales promotion, direct marketing, and public relations (see table 6.1).

Although these other marketing communications activities are not the direct concern of media firms seeking advertising expenditures, their existence is important to how media sell advertising, to how advertisers divide expenditures among media and other marketing communications activities, and for projecting the resources that media can expect in the future. To be effective, media personnel need to understand specific advertisers' strategies that integrate and coordinate all of these activities and how the strategies affect their willingness to purchase advertising, their objectives

TABLE 6.1
SELECTED MARKETING COMMUNICATIONS ACTIVITIES

Media Advertising	Direct Marketing	Sales Promotion	Public Relations
Newspapers	Catalogs	Point-of-sales displays	Publicity
Magazines	Flyers	Exhibitions	Product information
Free sheets	Direct mail	Sponsorships	Company information
Television/cable	Personal letters	Product placement	
Radio		Product Web sites	
Outdoor			
Cinema			
Online			

and goals for the advertising, and the importance of specific media in pursuing those strategies.

DIFFERENCES AMONG ADVERTISERS AND THEIR STRATEGIES

Although many observers think of advertisers collectively, they are differentiated in terms of their types, needs, and advertising behavior.

One can think of advertisers as being part of four major categories or types. First, national advertisers are typically producers of brand name consumer products or large national retailers. These advertisers need to reach audiences throughout the nation in which they are active. Second, there are large and midsized regional and local advertisers that tend to be retail establishments such as department and grocery stores, auto dealers, and real estate firms that are intent on reaching regional and local audiences. Third, there are small local advertisers that are typically smaller retail stores and business that need to reach audiences within their local market area. Finally, there are nonbusiness advertisers such as churches, organizations, and individuals that typically wish to communicate with local audiences.

Because of the different needs of these advertisers, and because different media provide different types of access to audiences, media firms get varying portions of their advertising revenue from the different types of advertisers. Television, cable systems, and consumer magazines are highly dependent upon national advertisers, whereas radio stations and newspapers are highly dependent upon local advertisers (table 6.2).

TABLE 6.2
AVERAGE SOURCES OF ADVERTISING INCOME FOR SELECTED U.S. MEDIA

	Local Television Station	Cable System	Radio Station	National Consumer Magazines	Newspapers
National	70%[a]	80%	25%[a]	95%	15%
Local	30	20	75	5	85

[a]Including spot ads.

These differences in sources of advertising income affect the levels of competition experienced for advertising expenditures at the local and national levels.

In addition to these general patterns, different types of advertisers employ different strategies to get their messages across to audiences. As a result, advertising agencies do not sell ready-made advertising campaigns to clients and spend a great deal of time determining which media and mix of media are best for reaching the audiences that are intended to respond to clients' advertisements.

The underlying purposes of these strategies are important in understanding why advertisers select different media in which to place their messages. Although most advertisers ultimately want to increase their revenue by spurring sales, specific advertising campaigns may have different purposes. Some are designed to directly promote sales by inducing consumers to purchase, telling them where to buy the product, or telling them about special offers. Other campaigns are designed to provide information about the attributes and availability of products and additional uses for them. Still other campaigns are designed to position products and services to establish or to change consumer perceptions about a product or to establish and maintain brand preferences.

Media, then, serve as a bridge between advertisers and audiences. The bridge is built by media content attracting audiences, by making it possible for advertisers to reach the audiences the media attract, and by providing mechanisms for targeting specific groups of people. Building and maintaining this bridge is not without problems and conflicts. Because commercial media are dependent upon income from advertisers, audiences must not see evidence that their interests are harmed by that dependence or they will lose confidence in the bridge and it will lose its effectiveness.

Media must seek to build and maintain stable relationships with both audiences and advertisers. As noted in the last chapter, media engage in a variety of activities, including subscriptions, audience clubs, and premiums. Similar methods are employed to strengthen advertising relationships. Advertisers are offered special prices if they enter into long-term contracts for quantities of space or time or regular purchases. A variety of customer service strategies involving proofs, pre-use information, preferential positioning, after-sales contacts, and follow-up information are offered by media companies. In addition, a wide range of advertiser events, tie-ins and cross promotions, advertiser publications, and advertising research are offered as means of strengthening relationships with advertisers.

Many media companies use key account managers to help solidify relationships with their most important advertising customers. Although this is done for a limited number of customers, they are typically the top ten to twenty companies that provide the bulk of the advertising income. Key account managers work to ensure consistency of service, understand the customers' businesses and needs, provide regular contact and information, and help develop strategies that mutually benefit both the media company and the advertisers and lead to long-term relationships. The Los Angeles *Times*, for example, uses key account managers for consumer sectors such as food and auto advertisers, and *CFO Magazine* uses key account managers for its top advertising clients as well.

Sat 1, the giant German satellite programming provider, offers its advertisers and potential advertisers *Sat 1 Report*, a monthly newsletter containing ratings data, information on future programming, and other topics related to television, television advertising, and Sat 1. Similar types of publications are offered free of charge to advertisers by many large media firms.

Responsibility for these activities is often divided among the advertising, marketing, and research departments. Only a few firms seek the benefits of creating unified advertising relationship activities.

EFFECTIVENESS OF DIFFERENT MEDIA

Media differ in their abilities to serve the wants and needs of advertisers because of differences in their characteristics, their relationships with audiences, and the way they are used by both audiences and advertisers.

Advertisers seeking to nurture a brand image for their products and services typically find that television, magazines, and outdoor advertising best suits that purpose. Advertisers, especially retailers, that want immediate sales typically turn to newspapers, free distribution sheets, or direct mail. Advertisers that are intent on providing information about their products, services, and locations tend to turn to magazines, direct mail, and telephone directories. The reason for these choices is that each medium has different strengths and weaknesses (see table 6.3) from among which advertisers select media that best suit their purposes.

Because individual advertisers serve different wants and needs at different times, they tend to use a mix of media, rather than only one medium, as a means of reaching and influencing audiences.

These choices are also dependent upon whether advertisers wish to reach broad or narrow geographical coverage and mass or differentiated audiences. As shown in figure 6.2 on page 130, advertisers that want to reach mass audiences with narrow or broad geographic coverage have a variety of media choices available that permit them to implement a selection of strategies for choosing and mixing the media that best suit their needs. If differentiated audiences are sought, the number of choices are more constrained, but the variety of choices and strategies available are greater when advertisers need to cover a broader geographic area.

Mechanisms of Advertising

Commercial media operate advertising departments designed to sell space or time in the product offered to those wanting to buy access to the medium's audience. These departments prepare a variety of sales promotion materials describing the product or service and its audience, and providing other information designed to produce sales.

Advertising departments engage in both direct sales and various forms of surrogate sales. Sales personnel call on potential advertisers in an effort to generate sales and then manage customers and orders that are produced. When relationships with major advertisers develop, these relationships are typically handled by experienced key account managers.

TABLE 6.3
STRENGTHS AND WEAKNESSES OF SELECTED MEDIA FOR ADVERTISERS

	Strengths	*Weaknesses*
Television	Broad coverage Ability to repeat messages Highly visual Good for image development	Market targeting limitations Ignored messages Advertising clutter Limited information content possible High cost
Radio	Ability to target local markets Formats attract different audiences Audiences uses in mobile situations Rapid ability to change message Low cost	Narrow audiences Audience instability Ease of station change Limited information content possible
Newspapers	Target market coverage Ability to change size and type of advertisements High frequency Cost advantages High information content possible	Advertising clutter Audiences read quickly Reproductions quality limited Short lifespan
Magazines	Target audience selectivity Excellent reproduction Long lifespan for advertisement High information content possible	Low overall market penetration Long lead time for ad changes
Online	Interactivity Immediacy Easy to change advertisements High information content possible	Low market penetration Low response rates

Figure 6.2. Matrix of Advertising Choices

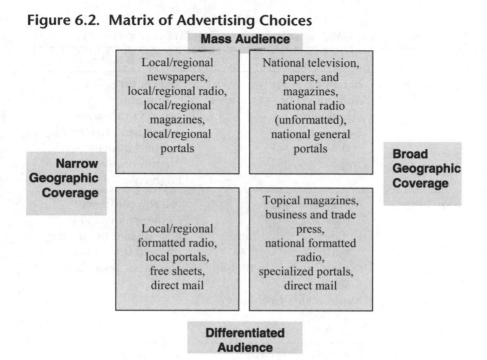

Mass Audience

Local/regional newspapers, local/regional radio, local/regional magazines, local/regional portals	National television, papers, and magazines, national radio (unformatted), national general portals
Local/regional formatted radio, local portals, free sheets, direct mail	Topical magazines, business and trade press, national formatted radio, specialized portals, direct mail

Narrow Geographic Coverage (left)
Broad Geographic Coverage (right)

Differentiated Audience

Some companies also take part in sales networks that involve a number of units of the same medium. When these networks generate sales, a percentage of the income from those sales is paid to the network. Advertising sales networks in the newspaper industry, for example, make it possible for advertisers to purchase space in some or all newspapers in different geographic areas through one organization, thus reducing their transaction costs.

Within the advertising industry advertisers contract with advertising agencies that provide a variety of research, planning, creative, and purchasing services. Sales personnel for media call upon those who place advertising in these agencies and on specialized advertisement placement firms in an effort to attract advertisements. Agencies that place advertisements in media receive part of their compensation in the form of commissions paid by the media firms.

Media also provide extensive information to specialized firms that publish information about the services, prices, and requirements of media firms.

Advertisers expended an estimated $236 billion on advertising in the United States during 2000. The United States alone accounted for 38 percent of global spending (figure 6.3).

Different patterns of advertising expenditures exist among nations, reflecting the availability of media, domestic media use patterns, and other market conditions. In the United States, the share of expenditures for television, cable, and direct mail grew steadily in the last decades of the twentieth century to become nearly equal rivals with newspapers as the primary choices for advertisers (fig. 6.4).

Internet advertising has grown rapidly in recent years, but by the year 2000 it accounted for only about 4 percent of total advertising spending. Although this represents a significant amount of funds upon which to base Internet business models, it has not yet taken significant amounts from other advertising expenditures on specific media. In most cases advertisers have used other marketing funds or increased advertising expenditures in moving to the Web, but they may begin allocating funds that were previously used for other advertising in the future.

It should also be noted that online firms are primary contributors to online advertising expenditures. Dot-com firms, for example, accounted for 68 percent of online advertising expenditures among the top 200 online advertisers in 2000, and that advertising accounted for 77 percent of impressions. Dot-com firms also made heavy expenditures in television, magazine, and newspaper advertising between 1998 and 2000, spurring the growth of advertising in those media in that period.

Figure 6.3. Percentage of Global Advertising Spending by Area

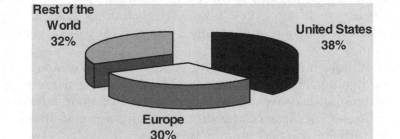

Rest of the World 32%

United States 38%

Europe 30%

Figure 6.4. Shares of U.S. Advertising Expenditures by Media, 1970–2000

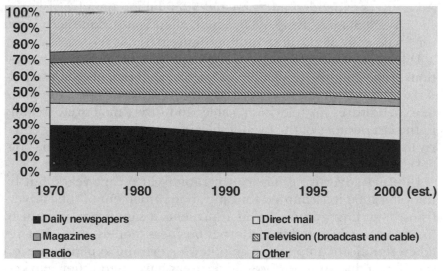

DEMAND AND PRICING OF ADVERTISING

The needs of manufacturers, service providers, and retailers drive the need for advertising, and those needs fluctuate depending upon the extent of product supply and consumers' purchases. Because of the dynamics of the market, supply and demand are rarely perfectly equal, and this produces periods in which more or less advertising is necessary.

In addition, advertisers have periods during which the majority of their commerce occurs that affect the extent to which they advertise. Although sales of groceries and other basic household products remain relatively stable throughout the year, retailers of other goods have periods when higher sales take place. There are months in which auto sales, home sales, clothing sales, and gift purchases are higher, and retailers increase advertising during these times.

In addition, business cycles and economic developments affect advertising demand. When economies slow, advertisers receive less income and, consequently, tend to reduce their advertising expenditures. Because of the differences in types of advertisers and advertising carried among media, print media advertising

132

Advertising on the Web

Advertising on Internet sites is developing a different approach than that found in traditional media. This new approach developed because of advertisers' unease with the penetration rates of Internet services among the population and because of difficulties in measuring audience size and characteristics.

In traditional media, in which future audience sizes and characteristics can be predicted at the time of sale, a simple fee for agreed-upon amounts of time, space, or audience rating is the norm. As Internet advertising began to take hold, major Internet portal companies such as Yahoo!, America Online, and MSN began offering similar types of arrangements to manufacturers, retailers, and e-retailers.

Because interest in the Internet was strong and major portal and topic sites generated significant use, they were well positioned to induce many companies to sign advertising contracts at fairly high rates and, in some cases, to accept multiyear contracts. In 1998, for example, ESPN Sportzone was achieving 20.5 million hits each week and offered banner ads for $100,000 for three months or $300,000 for one year. Yahoo!, which was receiving nearly three million hits per month, offered deals at $20,000 per million impressions.

Sites with fewer users were not able to command such high fees and could only offer relatively low rates based on the number of page views. As a result they began to seek new ways of charging advertisers based on the interactive aspects of the Internet. Many advertisers found these to be attractive offers.

Some sites began carrying clients' ads and taking transactions fees of 3 to 12 percent for e-commerce generated, while others began to offer flat rate fees in the $5,000 to $50,000 per month range or to base fees on the number of click-throughs (often in the range of $6 to $8 per click-though). Over time these have had the effect of creating a culture of performance-based fees for Internet advertising.

The move away from traditional media pricing, slower growth of Internet penetration, and the reduction of Internet expectations has now pushed costs for many advertisers downward. In addition, the diminished willingness of advertisers to pay high prices for general exposure, developments in hardware and software that have made it easier for advertisers to target audiences, and flexible buying systems that enable advertisers to purchase exposure in specific areas of the portals rather than throughout have affected prices of Web advertising. As a result, between 1998 and 2000 the costs for advertising on portals fell about 75 percent for many advertisers.

Because of the increasing interest in the Internet as an advertising vehicle, however, overall Internet advertising expenditures in the United

States grew to $4.6 billion in 1999 (fig. 6.5). The slowing growth of Internet penetration and the downward trend of advertising prices, however, created a slowing of the growth rate for Internet advertising, ending the boom that was experienced as it was introduced.

Figure 6.5. U.S. Internet Advertising Expenditures (U.S.$ Billions) and Growth Rate

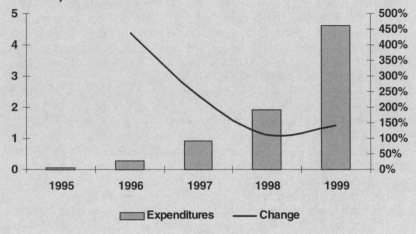

tends to be reduced more as economies slow than does broadcast media advertising.

There is a relationship between size of media audiences and advertising rates because advertisers of products and services intended for general use are willing to pay more to reach larger groups of people. Although other factors influence demand, the size of the audience is generally seen as the primary factor in the pricing of advertising space or time.

Because advertisers are seeking access to audiences and larger audiences tend to serve the needs of the largest advertisers, as well as many smaller firms, the price of advertising rises with audience size when the size or length of an ad, placement, and discounts are equalized.

Another relationship linked to price and audience size involves the cost per person. It is generally understood that this cost declines with increasing audience size, but the decline is not continuous.

MEDIA COMPANIES

The relationships between advertising prices and audience size can be seen in figure 6.6, using a newspaper industry illustration. The figure illustrates that advertising price rises with circulation, but that cost per thousand persons as measured in milline rate (cost per line per million circulation) declines to a point and then rises. It reveals that advertisers' ability to achieve the greatest cost efficiency occurs in a relatively small area to the right of the point at which advertising rates and cost per thousand cross but before cost per thousand rises. Similar dynamics exist for other general content, mass media such as television, and general consumer magazines.

For media with specialized audiences, advertisers are willing to pay a higher cost per thousand than is available in mass media because the media are able to deliver audiences with specific characteristics that the advertising may be targeting. Thus, a manufacturer of snowboarding equipment will be willing to pay a higher cost per thousand to advertise in a snowboarding magazine than in a general magazine because the snowboarding magazine deliv-

Figure 6.6. Relationships between Advertising Price and Newspaper Circulation

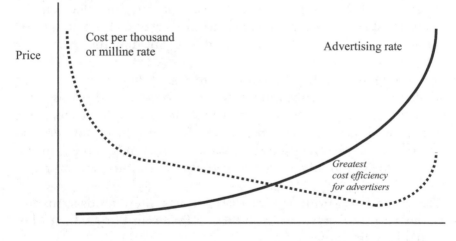

Source: Robert G. Picard, "A Note on the Relations between Circulation Size and Newspaper Advertising Rates," *Journal of Media Economics* 11, no. 2 (1998): 47–55.

ers an audience committed to the manufacturer's product and thus increases the effectiveness of the ad.

MEDIA SUBSTITUTION BY ADVERTISERS

Because of the different types of audiences delivered and the characteristics of messages that can be carried in various media, media tend to coexist rather than directly compete for advertiser expenditures.

Little real estate advertising is carried on radio and television, for example, because print media provides a better ability to convey information about specific homes and buildings available for sale or lease. Similarly, major fast food restaurants tend to use broadcast media rather than newspapers to convey their messages because the messages are primarily brand images, which are conveyed best through the audio and visual characteristics and repetition possibilities of television and radio.

In addition, the choice of which media to use tends not to change based on the prices offered. Price changes for television advertisers, for example, do not have a significant effect on demand for direct mail. And changes in the prices of Internet advertising do not have a significant effect on demand for radio advertising.

This is not to say that there is not substitutability of media among advertisers, but the substitutability tends to be over the long term rather than the short term. Direct mail, for example, has become a growing choice for newspaper advertisers as household penetration of newspapers has declined. Cable television became a substitute for television advertising as cable penetration and audiences increased.

Advertiser substitution of media products, then, tends to involve media with similar types of production forms and functions rather than all media equally.

Within specific media markets there is often a must-buy phenomenon that reduces the choices available to advertisers and reduces the amount of money that can be spent in other advertising media. The phenomenon occurs when the audience size or qualities offered require an advertiser to use a particular advertising medium or outlet as their primary choice.

For advertisers marketing to mass consumers, media or media units that reach the biggest audience become must buys. For advertisers marketing to specialized or niches of consumers, media or media units that reach the greatest numbers of those consumers become must buys. In these cases, access to the target audience becomes the primary factor in demand rather than price.

The end result of this requisite purchase of advertising in a dominant medium is the reduction of funds available for advertising in other media or units of the same medium. As previously noted, no one media or media unit can perfectly serve an advertiser's needs, and they must typically seek a media mix to effectively serve their purposes. When the advertising budget is constrained by the must-buy phenomena, an advertiser is forced to diminish the amount of advertising expenditures used to achieve the mix, reduce the number of media in the mix, or reduce the outlets of each media in the mix from which advertising space or time is purchased.

Media as Advertisers

Also note that media themselves are increasing becoming advertisers. In the past media rarely purchased paid advertisements, relying primarily upon nonpaid promotional ads internal to their own media product, along with some point-of-purchase promotion and direct mail marketing. This occurred because competition was typically limited in media markets and markets were saturated. As a result, making advertising expenditures produced few results.

In recent years, increases in the number of television and cable channels, radio stations, magazine titles, and online companies have produced heavier competition for audience time and monetary expenditures. Declining household penetrations for newspapers have also produced efforts to stabilize and increase readership. These factors have led to increases in purchased advertisements in other media and are making media not only purveyors, but consumers, of advertising services.

SUGGESTED READINGS

Davis, Joel J. *Advertising Research: Theory and Practice.* Upper Saddle River, N.J.: Prentice-Hall, 1997.

Jones, John Philip. *The Advertising Business: Operations, Creativity, Media Planning, Integrated Communications.* London: Sage Publications, 1999.

Jugenheimer, Donald W., Arnold M. Barban, and Peter B. Turk. *Advertising Media: Strategy and Tactics.* Dubuque, Iowa: Brown & Benchmark, 1992.

Reekie, W. Duncan. *The Economics of Advertising.* London: Macmillan, 1981.

Schmalensee, Richard. *Economics of Advertising.* Amsterdam: North-Holland, 1981.

Schultz, Don E., and Beth E. Barnes. *Strategic Advertising Campaigns.* 4th ed. Lincolnwood, Ill.: NTC Business Books, 1995.

Tellis, Gerald J. *Advertising and Sales Promotion Strategy.* Reading, Mass.: Addison-Wesley, 1998.

7

Competition in Media Markets

COMPETITION in media markets represents the rivalry of media firms to provide products and services. Many media managers believe their firms face high competition in their product markets, but in reality the competition they face is relatively moderate or low, depending upon their product and location. By comparison to other industries, the degree of competition among media products is not very high because of limited choice. In many cases, competition is noticeably low.

Media firms face little product competition by comparison with producers of undifferentiated agricultural products such as milk or pork and lower competition than that faced by dishwashing detergent manufacturers, shoe retailers, and beer producers. The number of pizzerias in the United States is sixty times higher than the number of newspapers, there are three times as many soft drink brands as cable channels, and there are five times as many ice cream shops as consumer magazines.

The perception of heavy competition in media industries has developed in the past few decades as social, technology, and policy changes have increased the number of media and direct competitors and altered the relatively secure and profitable media markets and structures of past decades. These have created new choices for audiences and advertisers and have raised the level of competition felt by media and communications firms significantly.

Thus, direct competition among media, such as newspaper versus newspaper or magazine versus magazine, is really not very high. However, overall media competition for audience time and advertisers' expenditures is high, as is competition for resources such as capital and technology, and competition to be the market leader.

Nevertheless, the levels of competition experienced by media companies are constrained because of difference in technologies, formats, and audience use patterns, as well as product differentiation and differences in geographic markets served by firms.

COMPETITION AND MARKET POWER

A market exists where companies provide the same or highly substitutable goods to the same group of consumers. In media terms this means that firms that produce and disseminate similar types of media products to users in the same location operate within the same market. This chapter, however, will show the limitations on the degree to which media firms compete in markets and that there are a number of factors that limit substitutability of media goods and services.

The characteristics of media markets and the effectiveness with which they work are determined by a number of factors, including the number of media users, their temporal and monetary expenditures, the number of media firms, cost structures of the firms, barriers to entry, product differentiation, and a variety of other factors.

Historically markets have been local and national, but they are increasingly becoming international as well. However, all media do not participate in the potential markets or seek access to all potential audiences. In the United States, for example, 99 percent of cities are served by only one daily newspaper. The newspapers in these cities focus on their home market and do not attempt compete in the other cities. Similarly, there are 210 television markets. Television stations broadcasting in one market do not compete in other markets, so their direct competition is limited to the other stations in the market in which they operate.

It must be noted that the size of markets varies widely depending upon the size of the metropolitan area or city encompassed by the market. Most markets are small- to medium-sized, and the number of competitors serving them is constrained by the economies of the markets. Some markets are very large, and media in them experience much stronger competition because those markets can support many more competitors. The top ten cities in the United States, for example, account for one-third of the nation's population (table 7.1), and the top twenty-five markets account for 46 percent.

Within markets there are different levels of competition, and the degree to which any firm or small group of firms controls or influences activities such as pricing and production affects the effectiveness with which that market operates. The more market power that any firm has, the less effectively a market operates, thus making it possible to do harm to competitors and consumers.

As noted above, the degree of power is related to the level of competition present, but it is also affected by the level of dominance of leading firms. In a market with ten television stations, for example, if any one firm gains 40 percent of the viewers, it can effectively control much of the market's activities. This occurs because the leading firm becomes a "must buy" for advertisers. If they wish to reach the largest portion of the viewing audience, they are forced to purchase advertising at the price set by the leading television station, which provides it the financial resources to obtain and produce more desirable programming to continue as the leading station. At the same time, the "must buy" expenditure reduces the amount of advertising budgets available for other purchases. Ultimately this reduces the financial resources available to the station's competitors, diminishes their ability to obtain desirable programming, reduces their profitability, and can even result in bankruptcy.

TABLE 7.1

THE TOP 10 GEOGRAPHIC MARKETS IN THE U.S. AND
THEIR PERCENTAGE OF TOTAL U.S. POPULATION

City	Percentage
New York	7%
Los Angeles	6
Chicago	3
Washington/Baltimore	3
San Francisco	3
Philadelphia	2
Boston	2
Detroit	2
Dallas/Ft. Worth	2
Houston	2

Although it is not illegal to become successful or reap the harvest of that success, oversight agencies and policy makers seek to ensure that market power is not used illicitly or cannot develop to the point that it damages markets. Antitrust regulations are used to limit a wide variety of activities that harm markets through the creation or damaging use of market power. This includes actions against mergers or acquisitions that create high market power, predatory pricing, and other anticompetitive behavior. Legislative bodies and regulatory agencies often place limits on number of media units owned, cross-ownership, and percentages of audience served by media firms as a means of constraining the development of unhealthy market power that limits competition.

PRODUCT AND AUDIENCE DIFFERENTIATION CONSTRAIN COMPETITION

Product differentiation is a strategy used by firms to make their products unique or to give them different properties than those of competitors. This process is designed to reduce the substitutability among products and limit the level of competition they encounter because the differentiated products are no longer equal choices.

In media, differentiation tends to focus on choices involving content, the time when content is made available, and production choices. Such differentiation gives firms a means of targeting specific audience groups based on demographics, place of media use, and sales methods. Even simple differences in design and presentation tone are widely used in print media to create publications that appeal to different audiences. This is seen in the differences between broadsheet and tabloid newspapers such as *The Times* of London and *The Daily Mirror* and the New York *Times* and New York *Post*. It is also illustrated by the differences between women's magazines, such as *Cosmopolitan* and *Woman's Day*.

Media can also chose to differentiate themselves by the characteristics of the audience they wish to attract. One medium or media unit may chose to attract general audiences, whereas another may decide to seek a well-defined and narrow audience. A magazine, for example, may seek an audience of male music lovers, who are between the ages of thirty-five and fifty-five, who earn high incomes, and who live in urban areas only in the northeastern portion of the country. In order to attract a differentiated audience, all personnel in the media company will have a clear understanding of that audience, and the activities of the editorial, marketing, advertising, and circulation departments must all work to serve and reach that target audience.

The number of differentiation choices available to media depends on the variety of elements related to content, format, sales, and distribution that can be controlled. Thus, the degrees to which differentiation strategies can exist depend upon the characteristics of the media and markets. Some of the types of choices that can be made in creating strategies for different media are shown in table 7.2.

A product differentiation strategy obviously influences the audience achieved, and a audience differentiation strategy influences the product offered, so both strategies must be coordinated and pursued simultaneously.

The ability to differentiate content in multiple ways is being heightened by information and communications technologies. This is increasingly allowing media firms to personalize content to the interests and needs of specific customers or customer groups and for customers to request specific types of content. The primary media taking advantage of these abilities today are magazines and online content providers, but television service firms are expected to take advantage of the potential when digital television penetration and broadband distribution capabilities increase.

THE ROLE OF GEOGRAPHIC MARKETS

Geographic markets are particularly important in understanding competition involving media because of the strong links of audiences and advertisers to particular locations. As noted in chapter 6, advertisers need to reach specific audiences that are often defined by geographic locations adjacent to stores they operate or geographic areas in which their products or services are distributed to retailers.

Thus, different types of media and different units of the same medium tend to provide services intended for specific geographic markets. In the magazine industry, for example, a national publi-

TABLE 7.2
PRODUCT AND AUDIENCE DIFFERENTIATION STRATEGIES FOR SELECTED MEDIA

	Product Differentiation	*Audience Differentiation*
Radio Stations	Programming offered	Target listeners
	Music (rock, jazz, classi-cal, urban, etc.)	General
		Demographic group
	News	Place of use
	Talk	Home
	Sports	Office
	Broadcast time	Commuting
	Length of day	Segmentation by program
	Counterprogramming	Geographic location of audience
	Language use	
Magazines	Product type	Target readers
	Consumer	General
	Trade/professional	Demographic group
	Content type	Interest group
	General interest	Geographic location of audience
	Specialized interest	Zoned editions
	Frequency	State/regional magazines
	Language use	National magazines
	Production choices	Sales Method
	Size	Subscription
	Inks	Single copy
	Paper	Both
Newspapers	Distribution time	Target readers
	Editorial orientation	Mass
	Coverage	Specialized
	News focus	Place of use
	Presentation tone	Home
	Readability level	Office
	Graphic/photo use	Commuting
	Production choices	Geographic location of audience
	Size	Local
	Inks	Zoned editions
	Paper	Statewide
		National
		Sales method
		Subscription
		Single copy
		Both

	Product Differentiation	Audience Differentiation

Television/Cable Networks or Channels	Programming offered
	  Variety
	  Specialized
	    Sports
	    Movies
	    Music
	    Lifestyle
	    Cultural
	  Broadcast time
	    Length of day
	    Counterprogramming
	  Language use
		Target listeners
		  General
		  Demographic group
		Segmentation by program
		Geographic location of audience

cation devoted to travel and tourism will include content on both national and global possibilities and attract readers nationally and advertisers nationally and globally. Another travel magazine, however, will target a region or a state for its coverage, readers, and advertisers. Still another publisher may produce a local travel or tourism magazine for a city filled with local content and local advertising and intended for persons who visit or live in that city.

Geographic markets are critical to the survival of multiple media units because they make it possible for multiple media units to exist without competing with each other. This is seen in the fact that there are about twelve thousand radio stations in the United States. These stations, however, are spread throughout the country, and the number that can be readily received within any one city is limited and exceeds two dozen in only a small number of metropolitan areas.

Geographic markets also limit the degree of substitutability of media products. *USA Today,* for example, is a national newspaper available in all fifty states and internationally. That paper does not provide the range or types of news coverage necessary to understand the events and developments in the community in which a reader lives, however, and it cannot provide useful access to the readers that most local advertisers want to reach.

The degree of competition experienced in any market can change if market conditions are altered. In general, competition increases whenever new competitors enter the market, the number of competitors is high, the market is well divided among the competitors, the market involves undifferentiated products, and the market is mature or growing slowly. In media markets competition tends to be increased if the content provided is similar, if audiences can easily choose among competitors' content, and if advertisers can gain access to similar audiences with different media products.

Benefits of Competitive Advantages

Competitive advantages are factors that give one firm advantages over another in a competitive situation. These advantages exist for a limited period of time, however, because competition is dynamic and constantly evolving. There are always new products and new market strategies put in place by competitors, and unless a firm is constantly working to capitalize upon and maintain advantages, these competitive advantages can be lost.

Advantages arise from constant efforts to improve firms' performance and upgrade products and services. In order to achieve advantages a firm needs an internal atmosphere and value system that support change and innovation.

Competitive advantages include the ability to produce the product or service less expensively than competitors. For example, book printers in countries such as the United States or Germany tend to have higher cost structures because of labor organizations, social costs, and taxes than do book printers in Singapore or Mexico.

As previously noted, product differentiation is a method of reducing competition, but it also is a competitive advantage, especially for differentiated products commanding a high price in a segmented market. Bang & Olufsen audio systems, for example, have competitive advantages related to their design innovation and differentiation over other audio products.

Another advantage is a proprietary asset such as a specialized process, technique, or patent that is not available to other providers of the good or service. Quality is also a competitive advantage when consumers perceive one product or service as providing higher quality. Other advantages come through advanced features and innovations, more efficient production that reduces costs, and the ability to develop new products more rapidly so that a company can respond to changes in demand faster than competitors. A television channel that can control its programming production methods so that it can commission and begin broadcasting a new program within six months, for example, has distinct advantages over a channel that requires twelve to twenty-four months to do so.

BRANDS AND BRANDING AID IN COMPETITION

The concepts of brands and branding are increasingly associated with media products and services, but their use is often merely the use of a contemporary industry buzzword rather than one of understanding of the competitive advantages of a brand and its further use.

The concept of brands has moved into communications from the retail and service industries, where it has been used to induce customers to purchase a variety of vegetables available under the Green Giant brand, because of the brand's image of freshness, size, and high quality. Branding is also used to build preferences for services like FedEx delivery services through creating and supporting an image of speed and reliability.

Brands are names or designs that help distinguish products and convey attributes or images of the product that are designed to attract and maintain customers. Both users and nonusers of a product and service recognize effective brands. The importance of brands is shown in that strong brands for retail products and services maintain loyalty, are linked to repeat purchases, and give advantages to the firm as it grows. Having a strong brand is especially important to a firm as the number of competitors increases, so it is no accident that the concept was adopted in the media and communication industries as the number of competitors exploded at the end of the twentieth century.

Although new to many media firms, branding has been used for many years in the magazine industry, where it was first introduced in the internationalization of magazine titles. *Reader's Digest*, for example, established its title in many nations in local languages, taking steps to ensure that its editorial profile of stories on human triumphs, condensed readings, clean humor, and inspirational readings were maintained across the titles despite localization of the content.

In addition to the names of the product or service, media companies have made a variety of uses of subbranding. The American Broadcasting Company (ABC) was one of the first to do so when it branded its Friday night programming using "TGIF Friday" to brand a family-friendly evening of programming that could be marketed as a package rather than individual programs. Later, the National Broadcasting Company (NBC) attempted the same by introducing "Must See TV" for its Thursday night lineup, and Discovery Channel branded "Shark Week" for an annual week of programming devoted to documentaries about sharks and a related Web site.

Branding can also use a variety of techniques to visually separate some products from others. The *Financial Times* newspaper, for example, uses salmon-colored paper to help rapidly identify it on newsstands and so that people recognize the paper when they see others reading it. Visual branding is used to carry the image across multiple media products. NBC, for example, uses its well-recognized color peacock across its products, including the NBC Network, CNBC, and MSNBC, thus conveying the strengths of the brand image to all its products.

Brand images are best established, developed, and maintained when companies consistently strive to solidify the images in all production, distribution, marketing, and customer service activities and by communicating the image in all marketing activities including logos, slogans, advertising, sales promotion, and direct marketing.

Brands can also be extended to include more than the original product under brand name and image. This provides particular competitive advantages to firms launching new products or services because it encompasses the secondary product or service with the same brand identity of the established primary product or service.

ESPN, the leading cable sports channel, expanded its brand by starting a second cable channel ESPN2 to carry even more live events. It then expanded its brand through the establishment of regional sports networks such as ESPN West to provide more intense regional coverage and ensure that regional team games could be viewed even if they were not on its national channels. The firm further expanded its brands with the establishment of ESPN Classic Sports to rerun notable games it had previously covered on its live networks. Ultimately it expanded out of cable to establish the *ESPN* sports magazine, ESPN sports radio network, and an ESPN online operation.

The French magazine *Marie Claire* expanded its products by transferring its editorial profile of fashion and living coverage for affluent working women to national editions published in countries ranging from the United Kingdom to Japan. It also began brand expansion into other magazines on related topic such as *Marie Claire Maison,* a home magazine designed for the same readers as its primary magazine.

Brand extension can be a successful way to more easily establish and development audiences for new media products. However, managers of media firms must be careful with brand extension because it loses effectiveness when products and services embraced by the brand are less central to the core brand identity or if lesser products or services are encompassed that weaken the brand image of the original product or service.

COMPETITION AMONG AND BETWEEN MEDIA

The nature and structure of media markets and the kinds of products provided influence the degree of competition each firm faces. Because true monopolies are rare in media today, competition among media units range from low to moderate to fierce depending upon the specific market. It has been argued that the fiercest competition tends to arise when there are many firms, low entry barriers, and less product differentiation, and that these have negative effects on content (table 7.3).

Competition among and between media can be understood as intermedia and intramedia competition. Intermedia competition involves the competition that takes place among different types of media such as television and radio, whereas intramedia competition involves competition among units of the same medium, such

TABLE 7.3
COMPETITIVE STRUCTURE AND COMPETITIVE CONDUCT IN MEDIA

Competition	Structure	Conduct
Moderate	Small number of media organizations with significant market power	Product innovation
		Strategy is based on product rather than price
	High barriers to entry and exit	Efforts are made to attract different groups of consumers
	Media operate in market niches	
Fierce	Many media organizations (some of them rivals for the same audience)	Process innovation
		Strategy based on price
	Low barriers to entry and exit	Following public preferences, competing for the same (mostly dominant) audience group with other media
	Absence of economically significant market niches	

as two radio stations. The two occur simultaneously, as illustrated in figure 7.1.

Intermedia Competition

In the content product market, intermedia competition primarily involves competition for the attention and time of audiences and

Figure 7.1. Intermedia and Intramedia Competition

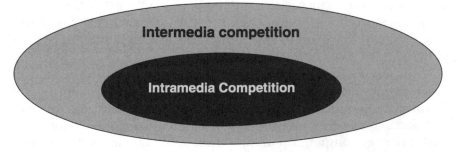

MEDIA COMPANIES

sometimes for expenditures by consumers. The competition among media is not equal, however, because of wide differences in availability and demand factors. As shown in chapter 5, these produce wide differences in the penetration of media in average households, in the amount of time that is allotted for use of different media, and in the purposes for using different media. These factors limit the degree to which different media directly compete, and it is useful to think of the existing competition in broader terms of gaining a portion of the overall use of different types of audiences.

In the market for providing access to audiences for advertisers, competition is limited by audience acquisition and use issues as well as by the characteristics of different media and their ability to deliver certain types of advertising messages. As a result of such factors, intermedia competition is constrained, and advertisers typically purchase advertising in more than one type of media. The primary competition among media almost always involves the size of the share of the advertiser's expenditures rather than an all-or-nothing choice among media.

A useful general rule for understanding audience and advertiser competition is that the more common characteristics there are among media, the more intermedia competition that will exist. Thus, audiovisual content delivered by terrestrial television channels will experience more competition with content delivered by satellite systems than a magazine will with content delivered by radio broadcasts. These differences, however, are being eroded as more and more physical products and services move some of their operations into electronic format for online distribution, as seen in figure 7.2. In doing so, they also alter the amount of competition that they traditionally faced.

Intramedia Competition

The highest levels of competition for audiences and advertisers' expenditures take place among units of the same medium, particularly if they serve the same audiences in the same location. Two Internet portals serving the same metropolitan region, for example, will be engaged in heavier competition than two portals that operate in separate metropolitan markets because of the choices of

Figure 7.2. Limitations on Competition are Eroded by Digitalization and the Movement from Physical Form

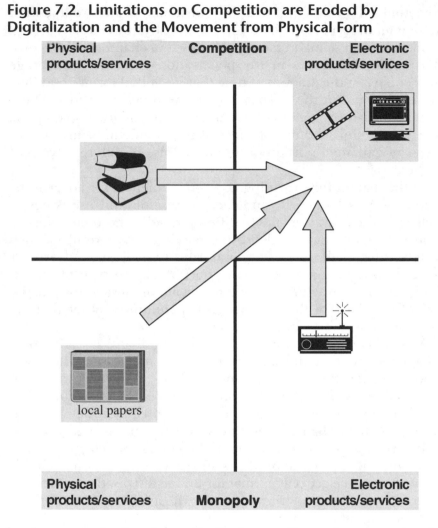

local users and advertisers. Similarly, a radio station operating in a market with twenty stations will face far greater intramedia competition than if only ten stations existed in that same market.

The nature of intermedia competition is determined within specific markets, and the number of competitors, the population, the number of potential advertisers, and the degree of market power held by market leaders must be considered in each individual case. As noted above, twenty radio stations face greater competition than ten stations in one market, but another market with ten sta-

MEDIA COMPANIES

tions may have greater competition than that market with twenty stations because of differences in the market characteristics.

Summary

Managers and observers who wish to comprehend the nature of media markets need to assess accurately the amount and degree of competition among units of the same medium and media as a whole. With that knowledge they can then develop appropriate strategies and make informed choices that limit the competition, utilize advantages available to them, and make them more effective in their competition against others.

Suggested Readings

Blunden, Brian, and Margot Blunden. *Electronic Publishing Strategies*. Surrey: PIRA International, 1997.

Brock, Gerald, ed. *Toward a Competitive Telecommunication Industry*. Mahwah, N.J.: Lawrence Erlbaum Associates, 1995.

Compaine, Benjamin M., and Douglas Gomery. *Who Owns the Media: Competition and Concentration in the Mass Media Industry*. 3rd ed. Mahwah, N.J.: Lawrence Erlbaum Associates, 2000.

Eastman, Susan Tyler, Sydney W. Head, and Lewis Klein. *Broadcast/Cable Programming: Strategies and Practices*. Belmont, Calif.: Wadsworth, 1989.

Johnson, L. L. *Toward Competition in Cable Television*. Cambridge, Mass.: MIT Press, 1994.

Koff, Richard M. *Strategic Planning for Magazine Executives*. Stamford, Conn.: Folio Magazine Publishing, 1987.

MacFarland, David T. *Future Radio Programming Strategies*. 2nd ed. Mahwah, N.J.: Lawrence Erlbaum Associates, 1997.

Norberg, Eric G. *Radio Programming Tactics and Strategy*. Woburn, Mass.: Focal Press, 1996.

Porter, M. E. *Competitive Advantage: Creating and Sustaining Superior Performance*. New York: Free Press, 1985.

Todreas, Timothy M. *Value Creation and Branding in Television's Digital Age*. New York: Quorum Books, 1999.

Wilkinson, Earl J. *Branding and the Newspaper Consumer*. Dallas: International Newspaper Marketing Association, 1998.

8

Concepts in Media Financing and Financial Management

FINANCING involves meeting the monetary needs of a firm so that it may be established, operated, and developed. Issues of financing range from creating sufficient funds to establish a firm, to obtaining money to pay for operations, to gathering funds to fund growth.

Certain types of financing tend to be available only at particular stages in company or product development. Those intent on creating and developing companies need to understand the constraints and relations that result from seeking capital at different stages.

The research stage represents the point at which ideas are pursued and elements that are necessary to make them into workable products and services are brought together to determine whether the product or service can be effectively produced and offered.

Media companies are rarely active in basic research but typically leave such efforts to suppliers and other hardware firms and then later find ways to exploit new communications inventions. The primary types of research done in media firms involves market research to improve the effectiveness of marketing existing media products or to find markets for new products such as a new magazine, cable channel, or online service.

In the research stage there is a highly negative cash flow because nothing is being sold and producing a source of revenue. As a result this process is typically carried out by inventors or in the research and development activities of companies and funded by those individuals and firms. Without the investment of that funding and support, the equipment, personnel, and supply costs necessary for the research could not be carried out.

Once research is completed, efforts must be made to develop the concept into a workable product or service. This development stage includes assembling the personnel and equipment needed and then preparing the product or service to be offered to the public, and creating the managerial or company structure for its operation. This stage also includes the preparation of an introductory issue of a new magazine, the construction and preparation of a new radio station, and the preparation of content and planning for marketing and operation of a new Web site.

During this development stage, in which the negative cash flow continues because nothing is being sold, funding typically comes from the entrepreneur or company involved or from venture capital firms. Very little outside funding has traditionally been available for media firms at this stage. In recent years, however, a number of venture capitalists and public-private joint ventures have created "new media incubators" in the United States and Europe to help fund the creation of new products and services and to provide a variety of managerial and marketing services and expertise to start-up firms.

The third stage is the introduction period, in which the new product or service is first offered to the public. During this stage there is a large and highly negative cash flow because the company must be fully operational and make large marketing expenditures. There is no guarantee that the market will accept the product or service, and the revenue stream develops slowly as the market initially responds.

At this stage funding comes from the entrepreneur or parent companies and any trade credit the firm may obtain from suppliers. Unless the product or service has unusual potential for high returns, only a limited amount of venture capital or risk funds will be available, because such investors tend to pursue products and services with high yield potential.

If a product or service survives its introduction, cash flow begins to become positive as the product gains acceptance and improvements are made. In this establishment stage stock markets and some traditional lenders such as banks begin to make capital available to help fund growth of the firm and further exploitation of markets.

When the product has achieved broad acceptance and has a highly positive cash flow and profitably, the firm can employ bond markets and a wide range of conservative lenders to obtain financing.

UNDERSTANDING FINANCIAL FLOW

Critical to understanding the financial needs of media firms is an understanding of how money flows within and around firms. Figure 8.1 illustrates the flow in a media firm, and central to the flow is cash, that is, money that is available to spend.

This cash, of course, must have come from an original source, and this may be the owner's contribution or debt. It is this cash that allows the firm to pay for facilities and equipment, labor, and supplies and services needed to produce the media product.

The media product is then sold to consumers and advertisers, producing cash through direct sales or accounts receivable. This cash can be returned to the process to create the next issue of the media product.

Additional cash is used to make payment on debts and, if there is excess cash, returned to the equity of the owner.

The amount of money regularly returned to the production process depends upon the medium and management choices. Newspapers, magazines, and broadcasters must regularly return large portions of the cash obtained from sales to the production process because of the frequency of their operations. The amount returned, however, is more variable for book publishers and motion picture and multimedia producers, who tend to produce discrete separate products and must make specific decisions about what and when to produce.

PROBLEMS OF FINANCING A NEW FIRM OR PRODUCT

As noted above, the financing issue for new companies and products is very important, because in the research and development stages there is no income from consumers, and income begins slowly in the introduction stage but is generally insufficient to cover costs. This process is illustrated in figure 8.2, which shows that the company's cash flow is continuously negative during the

MEDIA COMPANIES

Figure 8.1. Financial Flow in Media with Revenue from Advertising and Circulation

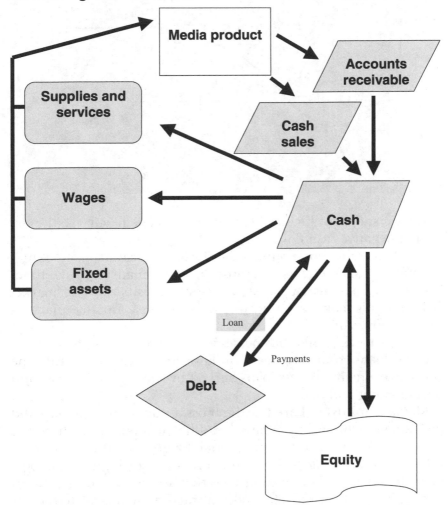

initial stages but then begins to rise and achieves positive figures if the introduction is successful and maturation occurs.

This is particularly problematic for the establishment of new companies. It means not only that persons intent on establishing firms must identify market needs that their companies will meet and have clear and reasonable business plans, but that they must

Figure 8.2. Cash Flow during Development and Introduction of a New Product or Service

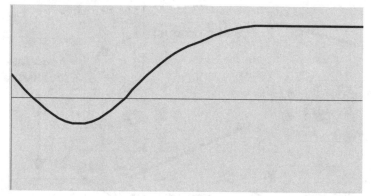

also have sufficient financial resources available to survive the period of negative cash flow.

The problem is compounded because the great majority of new businesses fail, sometimes because of poor financing, sometimes because of poor management, and sometimes because of market reasons. This makes such start-up enterprises generally unattractive to sources of capital.

As a result, most new businesses are financed out of the owner's savings, loans from relatives or in-laws, and occasionally with the support of small business loans backed by some governments and development authorities.

Media firms overall are not the most attractive for start-up and development financing because traditional media industries are not perceived as having the potential for growth. Most tend to be relatively unexciting to investors compared to high-technology, biotechnology, and other industries that are perceived as modern and rising industries. The most attractive media-related firms today are those involved in online and other new media activities, despite problems in their current performance.

These perceptions are important because they mean that most media firms fall under traditional business analysis when it comes to financing and financial issues, and that sources of venture capital and other forms of risk capital are not likely to see their potential for producing rapid growth through innovative products that can well reward high-risk investment.

158

Media firms are also affected because most survive as small enterprises or can grow only to become midsized firms. Only a few develop into large firms.

The establishment pattern for media and communication firms, then, is to start as a traditional small firm built and operated with equity capital from their owners, with little credit or other financing available from suppliers and capital sources. As the firms become more established and grow, they are able to obtain greater amounts of trade credit and secured loans that reduce their dependence upon revenue and their owners' financing.

These factors are important in terms of financial management because small firms tend to have more of their assets in cash, receivables, and fixed assets and less in fewer inventories than larger, more established firms do. Simultaneously they tend to have more of their liabilities in accounts payable and less net worth than larger, more established firms do. This means those smaller firms have to pay greater attention to issues of working capital, rapid collection of accounts, and liquidity of assets.

Cash-flow issues are not only encountered by start-up firms and small- and medium-sized enterprises, however. Established and successful firms also face the problem of negative cash flow when introducing new products. A record company, for example, will be spending money without offsetting income as it selects, records, masters, manufactures, distributes, and begins marketing a recording artist's CD. When sales begin, revenue begins to offset the costs, but initially not so much as to pay for expenses. If the artist is successful, the cash flow moves into positive figures, and the company will benefit if revenues exceed costs and the CD reaches profitability.

This negative cash-flow process in the introduction of new products is complicated by the introduction of upgraded products or multiple new products, because more than one product can have a negative cash flow simultaneously and create a significant drain on financial resources. If the company has insufficient cash resources, it will run out of working capital before the new products have the opportunity to become successful. This problem can be seen in figure 8.3.

The problem of insufficient working capital has been particularly difficult for emerging multimedia and software companies,

Figure 8.3. Cash Flow during Development and Introduction of Upgraded Products and Services

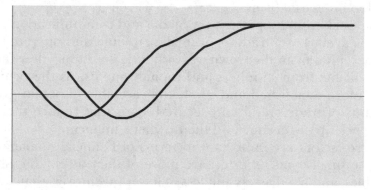

who must often introduce upgrades to their products or additional products before their initial product or products have reached positive cash flows or profitability. The same problem often presents difficulties for small independent book publishers and video producers.

In the late 1990s, however, because of the enthusiasm of venture capitalists and other investors for dot-com firms, many start-up firms were able to obtain large infusions of capital by having their shares publicly traded or through other financial arrangements with investors. The sudden growth of financial resources in these firms led to a situation in which many managers with little experience managing cash believed their firms had huge and endless amounts of money and made many mistakes that caused numerous firms to face financial crises and close.

FINANCING CONTINUING OPERATIONS

Once a firm is established and cash flow has developed, it is still not unusual for revenue from sales to be insufficient to meet all the financial needs of the firm. This occurs because the firm may need to invest in expensive equipment or purchase buildings, because the firm may experience seasonal fluctuations in income that do not provide sufficient revenue during some parts of the year to cover operating expenses, or because it may obtain an order that

160

requires making a large initial expenditure that will be recouped only when the order is completed.

A videotape reproduction studio, for example, might receive a manufacturing order from a motion picture studio to produce 500,000 video copies of a motion picture for sales and rental with payment being made upon delivery. This would require the reproduction studio to spend more than $1 million on videotapes, covers, employee time, and other costs prior to receiving its payment from the film company. Unless the firm already has sufficient cash to pay for those expenditures, it will need to find financing to cover the costs.

A magazine company may find that it obtains the bulk of its advertising revenue in two months during the spring and two months during the fall. If it has not reserved sufficient income from those months for the lean months, it may need to seek financing to pay expenses during some of the other eight months of the year.

CREDIT MANAGEMENT

Credit management in media firms involves controlling sales credit for customer purchases of advertising space and time, and service credit for purchases of subscriptions for media products by audiences.

Advertising sales account for the majority of income in most media firms. Purchases of advertising on credit create a need for significant attention to developments in those accounts. This need is particularly strong in commercial radio and television, newspapers, and most magazines. Cable systems and some magazines rely most heavily on sales of the media product to consumers, and credit management in these firms tends to focus more on the customer accounts for services provided but for which payment has not yet been received. Because circulation sales are also important to newspapers, magazines, and cable systems, management of these customer accounts also receives attention in those industries.

Credit management involves deciding whether to issue sales or service credit, controlling the use of that credit, and collecting the accounts. Newspapers, magazines, and cable systems risk only a

Obtaining Financing through Secured Debt

When a company is new and not well established, or if an existing company's ability to pay debts is uncertain, it is still sometimes possible to obtain financing for some activities by securing the debt with something of value that the lender can collect upon if the debt is not repaid.

Some common types of security are collateral, loans against inventory, and receivable assignment.

Collateral Lenders secure debts with assets they believe have market value equal to or exceeding their loan. The lender receives a security agreement describing the collateral, and it is filed with a public official giving notice of the lender's claim to the asset. Collateral is typically assets that are fairly easily sold such as land and buildings, machinery and equipment, vehicles, etc.

Inventory Loans If a firm is storing inventory that it has already purchased, that inventory has value, and some inventory can be used as security for debt if it is deemed relatively unperishable and easily marketable. Depending upon the circumstances of the firm seeking a loan, there are a variety of types of arrangements in which the inventory can be kept in the firm's storage facilities, or it may be required to be moved to an independent facility.

Accounts Receivable Because these are liquid, current assets, the assignment of some accounts receivable are accepted for security on debt by lenders, typically for no more than about three-fourths of their value. Such financing is sometimes used to help firms fill unusually large orders for which they do not have sufficient internal resources to produce or to increase cash on hand while awaiting payment from customers.

little money each time they send issues or provide service to a customer who is billed after the service is provided. However, television stations, newspapers, magazines, and other media risk amounts totaling hundreds of thousands of dollars when they provide advertising services on credit to large advertisers or advertising agencies. As a result, these financial management functions are critical to the survival and profitability of media firms.

Many media companies operate unified credit departments to handle these functions, but some choose to divide the credit functions among several departments. When a unified credit department exists, it may deal with both the advertising and media product sales credit. In other situations, typified by newspapers and magazines, the credit department will usually deal only with

Some Important Types of Short-Term, Unsecured Debt

Media firms use a variety of arrangements to acquire capital for operations. Money used for this purpose is called *working capital*. If a firm does not have sufficient cash on hand in current assets and retained earnings and it is an established, credit-worthy firm, it may arrange several forms of short-term unsecured debt to acquire the working capital it needs for continuing operations.

Commercial Loan. A commercial loan is designed to providing working capital to purchase supplies or finance production or distribution of products. It typically comes from a bank with whom the firm has a regular working relationship. It is a short-term loan, often ninety days, that is shown as a notes payable in the current liabilities section of the company's balance sheet.

Commercial Paper. Large, well-established business, including some media conglomerates, have the ability to issue these unsecured promises to pay a debt and interest. Companies use these as a means of raising short-term cash at a rate lower than bank interest rates. Those who provide the cash in exchange for commercial paper benefit from greater flexibility in maturity dates than is available in other investments, which allows them to invest excess cash for a short period of time.

Line of Credit. This is a form of debt in which a bank and customer agree on an amount of credit that the firm may obtain to meet temporary cash needs or respond to seasonal variations in revenue. The agreement is usually made for a year, and the customer usually pays for the creation of the line of credit, whether it is exercised or not.

Revolving Credit. This type of credit between a bank and customer operates much like a credit card, with the customer borrowing and repaying up to a limit established by the bank and according to agreed-upon terms for interest and payment dates.

Trade Credit. This is the most common type of debt for companies and is based on open accounts for goods and services from suppliers. This debt is a form of working capital extended to the firm by suppliers, because the firm can pay interest if it postpones payment of some or all of the account beyond the normal due date.

advertising sales credit. In these media, credit managers for the circulation departments typically handle subscription service credit.

In either case, those managers responsible for credit functions need to work closely with advertising and service sales departments to set policies and to ensure that credit activities help rather than hinder the overall marketing program of the company. Co-operation between the various departments is essential.

Regardless of the organization's structure and where responsibility for credit activities is located, credit management issues are similar. They involve credit evaluation and determination, credit risk management, and collection.

Credit Evaluation

The decision to extend credit to a customer is made by evaluating the ability of the customer to pay for purchases made on credit and the willingness of the customer to pay as shown in past behavior involving credit purchases. Media managers use a variety of means by which to make such evaluations, including credit applications and credit investigations.

In some types of sales, no significant evaluations are made. This is particularly true in the case of service credit requests for cable service or subscriptions to newspapers or magazines. Little investigation is made because the credit for service between the time the order is placed and when payment received is small and the cost of an investigation outweighs the potential loss.

Because the potential losses from unpaid advertising time or space are greater, credit managers spend a significant amount of time considering the credit worthiness of new advertisers by requiring them to provide information about themselves or researching such information before extending credit.

In some cases a credit manager may request a specific credit investigation beyond the information reported on the application. Because of the expense involved, this is usually done only with new customers who are expected to purchase significant amounts of advertising and who request extensive credit. Such investigations usually involve seeking reports from credit bureaus or credit databases. In some cases a major investigation may be warranted and involve significant analysis of the assets of firms as well.

Once the credit manager obtains information about the firm, he or she can make a rational decision. Every firm has its own guidelines for determining whether to extend credit and how much to provide. Such determinations involve weighing the performance of the applicant in past credit arrangements and the financial strength and stability of the applicant. The credit manager uses information on the application form and from credit investigations to evaluate the credit worthiness of the applicant. There is no easy way to determine what credit to extend, but experience gives credit managers a "feel" for what is appropriate, and these experiences as well as industry guidelines are used to form company policies.

Decisions to grant or refuse credit, of course, must be made in accordance with appropriate laws and regulations. Similarly, laws and common sense require that credit conditions and terms must be made clear in the credit applications, purchase orders, and billing statements. In most cases these include provisions for the assessment of late charges and collection.

Credit Risk Management

Risk management involves controlling and lowering the risk that the customers will not repay credit that has been extended. Although sales personnel have incentives to sell as much advertising and as many subscriptions as possible, credit managers must ensure that payment is received. Most managers help manage advertising sales credit by treating certain types of advertisers differently and placing special requirements upon some.

In the case of advertising, credit managers generally set credit limits for classes of advertisers, and companies are not allowed to make purchases above that limit. Limits are often set based on the amount of time the customer has been in business or been a purchaser of advertising. Some credit managers establish limits based on the operating budgets of a firm or some other estimate of how much a firm should spend on advertising. When dealing with large, regular advertisers, managers usually set separate individual limits based specifically on the companies' past performance in paying for advertising purchased on credit.

Collection

Media firms make collection efforts internally and externally. Collections involve getting timely payments from customers who are slow in paying on their advertising sales credit or service credit accounts, and getting payments from customers who have not paid. The collection process begins whenever an account is billed and payment is not received by the due date.

Because media companies value customers, and a variety of factors may account for late payment, collections involve several different and progressively coercive steps. Company employees make the initial steps, but final collection efforts are often done outside the media firm. Sending an account outside the media company is generally considered the last resort for nonpayment. Turning the account over to an attorney or collection agency is expensive, because in many nations collection agencies keep as much as one-third or even half of what they collect as their fee. A variety of national and state laws cover collection efforts, so companies engaging in collections internally and externally must be familiar with the range of permissible collection efforts and those activities that are forbidden. If collection efforts fail, media companies may sue advertisers or persons responsible for accounts in courts of law but typically do so only when the amount of money owned warrants the additional costs of legal action.

Bad Debt

When collection steps ultimately fail to generate payment, the company must deal with the account receivable that cannot be collected. In order to take it out of the accounting system, the uncollectable credit account is transferred to the bad debt account.

Media firms maintain bad debt accounts as a budgeted operating expense item. Obviously it is in the interest of the firm to keep bad debt as low as possible because of its effects on operating expenses and the profitability of firms. Although bad debt losses are generally written off as tax-deductible business costs, the benefits of doing so are far outweighed by the costs. In order to help minimize bad debt, media credit managers track bad debt carefully and make regular comparisons to past performance as a means of evaluating collection effectiveness.

Internal Credit Management Reports

In order for the manager to efficiently manage credit operations, he or she needs regular reports about the condition of accounts.

Important management information is found in aging reports, delinquency reports, and bad debt reports. Many media companies have computer programs that automatically generate such information.

Aging reports provide a look at the status of all the accounts and provide data on credit outstanding, payments received, and payments due. Many companies use aging reports to produce delinquency reports, special reports that show which accounts are overdue or delinquent.

A standard calculation used to indicate the efficiency of a credit department and the rate at which accounts receivable are paid and collected is "days sales outstanding" (DSO). This figure factors in credit sales and receivables and is normally calculated monthly, quarterly, and annually. DSO figures are used for comparative evaluative purposes to show performance of the credit department over time and as indicators of usually contemporary developments in credit management. One widely used DSO calculation is the average trade credit receivables for the last three months times ninety, and then that amount is divided by the total credit sales for last three months This figure provides an indicator of the quantity of the daily sales outstanding. Media firms are operating most efficiently when the DSO figure is low.

Bad debt reports indicate those accounts that cannot be collected and thus are losses to the company. Bad debt is generally reported as a percentage of credit or service sales, total sales, or service revenue for comparative purposes. Most media companies break down bad debt reports by source to gain a better understanding of where problems are developing.

CASH MANAGEMENT ISSUES

In addition to the capital and debt issues faced by companies, they also encounter issues involving cash that the firm receives from investors and operations. Capital and revenue received must be controlled to ensure its availability to pay for assets and future expense payments. Cash management involves the control of this cash in a firm's accounts in such a way that it produces the best possible results for the company.

This involves making choices about cash availability (liquidity) and interest income and choices about when to use the funds and for what purposes. Decisions are made regarding cash coming into a firm, cash leaving a firm, and cash held or invested.

Companies with significant daily income arriving by mail, for example, may choose to utilize banking arrangements whereby the bank picks up the money several times during the day from the post office, collects the funds as rapidly as possible, and then posts the payments to the firm's accounts. This process is speeded up if the firm employs electronic payment systems by which customers make payments directly to the firm's bank accounts.

The virtue of this type of incoming cash management is that it reduces the time between the arrival of payments and when it is converted to cash that can be used by the firm. Accelerating the collection of payments can reduce the amount of cash that a firm must keep on hand to pay day-to-day expenses, allowing that cash to be used more effectively elsewhere.

Outgoing cash management is designed to delay payments that the firm must make in a way that permits it to use the cash but without harming its relationships with suppliers and others whom it must pay, or its rating with credit reporting agencies. In order to achieve this goal, cash managers track payment due dates and time payments to arrive at the debtor only when it is due, a process easier to manage when a firm can use electronic fund transfers rather than checks. Managers also attempt to maximize the float time between when checks are written and when they will be cashed, and to determine and maintain the lowest possible cash balances and compensating balances in bank accounts.

The combination of the tactics of rapid collection of incoming funds and slow payment of outgoing funds maximizes the cash that a firm can have on hand to finance operations and obtain income.

Cash management also becomes an issue for firms when they have excess cash from capital or current operations but wish to save that cash for future operations. The need to preserve cash may be for either the short or long term, but because the firm does not wish to have funds sitting ineffectually in checking accounts, finding appropriate methods to achieve a return from the cash while preserving necessary liquidity requires special attention.

The problem of handling large amounts of cash from capital is illustrated on pp. 170–71. Decisions on cash management are usually made by the manager of the firm or delegated to the accounting or treasurer's office. Depending upon the length of time that cash can be used for income production, a variety of arrangements are possible, ranging from the use of money market accounts or investments in certificates of deposit, bonds, commercial paper, or other investments.

SUMMARY

Financial issues play an important role in the development and operation of all media and communications firms and require that managers throughout the firms understand issues associated with capital, income, expenditures, and debt. Companies of all sizes require knowledgeable financial managers. That need is especially strong in start-up firms, public firms, and firms coping with large cash flows.

The need for skillful financial management dictates that managers with special education and experience are in place to serve the needs of firms effectively. Other managers in the firm, however, also need to have a basic understanding of the issues and importance of these functions, because their strategies and operations are dependent upon effective management of the financial resources available.

SUGGESTED READINGS

Broadcast Cable Financial Managers Association. *Understanding Broadcasting and Cable Finance: A Handbook for Non-financial Managers*. Des Plaines, Ill.: Broadcast Cable Financial Managers Association, 1994.

Gitman, Lawrence. *Principles of Financial Management*. 9th ed. Boston: Addison-Wesley Publishing, 1999.

International Newspaper Financial Executives. *Newspaper Financial Management: An Introduction*. Reston, Va.: INFE, 1993.

Myddleton, David R. *The Essence of Financial Management*. Englewood Cliffs, N.J.: Prentice-Hall, 1995.

Van Horne, James C. , and John W. Wachowitz. *Fundaments of Financial Management*. 10th ed. Englewood Cliffs, N.J.: Prentice-Hall, 1997.

Vogel, Harold L. *Entertainment Industry Economics: A Guide for Financial Analysis*. 4th ed. Cambridge: Cambridge University Press, 1998.

The Problem of Large Infusions of Cash

Although it seems contradictory, suddenly obtaining a large amount of capital in the form of cash presents significant problems for firms because it requires that managers spend a great deal of time and effort maintaining and properly overseeing those funds.

This difficulty was encountered by a large number of dot-com and multimedia firms in recent years that made initial public offerings in the stock market and suddenly had hundreds of millions of dollars in cash in their accounts. If care is not taken in managing such funds, one risks following the pattern of rapid diminishment of the cash that was seen in many dot-com firms in the 1990s as they spent wildly and did not replace what they spent with revenues from sales of products and services (fig. 8.4).

To avoid such problems, firms with sudden wealth must behave more like banking institutions than media companies, or they will misuse or mismanage capital that will be needed as much as four or five years after it is received. Managing such sudden wealth typically requires expertise not readily available in growing media and communication firms because the cash itself must be invested or lent as capital so that it is not wasted and accumulates appropriate returns before it is needed by the company.

In most cases it is appropriate for companies to hire a financial manager for these funds who has expertise in the management of cash capital, often a person from the banking or investment community. The company board and management also need to develop and implement specific policies to guide the utilization of the capital.

Even internally, companies benefit and make effective use of the capital by allocating it to growth and projects through processes similar to approaching investors or lending institutions. Decisions on what to fund and the amounts to provide internally should be made on the basis of sound internal business plans, research and development strategies, and other factors rather than less rigorous reviews or whims that lead to loss of cash capital or decisions that reduce the ability of the firm to make the most of its cash resources.

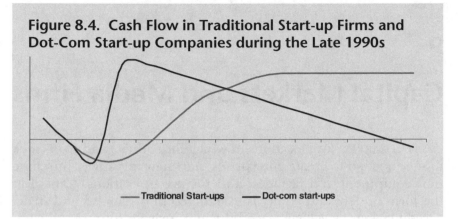

Figure 8.4. Cash Flow in Traditional Start-up Firms and Dot-Com Start-up Companies during the Late 1990s

———Traditional Start-ups   ———Dot-com start-ups

9

Capital Markets and Media Firms

CAPITAL MARKETS are locations in which individuals and firms seek money needed to create enterprises, start new initiatives, purchase new equipment and facilities, and finance operations. Capital in the form of debt and equity is exchanged in organized and structured markets as well as placed through private sources. All companies, including media firms, must have capital and access to capital to continue operations.

When individuals save money they can use that money to buy goods and services, or they can invest that money or lend it to others for a fee. Money that is saved can be placed in banks, investment funds, and other capital accumulation institutions, or lent directly to those needing capital.

The wealth of individuals or groups of individuals can be combined to create a firm and to obtain ownership or partial ownership of a firm. The existence of large amounts of capital through stock markets has helped create large companies that would have been impossible for individuals or small groups of individuals to create with their own capital alone and has made it possible for small firms to gain capital to introduce new products and services.

Those who obtain capital through ownership shares or borrowed capital use the funds to purchase raw materials, required materials and services, and the labor necessary to produce their own products and services, and to market, distribute, and sell them to purchasers. The income from the transaction is then used to repay the capital and the firm's costs of production, distribution, and administration.

WANTS AND NEEDS OF CAPITAL SOURCES

Those with capital to lend want the highest possible return for their lending of the capital, and, depending upon their strategies, they typically want that return in the short or medium term. They also pursue different strategies with regard to degrees of risk and may seek to maximize return and security across loans or investments in multiple firms.

The desire for a high return is tempered because the forces of supply and demand influence demand and supply of capital. If the price of capital rises, the number of borrowers and the amount of capital demand will decline. If the price declines significantly, those who have capital may use it in other ways that produce better returns, and the supply may also decline. The price of capital affects the demand for capital, but monetary and fiscal policies of central banks and governments and the condition of the general economy also influence the price.

In addition to return concerns, those who make capital available for use by others wish to preserve that capital and to have the value of capital increase because of the return from the rent or ownership obtained through its use. Different persons and institutions with capital have different strategies in how they approach their wants and needs, the degrees of risk they will take, and the amounts of capital that they will place in types of risk situations.

The strategies and degrees of risk can be seen in a financial pyramid of investment options (fig. 9.1). This pyramid also loosely represents the amount of financial resources available in capital markets for different purposes. More capital is placed and available in lower-risk investments because most persons are not willing to risk losing any or very much of their money.

The base is built upon funds placed in safe, relatively liquid investments with a reasonable rate of return. This often takes the form of investments in treasury bills, bonds, or notes issued by national governments or state and municipal bonds. The second level represents investments intended for growth of capital or income and typically includes stocks and bonds in established, financially stable, and growing firms that tend to be market leaders in their industries.

At the third and fourth levels the risks of no return or loss of investment increase significantly. Speculative investments are made usually in stocks, bonds, or debt with a possibility for high return if the companies in which such investments are made prove to be successful. These speculative investments are often made in

Figure 9.1. The Financial Pyramid of Capital Risk and Capital Placement

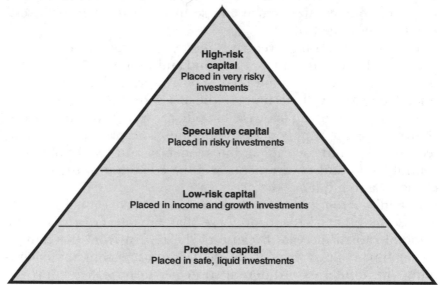

firms in emerging fields and often involve firms that are just changing from private to public companies. The highest risk investments, at the top of the pyramid, often take the form of venture capital in which return is uncertain but can produce very large rewards if a company or its products are successful. All of these strategies are used in providing different types of capital to both new and mature media firms.

VENTURE CAPITAL HELPS FUND NEW COMPANIES AND EXPANSION

Venture capital is a form of high-risk capital that is made available to provide seed money, finance start-up ventures, fund growth or expansion, or help reverse the fortunes of an existing firm in poor condition by providing the financial resources necessary to restructure and reinvest to improve its situation. Individuals and firms who provide venture capital typically invest only a small portion of their resources in venture capital and make it available only for short periods of time. These funds are typically provided to entrepreneurs who have a solid business concept and a product or service that may have a chance for success in the market.

The concept behind venture capital has existed for several centuries, in which consortiums of individuals funded potentially profitable enterprises. During the latter half of the twentieth century, however, this process developed more effectively as part of an emerging private equity market. Acceptance of the concept of venture capital and the development of methods for spreading risk led pension funds, insurance companies, holding companies, banks, and other organizations and individuals to place some of their funds with venture capital companies that invest and manage such funds or to become involved in direct investments in companies themselves.

Even the high-risk world of venture capital operates on principles of risk and reward, and different venture capitalists have different strategies about the types of firms and industries in which they will invest, whether they will fund product development or company start-ups, or whether they will get involved when companies first make shares available on stock markets.

Venture capitalists often seek a portion of the firm's profit, shares in the firm, or royalties from the innovative product or service for which financing is provided. In many cases they become partners in the management of the companies and seek positions on the board of directors so they can provide advice and other assistance and monitor the performance of the company.

Most media and communications firms in developed nations do not seek venture capital because they tend to be mature and in mature industries in which the risks are well understood. In recent years, however, online service and content companies and new media operations spun off from established firms have used venture capital to fund their development, start-up, and introduction to the market. Similarly, a good deal of venture capital has been placed with new online and mobile content firms whose ideas for new businesses have attracted interest.

In 1999, for example, about 40 percent of all U.S. venture capital was placed in Internet-specific investments and an additional 17 percent in other communications firms. A large number of such firms failed in 2000 and 2001, leading some venture capitalists to become more conservative in their funding choices, but venture capitalists still remain the primary funding source for a large number of new media ventures.

After their establishment, most small- and medium-sized enterprises operate along the lines outlined in chapter 8, generating profits that can be placed in reserves for later capital expenditures, such as new equipment or facilities, or for expansion through purchasing other firms.

This self-generation of capital is the primary means by which most firms develop and grow. Through creating wealth they make themselves more stable and valuable. When the capital needs are large, such as for purchasing land and constructing new buildings, such firms typically seek to borrow capital from traditional lending institutions.

Most media firms operate independently of venture capital and capital available from stock markets, following the pattern found in most small- and midsized firms. As a result, managers must make it a goal for the firm itself to be financially strong, developing its own wealth so that it can directly use that wealth either as capital or as the basis upon which capital can be borrowed.

This issue of generating money and making oneself strong so that one may borrow capital applies to both commercial and not-for-profit media, both of which have future capital needs if they are to develop, respond to changes in technologies, and improve the quality of their content and services.

A source of traditional capital has been banks and thrift institutions that invest customers' money by lending it to firms needing money for capital expenditures, to expand their activities, or to gain short-term financing for operations. These lenders have tended to be more conservative than other capital sources in terms of the amount of risk they will accept. As a result banks and other thrift institutions tend to make loans only to established, stable media firms or under conditions requiring significant security.

Banks and thrift firms create profits on loans by lending money to users at a higher rate than they pay their depositors, whose capital is pooled and used by the bank. The availability and price of capital from banks are thus affected by fluctuations in the amount of funds deposited, interest rates paid customers, and the state of the general economy.

The bank debt that a firm incurs through borrowing capital is typically distinguished by the length of time before full repayment is due. This is important because the two have different effects on the annual performance of a firm reflected in its accounting statements.

Long-term debt describes debt that is not expected to be paid within a company's fiscal year. Such indebtedness is often used to finance the growth and development of the firm and to acquire capital goods, machinery, equipment, and facilities needed for production. Because it is multiyear debt, only the portion due in a particular year must be repaid and will affect financial performance during that year.

A radio station, for example, might use a long-term loan to purchase a new building in which to locate studios and offices. An advertising agency might use long-term debt to acquire capital to purchase a Web-design firm, or a motion picture studio might use a loan to purchase equipment to update its editing studios.

Short-term debt from banks and thrift institutions tends to take the forms of financing designed to meet operation requirements of media firms. These typically involve various forms of loans that provide working capital such as commercial credit, lines of credit, and revolving credit as was discussed in chapter 8.

STOCK MARKETS SUPPORT LARGE MEDIA FIRMS

Stock markets are a means of capital accumulation that bring together persons and institutions with money to invest and companies that wish to sell shares of their ownership in exchange for that capital. Companies "go public," that is, list their companies on stock markets to obtain capital for growth and development, including the acquisition of other companies. In other cases, firms have gone public as a means of allowing its original private owners or heirs to obtain cash for other purposes and investments.

Major media companies worldwide are increasingly turning to

stock markets to meet their growing needs for capital as investments in expensive technologies and global expansion dramatically expand their need for capital. In creating or transforming themselves into public companies, firms make an initial public offering of the shares on the market of their choice. It is the first time that shares are given a market value that is based on projections of future growth and performance.

When a firm is transformed into a stock company listed for trade on public markets, it must comply with laws and regulations that govern such companies in the country of its origin. In addition, it must comply with procedures outlined in its articles of incorporation, by-laws, and other relevant managerial documents. The firm must also comply with relevant laws and regulations in countries in whose stock exchange its shares are traded. Thus, a firm in Italy is governed by Italian corporate law and, if its shares are traded in the United States, by U.S. securities laws.

Unlisted stocks can also be traded in what is called over-the-counter market. This type of trading is also governed by various national laws and regulations, but the requirements that must be met by companies are typically less rigorous than those for listed companies.

Shares in media companies are categorized as "cyclical" in stock market language because they are not recession resistant and are typically affected by the business environment. The performance of media stocks depends on multiple factors, including advertising volume, subscriptions and other sales, prices of essential resources such as paper or content, promotional spending patterns, labor relations, capital spending patterns, the availability of cash flow to fund new activities, cost-cutting moves, and consolidation in the industry. Obviously these factors are influenced by larger economic and environmental concerns, so media share prices respond to economic climates and to expectations about the future.

In the late 1990s investors worldwide expressed more confidence in the future of Internet and multimedia firms than in traditional media firms, so those share prices surged ahead of traditional firms. Following the realization in 2000 that the new media firms were not able to deliver positive returns even in the midterm, their share prices fell, but many remained overvalued compared to traditional media firms. Among traditional firms, companies with significant production of television programming and motion pictures have tended to have higher prices in recent years than those firms that primarily operate broadcasting stations or channels and print media.

Although new media shares have attracted large investments, they are viewed as having low financial performance but the potential for significant growth and future profitability. Because of the uncertainty of the firms, their capital has primarily resulted from the risk funds of institutional investors. Traditional media have been more attractive to institutional investors desiring capital preservation, income, and predictable growth.

Stock Market Operations

Domestic laws govern the operations of stock exchanges, and regulations are established by those who operate the exchanges. Generally, persons who wish to buy shares place an order with a broker, who sends the order to the stock exchange, where traders find a seller (a shareholder in the listed company who wishes to sell) who has made the shares available.

Before electronic communications the process involved direct contact between traders, but the use of sophisticated computers now makes most of the process automated, with computers keeping track of prices, individual trades, and a variety of other information that makes trading and record keeping much more rapid than in the past.

Investors primarily fall into two major categories: individuals and institutions. A third category, inside investors, can be either individuals or institutions. Individual investors are single persons who, depending upon their interests and wealth, purchase one or many shares in one or more companies. Institutional investors are the primary source of capital in stock markets and include pension plans, investment firms, insurance companies, banks, and other institutions that invest some or all of their available funds in stock markets on behalf of their clients and themselves.

Inside investors are individuals employed within a firm who own shares in that firm. The term *insider* is typically applied to those who manage or direct the company while owning shares, such as members of boards of directors, corporate officials, and company executives. Institutional investors are considered insiders if one of their executives is on the board of or an officer in a company in which it owns shares.

Different types of equity shares are offered on stock markets, providing different rights to managing and sharing in the financial performance of firms. The most important are common stock, classified stock, and preferred stock. In some cases convertible shares exist that permit holders of one type of share to convert them to another.

Common stock is the primary type of share available. It proportionally splits the equity in the firm and the rights to make decisions regarding the firm such as voting for directors and officers, making changes in the company charter, and approving new stock issues. Each share has an equal voice in the decisions.

Classified stock proportionally splits the equity in the firm but limits or removes voting rights in one or more categories of stock. This is often done to limit the control of shareholders of publicly traded shares. The founders of the firm or their heirs typically hold the most powerful shares, and these shares are not publicly traded. Among media firms, these are typically found more often in newspaper-based companies where strong social, cultural, and political orientations remain, and the original owners wish to protect that orientation—and sometimes their own pocketbooks—from the powerful influence of outside capital.

Preferred stock is shares that pay dividends at a specified rate and carry preference over common stock when dividends are paid or the firm is liquidated. Preferred shares rarely carry voting rights. Convertible stock is typically shares of classified or preferred stock that can or must be converted at a specific price and/or time to common stock.

Shares of firms are constantly traded, and the price of any firm's shares is dependent upon the willingness of investors to purchase at a given price based on their view of the economy, the performance of the firm, and its future prospects. The price of shares is important to companies because they typically retain portions of the shares themselves, and changes in price affect their wealth and the perception of their firms by investors.

Effects of Changes in the Price of Shares

The prices of shares in companies rise or fall depending upon the price investors are willing to pay for shares. That willingness is affected by perceptions of a variety of factors, including company profitability, dividends paid, company strategies, industry potential, and the general economy. Changes in the price of shares can both help and harm company strategies.

Stock market instability, for example, forced News Corp. to postpone plans to restructure the company by spinning off its digital television operations, including BskyB and Star TV, in the fall of 2000. The volatility in the stock markets was caused by investors' uncertainty over information and technology company shares. The plan to create Sky Digital Networks with a share flotation of Sky Digital Networks valued at $40 billion had been announced but was put off after the price for shares in News Corp. dropped 7.5 percent on October 18 alone, thus reducing the amount of money that would be raised.

Beginning in January 2001, Viacom began repurchasing shares in the firm. It bought back $1 billion in stock that month. On February 1 it announced it would buy up to $2 billion more in the coming months, and its share price rose 2.5 percent on the announcement.

Stock Markets Worldwide

Stock markets exist worldwide to facilitate the exchange of shares in public companies. Each operates with its own sets of rules and procedures and is guided by the laws and regulations of the countries in which it operates.

Today, the stock market featuring the largest number of media companies is the New York Stock Exchange. In most cases, shares in the largest media companies are traded on the largest stock exchange in their nation of origin, and they are sometimes traded in markets in other countries. The large number of U.S. media firms traded on NYSE has helped make it the location of the largest number of media stocks in one market.

Because of the complexities of securities laws in each nation, and because stock markets have traditionally provided sufficient capital for major domestic firms, these markets traditionally exchanged only shares of domestic companies. The growth of multinational firms needing capital worldwide, and telecommunications developments during the final decades of the twentieth century that permit rapid global communications and data exchange, however, have led some firms to list themselves on multiple markets.

The most important exchanges in the world are located in Frankfurt, London, New York, Paris, and Tokyo. Significant markets in other parts of the world include Buenos Aires, Hong Kong, Rio de Janeiro, Seoul, Singapore, and Sydney.

Major Media Companies Traded on Stock Markets

Shares in nearly every major media company in the developed world are now traded on one or more stock markets because few large firms have sufficient access to capital to keep them from becoming public. Among the hundreds of media firms in which investors can choose are companies such as Walt Disney, Dow Jones, EMAP, Fairfax, Gannett, Lagardère, News Corp., New York Times, Pearson, Quebecor, Reuters, Televisa, AOL Time Warner, Torstar, Viacom, and the Washington Post.

Although broadcasting and motion picture companies entered the stock market around the middle of the twentieth century, newspaper companies were reticent to do so, and most did not begin entering the market until the 1960s (table 9.1).

As media companies worldwide have increasingly turned to stock markets for capital, they have gained resources that have allowed them to improve their content and its presentation, upgrade facilities and equipment, begin new initiatives, and establish media products. They have gained funds that have helped them grow, acquire other companies, and create relatively large media companies and conglomerates. The interest in media firms can be seen in the value of investments in major firms. This value, of course, fluctuates as the prices of shares rise and fall.

Simultaneously, new pressures for increased company performance have been placed upon managers because of the obligations to shareholders whose interest is primarily the highest possible regular returns, and this has caused managers to work for increased cash flows, return on sales, and higher net profit margins. These market pressures have led to short-term thinking in some media companies in which the management has determined that the best possible short-term performance measures are the pri-

TABLE 9.1
Going Public: When Newspaper Company Shares Began Trading

Before 1960

	Dow Jones & Co.
1938	Times Mirror Co.

1960s

1967	Gannett Co.
1969	Knight Newspapers Inc. (merged with Ridder Publications in 1974 to form Knight-Ridder Inc.)
	Ridder Publications Inc. (merged with Knight Newspapers in 1974 to form Knight-Ridder Inc.)
	Lee Enterprises Inc.
	New York Times Co.

1970s

1970	Media General Inc.
1971	Washington Post Co.
1972	Harte-Hanks (privatized 1984)

1980s

1981	A. H. Belo Corp.
1983	Tribune Co.
1986	Pulitzer Publishing Co.
1988	McClatchy Newspapers Inc.
	E. W. Scripps Co.
1989	Central Newspapers Inc.

1990s

1993	Harte-Hanks Communications
1994	Hollinger International (American Publishing Co.)
1996	Providence Journal Co.

Market Capitalization of Media and Communication Firms

Market capitalization is a term used to determine the comparative value of firms traded on a stock market. The value is created by multiplying the market price and the number of its issued and outstanding common shares.

The largest media and communications companies have market capitalization and revenues in the tens of billion dollars range (table 9.2).

TABLE 9.2
MARKET CAPITALIZATION OF 20 LARGEST MEDIA FIRMS, 2000 (MILLIONS)

Company	Market Capitalization
1. Time Warner	$112,129.9
2. Disney	70,502.2
3. Vivendi Universal	45,133.5
4. CBS	42,275.3
5. Viacom	36,687.9
6. Cox Communications	25,788.4
7. Reuters	22,099.6
8. Pearson	18,734.6
9. Gannett	17,803.1
10. News Corp.	12,804.7
11. Reed International	10,809.0
12. McGraw-Hill	9,100.5
13. Lagardère	7,741.3
14. New York Times	7,229.0
15. USA Networks	6,756.2
16. EMI Group	6,524.5
17. United News & Media	6,249.8
18. Carlton	5,277.4
20. Times Mirror	5,271.9

mary objectives for the firm. This type of bottom-line orientation can result in management's not paying sufficient attention to the reinvestment needs of the firm and its needs to grow and develop.

Some media critics also argue that the major problem with stock ownership is that it causes many owners and managers to move away from a public-service orientation toward a commercial orientation equivalent to that of any big business, and that this affects the type of content and nature of service provided by public firms.

Shares in media companies can be categorized, in terms of the traditional classifications used on Wall Street, as "cyclical." Cyclical stocks are defined as stocks that are not recession resistant and typically are strongly affected by the business environment.

The performance of media stocks depends on multiple factors, including advertising volume, subscriptions and other sales, prices of essential resources such as paper or content, promotional spending patterns, labor relations, capital spending patterns, the ability to use cash flow to fund new activities, cost-cutting moves (which can result in operating leverage), and consolidation in the industry. Obviously these factors are influenced positively and negatively at various points by larger economic and environmental concerns. Media share prices respond to recessionary economic climates and to expectations for the future.

In recent years companies with significant production of television programming and motion pictures have tended to have higher prices than whose are primarily operating broadcasting stations or channels and print media. Although new media shares have attracted large investments, they are viewed as having low financial performance, but some have the potential for significant growth and future profitability. Because of the firms' uncertainty, their capital has primarily come from the risk funds of institutional investors. Traditional media have been more attractive to institutional investors desiring capital preservation, income, and predictable growth.

THE GLOBALIZATION OF MEDIA CAPITAL

A phenomenon in the last quarter of the twentieth century was the growing internationalization of capital as a whole. In practice this has meant that the location in which capital is produced need not be the location in which it is invested. As a result, capital accumulated in the United States can be invested in the Brazil, capital gathered in the Netherlands can be available in Japan, and capital collected in Singapore can be borrowed in Korea.

The reason for this international capital flow is that those institutions and individuals with capital look for opportunities to achieve the best returns or growth opportunities. Because of differences in national economies, those returns may occur in different nations at different times.

The desires of capital sources to find better returns have been supported by developments in communications and financial systems. As the mechanisms and processes for better information and capital flow matured, media firms began to feel the effects of the international capital market.

A prime example of these effects on U.S. media is the motion picture industry, which was primarily a domestically financed industry until the 1980s. As international capital became easily available, producers began to see it as a means of bringing new money into the industry. A large number of film productions began to be financed by capital from France, Japan, and the United Kingdom. The industry then became a target of direct international investment, and by the 1990s the majority of U.S. motion picture studios had been purchased by firms from Japan, Australia, and France.

European capital also flowed to the United States when companies such as Hachette Filipacchi, Lagardère, and Bertelsmann made massive purchases of American magazine and book publishing firms that catapulted those firms into the positions of the leading magazine and book publishers in the world.

Large amounts of capital flowed to foreign media firms from the United States as well. By listing their shares on the New York Stock Exchange, firms such as Australia's News Corp., Britain's Pearson, Japan's Sony, and Spain's Telefonica have gained access to billions of dollars in U.S. capital.

Capital also flowed abroad through investments of U.S. media firms. NBC, for example, invested $26 million and took a 1 percent ownership share of the number 2 Mexican broadcaster, TV Azteca, in 2000. The deal provided NBC further access to the Mexican market and to the Internet and telecom operations of the Mexican broadcaster. The previous year, the *Wall Street Journal* entered a joint venture with Pearson Plc, publisher of the *Financial Times,* and the Dutch media conglomerate VNU to finance and publish a Russian-language business daily in Moscow.

The globalization of capital is increasingly separating ownership of large media firms from the nations in which they were established and forcing managers to take a more international outlook and approach to their strategies and operations.

SUGGESTED READINGS

Bradley, Edward S., and Richard J. Teweles. *The Stock Market.* 7th ed. New York: John Wiley and Sons, 1998.

Dufey, Gunther, and Ian Giddy. *The International Money Market.* 2nd ed. Englewood Cliffs, N.Y.: Prentice-Hall, 1994.

Golis, Christopher C. *Enterprise and Venture Capital*. 3rd ed. London: Allyn and Unwin, 1999.

Harvard Business School Press. *Corporate Finance and Capital Markets*. Cambridge, Mass.: Harvard Business School Press, 1991.

Robertson, Robert J., and Mark Van Osnabrugge. *Angel Investing: Matching Startup Funds with Startup Companies—A Guide for Entrepreneurs, Individual Investors, and Venture Capitalists*. San Francisco: Jossey-Bass, 2000.

10

The Development of Large Media Companies

LARGE MEDIA COMPANIES result from the creation of an administrative organization that is used to pursue business strategies that include growth as a goal. Until the last half of the twentieth century, media firms tended to be small- and medium-sized enterprises. Even the companies operated by publishing giants such as Hearst, Northcliffe, and Pulitzer were relatively small enterprises in terms of revenue, employment, and facilities when compared to other industries.

The development of large media firms resulted from changes in technologies that produced additional types of media, from strategies of growth and expansion, and from the availability of capital, particularly through equity markets, to finance expansion and further development of media firms. In the United States, commercial radio networks begun in the first half of the twentieth century expanded into television and rapidly grew into large media firms by the 1970s. In the 1970s and 1980s, a number of newspaper companies began expanding, and many became large firms by emphasizing newspaper, magazine, and book publishing holdings before deciding to expand into other media. Similar movements can be seen among publishers in other major companies as cable and satellite developed and government policies permitted commercial television where it had not previously been authorized and other media opportunities.

Although important media firms have existed since the commercialization of newspapers in the nineteenth century, the rapid and seemingly unending expansion of communication conglomerates at the end of the twentieth century has fueled rhetoric that, taken uncritically, might lead some to believe that such conglomerates are self-sustaining, continually expanding, nearly immortal organizations.

This view, however, ignores widely differing degrees of success in media firms that result from differences in their strategies, organization, and operation. Some have used centralized management, whereas others use decentralized management; some require standardization among their media products, but others permit individuality. Some firms operate as single entities, others operate with divisions and subsidiaries; some are operated with a strategic vision, others are not. Some firms seek higher degrees of integration than others; some seek more product and geographic diversification than others. These types of factors create differences in behavior and the ability of communication firms to grow or survive, so one cannot view all media empires as similar and behaving in the same manner.

Media companies have grown in size for a variety of reasons. First, some have become large firms as part of the aspirations of strong leaders who have reinvested profits and often gathered new capital—in many cases by becoming publicly traded companies—to undertake strategies of growth and expansion. These leaders have sought out opportunities for expansion and exploited the weaknesses of other firms through acquisition or creating mergers. In recent decades this has been seen in the case of the Australian company News Corp., led by Rupert Murdoch, and the U.S. firm Gannett Co., which was transformed from a small, relatively unknown local newspaper company into one of the largest media conglomerates by Allen Neuharth. Similarly, the Walt Disney Co. has been developed into one of the world's largest media and entertainment firms under the leadership of Michael Eisner.

The growth of media firms is possible because of the ability of company leaders to translate their visions into actions. Large firms are not created only to serve the aspirations of leaders, however; sometimes growth is precipitated by the firm's regular need for some resources or resources to which it does not currently have access. In such cases it may purchase important suppliers such as programming production companies, paper companies, or distribution service firms.

Efforts to stabilize the finances of a firm also have played a role in the development of media firms. They increase their size and scope to help reduce the effects of changes in specific market seg-

Who's the Biggest? Does it Matter?

One regularly encounters listings of "the biggest" or "the largest" companies in media and communications. These are used to make all kinds of points about the industry and the management of the companies on these lists. Most observers accept these lists rather unquestioningly because size comparisons create nice, orderly means for simplifying the world. And they give the impression that the goal of business is to become as large as possible.

Listings of size can be problematic, however, because they are based on the specific accounting item selected for comparison. The indicator used produces important differences in the results.

One regularly used method of comparing firms is market capitalization. It is a perfectly good indicator of size, but it includes only those firms whose shares are publicly traded. It is also problematic because capitalization fluctuates, depending upon share prices in the market. In international lists of media firm capitalization, for example, the giant European media firm Bertelsmann does not exist because it is privately held (see fig. 10.1). The capitalization measure also presents problems in ranking companies that have significant media holdings but whose structures do not allow separate accounting of capitalization for their media operations.

Although revenue-based measures are more inclusive, they also present problems. The biggest difficulty is that the comparison ignores differences in cost structures and operations of firms, something that is never the case (see fig. 10.2, p. 193). As a result, some persons who construct rankings then prefer to use profits produced as an indicator of size for ranking to respond to that criticism. This produces results different from the capitalization and revenue measures. If one considers the top ten in that regard, two firms that were neither in the top ten in terms of capitalization or revenues appear: the American television network NBC (National Broadcasting Co.) and the Canadian printing and publishing firm Thomson Corp. (see fig. 10.3, p. 193).

The real issue with such rankings, of course, is what they tell us. Few observers really think about that question and whether being at the top of the list matters. If a firm is number 4 on a list, does that position give significant advantages over being number 6? Or if a company is in eleventh place and left off a ten-company list, is it significantly different from number 10? Ultimately one questions whether the length of the rankings matters: Should the list rank five, ten, twenty-five, fifty, or one hundred firms? And where do distinctions within the firms develop?

This is not to say that size doesn't matter at all, but that the basis for inclusion and the length of the list are factors that need to be considered when applying meaning to such lists. Being a major player clearly provides advantages in financing, producing, marketing, and distributing media and communication products and services.

Is it then undesirable to be a small- or medium-sized firm? No. Innovative companies, firms providing quality products, and enterprises delivering good customer service can be successful regardless of size. The managers of many firms deliberately choose not to seek largeness but rather to focus their firm's activities and markets to achieve the best returns possible and ensure competitiveness and sustainability.

Increasing company size alone, then, cannot be the overriding goal for a manager. Although there are sometimes excellent reasons for such growth, the choice to increase size needs to be driven by strategic reasons rather than merely the pursuit of size. This is especially true in an era in which media and communication products and services are being increasingly digitized, a process that removes many of the traditional economic incentives for size that existed in the past.

Largeness produces both advantages and disadvantages and is not the answer to all the pressures and issues that companies face. In the end, regardless of size, managers of successful firms must continually seek to make their companies the best they can become, to remain focused on customers and how the firms' products and services can be improved to meet their needs.

Figure 10.1. Largest Media Companies by Market Capitalization, 2000 (U.S.$ Millions)

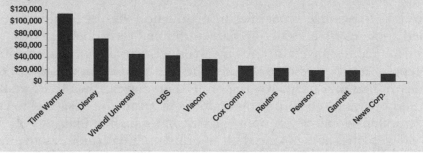

ments or market locations or to make themselves less dependent upon changes in prices by suppliers and distributors.

Because of the desire to stabilize resource supply, some newspaper firms have purchased newsprint mills. From the desire to stabilize distribution arrangements, some magazine companies have purchased magazine distribution companies. Expansion to reduce dependence on a single type of music or a few recording stars, as

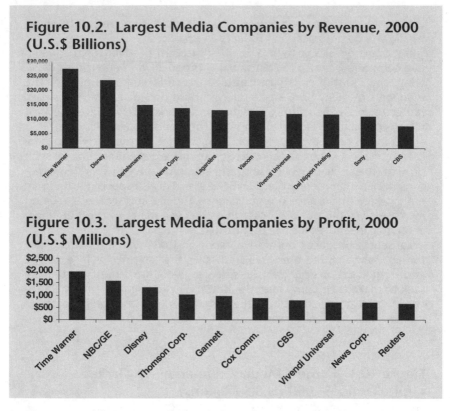

Figure 10.2. Largest Media Companies by Revenue, 2000 (U.S.$ Billions)

Time Warner, Disney, Bertelsmann, News Corp., Lagardère, Viacom, Vivendi Universal, Dai Nippon Printing, Sony, CBS

Figure 10.3. Largest Media Companies by Profit, 2000 (U.S.$ Millions)

Time Warner, NBC/GE, Disney, Thomson Corp., Gannett, Cox Comm., CBS, Vivendi Universal, News Corp., Reuters

well as to achieve economies in production and distribution, has led audio companies to purchase additional record labels.

Companies have also grown to reduce economic risks, seeking geographical diversity to reduce the effects of economic cycles or downturns in a particular region. Others have grown to diversify their operations by pursuing multimedia strategies designed to reduce their dependence upon a particular type of media.

Companies also expand their operations and diversify to acquire a greater share of the market and its profits, to enter industries and industry branches that offset slower-growing existing operations, and to move into emerging industries related to their operations that may have profitable futures.

Size is no guarantee of success. It is both an advantage and a disadvantage. It can both empower as well as constrain a manager's actions. Size can provide strength and economies of scale, but it can also make enterprises difficult to manage and cause inertia

192   MEDIA COMPANIES

or slow response when change is needed. Size can create greater dependence on outside capital or vulnerability to rapid economic changes.

As a result, it is important to understand the reasons for growth and the rationales and strategies necessary to guide that growth so the company can be successfully managed to gain the advantages of size while minimizing disadvantages.

GROWTH PRESSURES AND STRATEGIES

Questions of how a firm grows and the strategies it can employ for growth interest managers who are focused on developing their firms by increasing their size. Natural growth occurs when resources are used more efficiently and productivity is increased, or when firms offer new products and services that are successful in the marketplace.

Growth can also occur by using financial resources to expand one's market or by acquiring other firms. Because firms experience unequal growth, some firms grow larger than others and may have the ability to purchase some of the smaller firms. In other cases mergers are sought between existing firms to create an even larger enterprise.

Growth is sometimes sought as a means of reducing risk by diversifying a firm. This growth through diversification may be pursued in geographic terms as a firm expands the markets in which it operates to reduce the effects of economic fluctuations in any one market. The diversification may add subsidiaries that are not in the original business of the firm to reduce its dependence on one product or service.

Growth can also occur if a firm engages in vertical integration to control resources needed for its operations or to control or participate in the distribution or marketing of the end product or service. Growth can also occur as the result of special opportunities, such as those that force the sale or divestiture of other companies. Other factors promoting growth are

- Growing demand for a product or service
- New technology that increases productivity and market size
- Substitute products or services that can be offered by the firm

A Business View of the America Online–Time Warner Merger

Many social critics have used the takeover of Time Warner by America Online in the year 2000 to illustrate the power of large companies. To observers with a business perspective, however, the merger was more illustrative of weaknesses driving firms together than an exercise of raw corporate power.

The merger created a firm with $350 billion in market value and revenues in excess of $30 billion annually. AOL shareholders received 55 percent of the new firm, whereas Time Warner shareholders received 45 percent. The deal was certainly large enough to raise eyebrows everywhere, but when considered using questions from a business standpoint, it becomes understandable in a different way.

How could America Online take over a firm that had sales revenue five times larger than its own? Why was it possible for America Online to acquire a firm with net income almost 2.5 times higher than its own? How does a firm with 12,000 employees take over a firm with 67,000 employees?

The answer lies in the fact that both firms had significant impediments to their ability to compete individually in the emerging content-driven broadband distribution environment. It also lies, equally significantly, in the fact that America Online had capital. Its market capitalization was nearly twice that of Time Warner, thanks to the stock market's infatuation with Internet shares.

Although America Online was a preeminent U.S. Internet service provider and content organizer, it was vulnerable because it could not easily gain access to cable systems for broadband distribution services and because it was dependent upon Internet subscriptions. The company was established in 1985 and became the first Internet firm to make a profit in 1998, just two years before it became the dominant player in the merger with Time Warner.

The company had a strong understanding of Internet operations and markets, operating the AOL family of services that includes CompuServe, DigitalCity, and MovieFone. However, its own financial performance was weak by comparison to the price of its shares. At the time of the acquisition, AOL shares were priced at fifty-five times its earnings. AOL executives realized that the firm had vulnerabilities that could be ameliorated by acquiring or merging with a firm with hard assets and a large cash flow.

Time Warner was one of the largest media conglomerates and enjoyed the benefits of well-known media brands such as Warner Brothers, *Time, Sports Illustrated,* and CNN. Its strength as a content creator was also supported by its position as the second largest cable operator in the United States. But Time Warner also had weaknesses. Although the firm

194

was well known, it was perceived—as many traditional media firms have been—as being slow to respond to changes in communications technologies and unable to exploit opportunities in new media fully.

The firm has been carrying a huge debt load accumulated by upgrading its cable systems, financing the merger of Warner Communications and Time Inc., and paying for acquisitions made during the 1990s. It was also limited in its ability to move its content across different platforms because the Internet was becoming an important part of that ability and Time Warner did not have strength in Internet operations or expertise.

Joining the two firms thus simultaneously combined their strengths and eliminated significant weaknesses. It presented increased opportunities for online distribution and e-commerce in music, video, and other Time Warner content and additional opportunities for cross-marketing and brand enhancement.

But to make the deal, which involved a swap of shares, America Online had to discount the value of its shares by one-fourth, a clear indication that its management recognized that its shares were not worth their price in the stock market. With that discount the deal was palatable to Time Warner shareholders and still perceived as beneficial for AOL shareholders.

The value of the deal for Time Warner shareholders is seen in the fact that the day before the deal was announced, Time Warner shares were trading for $65 dollars. Under terms of the merger, shareholders received the equivalent of $110, about 70 percent more value than they had in the stock market.

News of the merger in January 2000 boosted AOL shares from $68 the day prior to the announcement to $74 on the day of the announcement. Time Warner shares shot up from $65 to $92. The following week, however, AOL shares dropped to $60 and Time Warner shares to $79. At the beginning of February, AOL shares had dropped to $55 and Time Warner to $77.

Part of the decline was due to a decline in share prices across the U.S. stock markets, but the initial buoyant reaction to the merger was also restrained when the deal was considered from a financial standpoint. In order to produce a real rate of return of 10 percent annually for investors, the combined company will have to grow at 15 percent per year for 15 years and maintain a price-earnings ratio multiple of about 30. To gain a 15 percent return, the growth rate would have to be in the range of 22 percent a year.

Although these are not impossible goals for the company, they will place a great deal of pressure on the management to increase cash flow, keep costs low, and ensure high operating profits.

- Available resources such as financial or managerial ability to create growth.

Factors impeding growth include

- Poor management
- Lack of capital
- Company traditions
- Lack of capacity
- Declining demand for the product or service
- Heavy competition from other producers of the product or service
- Policy and legal control on growth.

The rate of growth experienced by companies presents special problems for firms. Slow growth rates require that managers exercise great care in financial management and plan any debt increases or other company changes carefully.

Because slow growth is also indicative of mature markets or consumer disinterest in the product, media managers whose companies are experiencing slow growth need to consider carefully the reasons for the rate of growth and develop strategies to ensure they have sufficient resources or alternative products for the company to survive in the future. Newspaper publishers in North America and Europe, for example, are experiencing relatively lower revenue growth when compared to other media and no growth or negative growth in terms of the number of customers served. As a result, newspaper companies are implementing a variety of strategies to expand markets and products and spread costs across multiple products.

At the other end of the continuum is rapid growth. Although it presents a number of opportunities and is more desirable than negative or no growth, rapid growth presents critical issues that must be addressed or else firms can encounter disastrous managerial and financial conditions. The largest problems with rapid growth result from the inability of existing organizational structures or managers' abilities to respond to and control the growth effectively. This leads to inadequate financial planning and control, heavy financial leveraging, poor utilization of personnel, loss of focus, and growth taking the place of strategic planning. These problems have been experienced in recent years by a variety of online media and dot-com firms, cable and satellite television firms, and other companies that have benefited from rapid growth resulting from advances in information and communications technologies.

Growth or the lack of it thus create issues that require careful attention by managers if the company is to benefit or survive the growth environment in which it exists.

GROWTH THROUGH DIVERSIFICATION

Diversification is a strategy used by firms to smooth sales and profit fluctuations, stimulate growth faster than if they concentrated on a single product or service, and ensure that performance is not dependent on the economic cycles of one location or industry.

Decisions on whether and to what degree a company will diversify vary, but large media and communication firms typically diversify into a range of media and communication products and services. Company choices and investments change the pattern and amount of diversification. The Tribune Co., for example, was much more clearly a newspaper company in 1980 than it was in 2000 (see fig. 10.4), because of subsequent, significant investments in broadcast and entertainment activities during those two decades.

Figure 10.4. Example of Diversification Reflected in Revenue Sources of Tribune Co., 1980 and 2000

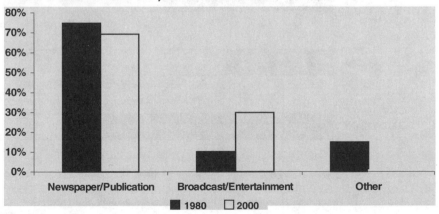

Patterns of diversification differ significantly among media firms (see fig. 10.5). Some newspaper companies are comfortable only diversifying into other print media or extending their publications online. Other companies choose to offer a wide range of media and communication products ranging from newspaper to magazines, from television to recordings, and from radio to online operations.

Diversification creates problems for companies if it is not based on the existing knowledge of managers. If top personnel do not understand the dynamics and inner workings of an industry, its culture, the production and distribution activities required, or consumer behavior in that industry, they can run into significant difficulties.

GROWTH THROUGH MERGERS AND ACQUISITIONS

Mergers and acquisitions combine companies by joining the companies together or through the purchase of one company by another. Despite the popular conception that such activities are designed merely to increase the size of firms, these fusions are use-

Figure 10.5. Examples of Different Diversification Patterns Shown in Revenue Sources of Three Large Media Firms, 2000

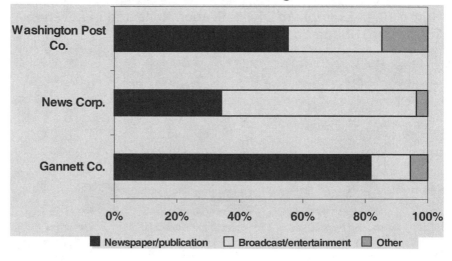

MEDIA COMPANIES

ful only if they are part of a strategy to increase the competitiveness of one or more of the firms involved.

Mergers and acquisitions are a strategic method to improve companies, rationalize operations, and gain access to resources needed to compete in larger markets with a greater number of competitors. In media industries, for example, many mergers and acquisitions have occurred as firms have responded to weaknesses resulting from globalization, entry of competitors, and changing technologies.

Acquisitions or mergers are a means, for example, to enter new geographic markets. A publisher in Italy might purchase a publishing firm in the United States so that it may benefit from the larger U.S. market as part of a strategy of increasing its cash flow and distributing American materials in Europe and European materials in America.

In other cases mergers or acquisitions can aid entry into a media product market in which a firm has not previously operated. In this type of activity, a newspaper publisher may merge with a magazine publisher to enter the magazine market without the risk of having to start new titles.

Firms also combine so that they can acquire and use innovative products. A dot-com company, for example, might merge with a software company so it can gain the right to use a unique proprietary software that improves its customers' abilities to personalize the information they receive.

The desire to shorten the time required for delivery or to find a mechanism to better serve customers may promote mergers or acquisitions. An American recording company, for example, may purchase a recording distributor in France to increase the efficiency with which European retailers can order its recordings and to reduce delivery time because the orders will be filled in Europe and not the United States.

Successful mergers and acquisitions need to serve clear business strategies goals, not mere growth, or they actually can harm a company. This is why some divisions or subsidiaries of the combined firms are sold shortly after mergers or acquisitions and why there seems to be constant trading of media firms and divisions. As companies try to rationalize all the elements acquired during a merger or acquisition, it is natural to shed those that do not serve corporate strategies and core business activities.

The primary value of mergers and acquisitions to companies, then, comes not merely from increasing their assets but from organizing the assets in a way that increases shareholder value. This occurs when the combined pieces are put together so that they are more valuable joined together than they were when they were independent.

John Malone, who guided the growth of TCI and made it the largest cable operator in the United States before selling it to AT& T in 1999 and now heads Liberty Media, has been both lauded and reviled for his willingness and prowess in trading assets as a means of increasing shareholder value. One of the era's best deal makers, Malone is highly adept at finding firms or portions of firms that fill needs within his own organizations or creating opportunities that are attractive to investors and increase the overall value of the firm.

Because consolidations designed to increase value are depen-

Making the Pieces Fit: Harcourt General, Reed Elsevier, and Thomson Corp.

Ensuring that an acquisition serves the needs of an acquiring company was starkly illustrated in 2000 when Harcourt General, the textbook and journal publishing company, was put up for sale by its owners.

Although both Reed Elsevier, the British and Dutch publishing conglomerate, and the Canadian publishing firm Thomson Corp. were interested in Harcourt, neither company wished to purchase all of its operations because they could not be integrated into the strategies of either one. In the end, the two companies made an unusual $5.7 billion joint bid and purchase in which Reed Elsevier purchased Harcourt and then passed on about half of that company to Thomson.

The arrangement occurred because strategic decisions within each company had placed them on divergent paths and each could not use large portions of Harcourt in those directions. As a result of the decision to divide the company, Reed Elsevier was able to focus its acquisition on Harcourt's medical and science holdings, including about five hundred scholarly journals, whereas Thompson was able to obtain Harcourt's higher education and corporate publishing activities that fit well with its publishing strategies.

dent upon the effects of the fusion of firms, whenever such mergers and acquisitions occur, managers need to increase the efficiency and effectiveness of the combined firms to produce the desired results. This necessity is often the impetus for restructuring through blending operations, modifying organization structures, and selling or ending some operations. These activities, of course, affect personnel. Sometimes they force job changes, layoffs, buyouts, retirements, and relocations. If restructuring is not handled sensitively or occurs too often, it leads to insecurity, resentment, career development concerns, reduced productivity, resignations of talented employees, and other problems that affect firms' long-term interests.

Similarly, financial performance of the merged or acquiring firm can be harmed if technology, organization structures, company cultures, compensation and benefits, accounting and management information systems, marketing activities, production equipment, and sales and distribution methods are not rapidly and effectively fused.

These force managers to confront rapidly how the pieces of the company get put together for maximum efficiency by taking advantage of economies of scale, scope and integration, and complementary products or services. Mergers and acquisitions require that a shared vision must be built and a clear strategy for the integration of the firms be present and effectively communicated.

Large mergers and acquisitions often create public opinion that these deals are limiting competition. The number of mergers and acquisitions and the size of the deals rightfully raise concern over the possibility of anticompetitive practices. If mergers and acquisitions create unhealthy levels of market power or barriers for new firms to enter, there certainly is reason for public concern, and the merger may attract the attention of competition authorities.

GROWTH THROUGH JOINT ACTIVITIES

Another form of company growth is seen in activities in which companies cooperate with each other through joint ownership in other companies, by creating joint ventures, or by establishing formal business networks.

Making Mergers and Acquisitions Work

If consolidating firms that are merged or acquired is not made a priority, internal conflicts and coordination difficulties will emerge among companies operating under one owner. As a result, acquisitions and mergers sometimes do not produce anticipated synergies, cost savings, or other advantages and may reduce the financial performance of the new larger firm. Other problems can result from issues related to company strategies, company organization and management, personnel, company cultures, and customer reactions.

Growth through merger or acquisition thus needs to be guided by process and strategy if it is to be successful. The overall strategy of the acquisition or merger involves choices such as whether the companies will operate independently or be integrated into one new firm and whether the acquiring firm will be active or passive in the operation of the acquired one. If integration and active management are the strategy, it means that senior management must work to increase the capacity and productivity of the entire organization, not just its individual parts. This requires a vision that will guide decisions and needs to be communicated to and accepted by personnel throughout the organization.

For a successful blending of firms, attention must be paid to the entire organization, not just the acquired firm. Managerial teams need to explore the effects on the technical and organizational system of the new, larger firm and the existing political and cultural systems of the existing firms. They need to explore differences and similarities in

- Management information systems
- Accounting systems
- Marketing programs
- Management styles
- Organization structures
- Work forces
- Production equipment and processes
- Customer bases and needs
- Competitors
- Types of products
- Distribution methods.

A variety of overall questions need to be asked and answered, such as "How do the firms differ in terms of structure and product lines?" "Can sales and marketing efforts be joined effectively for joint sales and cross promotion?" "Can joint purchasing and standardization of needed resources save money?" "Can some parts of accounting be centralized?" and "What is unique, good, and bad in each division or unit?"

202

Specific questions about operations also need to asked: "Are there differences in the costs of production and distribution for the products?" "Are employees treated differently in terms of compensation and benefits? Can and should those differences be standardized?"

Ultimately mergers and acquisitions are effective only if an integration plan is devised and implemented in a timely matter that addresses the methods for management to put the pieces together, to take advantage of economies of scale, scope, and integration, and to make products and services complementary. The strategies and pace of change need to be set and communicated to everyone in the organization to reduce uncertainty and fear.

To be fully successful, a new culture must be created that is not merely a blending of the existing cultures. It must have clear values, strategies, and expectations that promote improvement and innovation. Not only employees but also customers must understand how the changes will affect their relationships with the firms and what benefits they will accrue.

There are a variety of reasons that induce managers of large companies to engage in these cooperative activities. They often result from government policies, weaknesses in firms, or uncertainty on the part of boards and managers. These activities are sometimes used when government antitrust or policy regulations block greater ownership. Most often, however, strategies of joint activities are employed when managers of firms wish to respond to high-risk opportunities but cannot bear the risk alone or when firms have financial resource limitations and cannot afford to acquire a firm as a subsidiary on their own. They are also sought when the knowledge base about new technologies or applications—or the skills and abilities of personnel—in a firm are limited but management wishes to participate in and learn from a new media market because of its potential.

The entertainment and telecommunication giant Cablevision System Corp., for example, entered into a strategic alliance with Princeton Video Image in 2000 to gain access to an innovative television advertising technology. Cablevision made a $10 million equity investment in the smaller firm and received warrants allowing it to increase its ownership up to 45 percent, in exchange for licenses to Princeton Video Image's virtual advertising technologies and products that allow real-time video insertion into live broadcasts such as sporting events. The two also agreed to develop additional products and technologies jointly.

The partial ownership and other relationships that characterize joint ventures show that the participating firms are more *interdependent* than unconstrained powerful companies that are independent of outside influences. Although the relationships clearly show joint interest, these joint ventures in and of themselves are not evidence of the lack of competition between firms in other activities. Gaining advantages in that competition, as well as changing corporate strategies, is what leads to alliances through joint activities changing so often.

THE PURSUIT OF SYNERGIES

The idea of creating synergies through the combination of cross-media activities has been widely touted during acquisition and merger activities in recent years. Company executives, analysts, and industry observers have argued that combining firms that produce different types of content and operate different distribution capabilities can create synergies that will improve the performance of the combined firm.

After a decade of efforts to find synergies among media operations, the goal of reducing costs or increasing profits through synergies remains generally elusive. Efforts to create synergies in the content by "retooling" content for additional uses, trying to create successful cross-media concept products in film, books, and games, and using staff from one media operation to provide services to another have not generally produced the desired financial results. These efforts, however, have produced some advantages in terms of brand development and strengthening. Those factors are, of course, difficult to measure in terms of impact on company financial performance.

The most visible financial improvements resulting from mergers seeking synergies have occurred in noncontent areas of media operations. Some costs savings have been achieved through the combination of subscription marketing, billing, and distribution when magazine holdings have been joined. Cross-media synergies producing financial results through economies have also been possible

Joint Interest, Joint Ventures, and Competition

Many observers of the growing networks of activities among media firms, including partial ownerships and related joint ventures of subsidiaries, point to these webs of activity as evidence that competition is diminishing and that there is a convergence of interests among big companies that is leading to co-option and collusion. These critics often argue that joint activities are a means by which big media firms have become powerful companies that dominate communications in a cooperative manner. Such concern can be illustrated by examining the relationships that exist between two large Australian media firms.

Rupert Murdoch's News Corp. Ltd. and Kerry Packer's Australian Consolidated Press Holdings Ltd. (ACP) dominate much of the Australian media scene. Both own significant publishing, broadcasting, and news media operations.

When one takes a look at those operations, one finds significant relationships that link the firms. For example, the firms are joint owners of *TV Week,* Australia's leading television guide, and they also own equal shares of Foxtel, a subscription-broadcasting firm that distributes signals through cable and satellite delivery. News Corp. and Packer's ACP own half of Foxtel, and the other half is owned by Telstra, the public telephone company that is in the process of privatization. Observers who use these types of relationships as indications of the diminishment of competition and the rise of cooperation among companies might easily come to the conclusion that News Corp. and ACP have aligned their operations in a friendly sharing of the Australian market.

However, one cannot immediately accept all such examples of joint activities as evidence of co-option and collusion between firms. Anyone who is familiar with the Australian media scene knows about the extraordinary vigor with which the separate holdings of News Corp. and ACP compete and the explicit rancor between Murdoch and Packer and executives of their respective firms. There is anything but a cozy relationship with friendly market divisions among the firms; each firm actively pursues its own advantage and works to block the other from gaining any competitive advantage.

when the warehousing and distribution operations for books, audio recordings, and videocasettes/DVDs have been combined.

More recently, media executives have attempted to achieve synergies by joining traditional media firms with online firms. However, most of the initiatives launched do not really create synergies. Instead, these efforts usually represent a defensive mechanism against competitors, risk reduction in case of rapid acceptance of

Internet-based media and distribution, and the creation of new sales and distribution mechanisms. The extent to which these efforts are successful for different types of media and communications products and services remains to be seen.

ORGANIZATION AND MANAGEMENT OF LARGE FIRMS

As companies grow, it becomes difficult for corporate managers to focus attention on the wide variety of operations within their firms, so they often create divisions within the corporation that are headed by managers responsible for those operations. Sometimes they have subsidiary firms, semi-autonomous companies in which they have significant or controlling ownership, within the scope of their responsibilities.

Large firms can be either privately or publicly owned. Although there are some large privately held firms, public ownership is more common among large media and communications firms because of their needs for capital.

The typical corporate organization for large firms is based on a board of directors made up of the major owners of the firms and often other persons selected for their expertise or perspectives. Boards make major strategic decisions and typically determine company goals and objectives. Firms are typically headed by a chief executive officer (CEO), who is concerned with overall strategy and corporate development, and a chief operating officer who typically holds the president's title and is responsible for managing the implementation of strategies and overseeing the operations of the firm. Below these persons are managers of divisions or subsidiaries, who typically hold corporate vice presidential titles and presidential titles for their divisions or subsidiaries.

Different types of vertical and horizontal hierarchies are employed because every firm is unique and has varying managerial requirements. In large media corporations, however, it is typical to place responsibility for print and broadcast operations in different divisions because of the significant differences in their characteristics and the media-specific knowledge required. Large companies also differ in terms of their degree of centralization of decision making.

Company Cultures

Every company operates within its own culture that is created by its values, traditions, methods of operations, relations among management and employees, and other factors. This company culture is a particularly important factor in the ability of firms to grow, change, and integrate with other firms through mergers and acquisitions.

Synergies in growing companies may not be created because people may be used to operating in other company cultures and do not have experience working together and are not used to thinking about ways they can help other portions of the firm. The result can be differences in goals, in what is perceived as important, in how issues and problems are understood, and in varying levels of cooperation among the divisions or subsidiaries.

Within the same firm, even a small one, different cultures may exist in different departments, and this may result in problems in coordination and joint activity. The differences result from the types of persons and working environments in which they are located.

If one examines media firms, for example, one often finds some personnel working in an entrepreneurial culture, whereas others work in an administrative culture; some persons work in a creative culture, whereas others exist in a maintenance culture; some persons work within a sales culture, whereas others work in a production culture; and some persons work in a process culture, whereas others work in an outcome culture. Finding ways to work together and understand each others' perspectives is critical for achieving cooperation and success within the firm.

In order for companies, especially large companies, to operate successfully, managers need to understand the culture of their companies and departments. This is problematic because cultures are rarely explicit: that is, they are rarely written down and explained in company descriptions, handbooks, or employee orientations.

Managerial Conflicts

In large firms a certain amount of conflict among managers of the corporate parent, among corporate managers and divisional and subsidiary managers, and among the managers of divisions and subsidiaries is normal because of their different needs and responsibilities. That conflict can rise to unhealthy levels, however, and create significant problems. Strong personality conflicts, competition among managers, and differing visions among managers can reduce cooperation and the performance of the firm overall.

The problem that conflicting leadership styles can create was starkly illustrated in the relationship between Michael Eisner, CEO of the Walt Disney Co., and Michael Ovitz, who was brought into the firm to become its president. Eisner, who is reported to have an autocratic style, clashed with Ovitz's own strong personality. Ovitz left the firm within a year, taking with him severance package that cost the company more than $100 million. Within a few years in the late 1990s more than a half dozen senior executives left the firm, including its chief strategist, two chief financial officers, a senior executive vice president, and the head of its studio operations, to take top executive positions in other firms. Disney was obviously a good training ground for upper management, but many managers apparently were unhappy with managerial relations and did not see desirable upward opportunities within the company.

In order to avoid conflicts, leaders with strong personalities and visions often seek top managers whose personalities complement rather clash with their own. Al Neuharth built the Gannett Co. into one of America's largest media firms, and in his autobiography he characterizes himself as an SOB. The position of his second in command was filled by John Curley, who was not overly aggressive, did not seek the limelight, and was excellent at implementing Neuharth's visions. Curley became the CEO after Neuharth retired.

Managerial differences can also emerge after mergers and acquisitions if the leaders of both companies remain in the firm. Although Gerald Levin of Time Warner and Ted Turner of Turner Broadcasting made a workable arrangement that provided Turner the status and relative autonomy he desired when those firms merged, Turner's ownership share and influence within the firm was reduced when Time Warner and AOL merged. His management activities effectively ended with the AOL–Time Warner fusion.

Internal Conflict in Large Companies: Bertelsmann's Settlement of the Napster Litigation

Differences in perspectives about strategies and potential business opportunities can create conflicts within large companies. Managers of various divisions and subsidiaries have different perspectives and goals, and there is a rivalry among these different portions of the company for internal resources. Differences in the importance and influence of divisions and managers, as well as the personalities of managers, can also create conflict in the management team. If the conflict cannot be resolved through accommodation or compromise, it can become divisive and harm the continued pursuit of corporate goals.

In 2000 leading music industry firms filed copyright infringement suits against Napster, the online music file-sharing company. Before the case was concluded, however, Bertelsmann, Europe's largest media company, withdrew from the suit and announced it had reached an agreement for an alliance with Napster that would compensate the copyright owners of music traded. The arrangement was approved by company CEO Thomas Middlehoff, who determined that Bertelsmann's e-commerce division would work with Napster to create a paid file-sharing membership service.

The decision, however, was opposed by the executives of Bertelsmann's music operations who had brought the original suit against Napster. Their opposition reportedly included preferences for other online strategies, the wish to remain united with other major record companies against file swapping, and the desire not to be seen as rewarding Napster's previous copyright infringement. When Middlehoff approved the Bertelsmann-Napster deal despite their opposition, Bertelsmann Music Group CEO Strauss Zelnick and President Michael Dornemann resigned.

Middlehoff's decision to align Bertelsmann with Napster was part of a larger corporate strategy to become the world's leading music company and a leading online distributor of content, something it was already doing with books through its position as the world's largest book publisher. In making the deal with Napster, Bertelsmann made a significant alliance with the file-sharing firm, loaning it about $50 million and obtaining an option to purchase a large share of the company when settlements were reached with the other major record companies involved in the suit.

HOW LARGE IS LARGE?

Large media enterprises face a variety of financial, economic, and organizational pressures that are unique to firms of their size, as well as those pressures that are shared with smaller firms. However, it must be understood that the concept of size is relative and determined by comparison to other firms.

Although large media companies such as AOL Time Warner, Vivendi, Bertelsmann, and News Corp. arc larger than most firms involved in media, they are not among the top companies on any measure of company size. If one considers big media firms in terms of revenue, the numbers are clearly impressive (see fig. 10.6). Companies with billions of dollars in revenue can hardly be thought of as anything but "big."

Based on 2000 revenue, however, General Motors in more than twelve times as large as Bertelsmann, Exxon is eight times larger than Walt Disney, and WalMart is seven times larger than Time Warner (see fig. 10.7). Although media companies have significant size, when compared in business terms they are not as large, rich, and independent as some might assume.

Figure 10.6. Revenues of Largest Media Firms, 2000 (U.S.$ Billions)

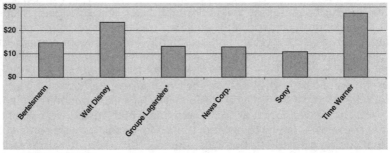

*Media operations only.

Figure 10.7. Revenues of Largest Firms, 2000 (U.S.$ Billions)

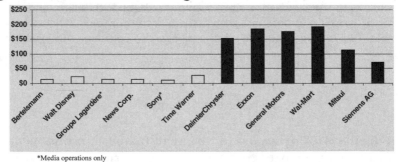

*Media operations only

MEDIA COMPANIES

Suggested Readings

Barnouw, Erik, ed. *Conglomerates and the Media*. New York: New Press, 1997.

Baysinger, B. D., R. E. Meiners, and C. P. Zeithaml. *Barriers to Corporate Growth*. Lexington, Mass: Lexington Books, 1981.

Gaughan, Patrick A. *Mergers, Acquisitions, and Corporate Restructuring*. New York: John Wiley and Sons, 1999.

Needham, Douglas. *The Economics of Industrial Structure Conduct and Performance*. New York: St. Martin's Press, 1978.

Penrose, E. T. *The Theory of the Growth of the Firm*. Oxford: Basil Blackwell, 1959.

11

Trade and Globalization in Media Products and Services

MEDIUM- AND LARGE-SIZED MEDIA COMPANIES are increasingly expanding their activities internationally as they attempt to benefit from additional opportunities and markets for their content and services. Even some small enterprises are finding innovative ways to operate globally. Their activities involve trade in their products and, sometimes, globalization of the firm by establishing itself in locations outside the country of its origin.

"Trade" is a term used to describe the movement of goods and services among countries and involves a number of activities ranging from shipping products to consumers outside the country of origin to establishing relationships with domestic distributors and retailers who make them available in other countries.

"Globalization" is a term used to describe the increasing internationalization of business activities by companies worldwide that involve more than mere trade in goods and services to include establishment of subsidiaries and joint ventures worldwide, as well as activities such as the acquisition of supplies and the manufacture of components or finished goods beyond the borders of a firm's home country.

A number of factors promote trade and globalization in media and communication product and services. The first is demand. Although media exist globally and some domestic production takes place in every location, large-scale content production capabilities—particularly in film and television—are not equally distributed and tend to be concentrated in a few countries. As a result, when there is a need for products and services that are unavailable domestically or there are desirable products elsewhere, firms in these nations look externally for content products they can use.

The uneven distribution of capabilities, amount of production,

212   MEDIA COMPANIES

and range of content production has occurred because domestic needs and financial support for production in large content-producing countries such as the United States has made it possible for content-creation clusters to develop. These involve financiers, producers, studios and equipment, directors, actors, and other necessary personnel and support services, and these have been used to create products and services to serve the domestic market and simultaneously seek additional uses in foreign markets.

Technical as well as policy changes worldwide have promoted trade and globalization in recent decades. Digitalization, global telecommunications, and transportation systems have combined to create mechanisms for easier distribution of media products outside their nation of origin. These changes have accompanied the liberalization of media and communications policies that has privatized much telecommunications infrastructure and created private commercial broadcast, cable, and satellite systems; increased the number of stations, channels, and networks; and generally heightened demand for information and entertainment products and services.

For some firms, globalization has occurred when ownership limits, antitrust regulations, or other governmental actions have blocked growth in a company's home country. Some firms globalize when saturated domestic markets offer few additional opportunities or when revenue and profit levels plateau or decline in domestic markets, and they seek horizontal and vertical integration opportunities elsewhere to increase revenue, reduce costs, or create economies.

Whatever the motivation for individual companies, trade and global expansion are becoming increasingly important activities for all sorts of media companies. In some cases they limit their activities to selected countries or regions. In other cases they engage in commerce worldwide depending upon their resources and strategies, and the demand for their media and communication products or services.

TRADE IN MEDIA PRODUCTS AND SERVICES

Trade in media products and services has occurred since the first person paid a publisher or contact in another country to send copies of books, newspapers, or other printed matter for personal or commercial use. The development of this trade often followed colonial lines. Colonists in Brazil and Indonesia wanted books published in their native Portuguese or Dutch. Colonists in North America and India sent to England for copies of books and pamphlets. The needs of financial and business communities in Europe and North America led to the creation of financial news agencies—such as Agence Havas in France, Wolff's in Germany, and Reuters in the United Kingdom—that began offering their information to clients outside their nations of origin more than 150 years ago. Today there is vibrant worldwide trade in all types of media and communications, ranging from news and information to recordings to books to advertising.

Media industries have fundamental differences that affect exportability when compared to general goods and services, however. The properties of products and services such as automobiles, vacuum cleaners, and water filters make them easily traded among nations, assuming there are roads upon which to drive, electricity, and water systems. There are differences, however, when media products are involved. The most important differences involve time sensitivity, language, and local/domestic content requirements.

Media products vary in terms of their time sensitivity depending upon their roles as information or entertainment providers. News and contemporary information must be disseminated rapidly to maintain its immediacy and currency to audiences. Information with less time sensitivity, such as feature materials and in-depth analysis as well as entertainment materials, can be disseminated at a more leisurely pace without losing its attractiveness to audiences.

Time sensitivity is important because it affects the amount of lead time that is available before production, where the production takes place, the distances to which the product can be distributed (and thus market size), and the general exportability of products.

Newspapers have the highest time sensitivity because they are typically published daily. Magazines and periodicals have medium time sensitivity because they tend to have monthly frequencies, but a segment of the magazine industry has higher time sensitivity because of its weekly publication schedule. Books, motion pictures, videos, and audio recordings typically have the lowest time sensitivity. Thus it is easier to export products with lower time sensitivity because the distribution time required in international trade does not make the product less valuable.

Language is also a significant factor affecting trade in communication products and services. Although many persons worldwide are bi- or multilingual, many others speak only their native language, and most persons prefer content in their mother tongue. The result is that the majority of readers prefer printed news, information, educational, leisure, and cultural materials printed in their own languages, although this preference tends to be less strong with materials of a scientific, professional, and technical nature. Audio recordings have been the most successful media product exported in their original languages, and motion picture and television programming producers have overcome linguistic problems by dubbing, subtitling, and other methods.

Media products, however, are not homogenous products that are relatively interchangeable once basic style and quality requirements are met. Because audiences use media for local news and information, and advertising associated with a particular city or region, information and advertising media such as newspapers are not easily substituted with products from abroad. Most magazines exist within a domestic framework, providing information that reflects a domestic culture and preferences. Domestic as well as foreign advertising is also served by this mechanism. The book industry also experiences strong domestic content pressure because literature, social commentary, current events, and history are domestic interests.

Acceptance of international audio recording artists is high, but domestic recording industries exist worldwide, providing music that reflects domestic culture and issues. The motion picture and television programming industries also produce highly exportable materials, particularly from countries such as the United States, Canada, the United Kingdom, Germany, France, Australia, Japan, Hong Kong (China), Egypt, Mexico, Spain, and Brazil. Despite this trade, domestic production exists in most nations, although financial and talent issues often limit the amount of material available.

These issues of domestic content needs, language, and time sensitivity combine to affect the exportability of media products. The relative exportability is shown in figure 11.3 on page 218.

European Trade in Recorded Compact Discs

Europe has played an active role in the global recording industry for the past forty years. European artists have enjoyed significant success worldwide and have heavily influenced the rock, pop, and dance genres. All major recording industry firms are present in Europe through subsidiaries at the regional and national levels, and two large European firms, Bertelsmann Music Group and EMI Group, are among the global top five, which also includes Warner Music Group, Sony Music Entertainment, and Universal Music Group.

European artists such as Eros Ramazzotti, Oasis, U2, Björk, Patricia Kaas, Darude, the Cardigans, and the Corrs have had great success outside their nations of origin in recent years and made important contributions to the success of the industry. Consumption of recordings is high in the European Union with widespread acceptance of European recordings, as well as recordings produced in the United States and elsewhere.

Recordings of European artists are typically made by domestic subsidiaries in the nations of those artists who then release the recordings in their nation. If the group has the potential for European or global success, the firms grant licenses to companies in other major countries to release and market the recordings there. Recording firms also engage in direct export of CDs they produce.

Because of a strong market for recordings within Europe and elsewhere, there is a positive trade balance for recorded CDs in the EU nations. In 1997, for example, total imports of CDs to EU countries (including those from other EU nations) totaled 1.1 billion ECU ($1.3 billion), and total exports from EU countries (including exports to EU nations) totaled 1.4 billion ECU ($1.6 billion). This produced a positive total trade balance of 322 million ECU ($377 million) (fig. 11.1).

If only trade with nations outside the EU is considered, imports into the EU were valued at 172 million ECU ($195 million), and exports from the EU were valued at 400 million ECU ($454 million). This trade created a positive trade balance of 232 million ECU ($263 million) as shown in figure 11.2.

Because these are trade figures, the amounts represent only the value generated by sales moving out of the countries of origin of the CDs. They do not include the value generated by the domestic sales of domestically produced CDs or the trade in licensing rights.

When a firm chooses to engage in trade, the number of factors affecting success rises rapidly and requires specific managerial attention. The company will now be affected by economic, social, and political developments in more than one nation. Therefore,

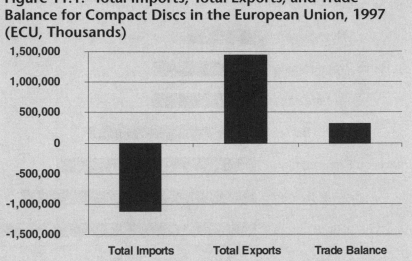

Figure 11.1. Total Imports, Total Exports, and Trade Balance for Compact Discs in the European Union, 1997 (ECU, Thousands)

Figure 11.2. Extra EU Imports and Exports and Trade Balance for Compact Discs, 1997 (ECU, Thousands)

its ability to conduct trade will require different types of financial structures and partners, additional planning and logistics, new marketing efforts, and a variety of changes in company strategy and organization.

Figure 11.3. Relative Exportability of Different Media Products and Services

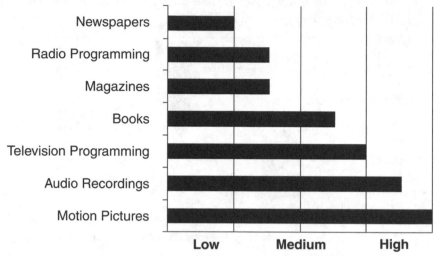

For many companies there are numerous benefits in internationalization. However, risks are also present, and companies need to be mindful of those risks when making decisions about how to engage in trade.

BARRIERS TO TRADE IN MEDIA PRODUCTS AND SERVICES

Trade barriers is a term typically used to describe the results of public policies that limit or halt the importation of products into a nation from another nation or the ability of foreign individuals or firms to do business or invest in a country. These are forms of barriers to entry. Most trade barriers emerge from good intentions of domestic policy makers, but some are erected as the result of poor intentions. Some barriers harm the global economic market by artificially harming competition within it. Others harm the competition for ideas by limiting the availability of ideas imported into a nation.

For the most part, trade barriers to transnational communication result from domestic efforts to respond to economic, cultural, and health and well-being issues. The primary economic rationales

218

Strategies for Volatile Export Markets

The globalization of media company operations has created many opportunities for expanding the market base of companies. But the development has also created the new problem of handling volatile export
markets. The decision to engage in foreign trade presents many additional challenges: new marketing and transportation needs, linguistic issues, banking and foreign exchange issues, dependency on trading
partners, and the effects of changing foreign economies.

Each and all of these factors simultaneously tend to make foreign sales
of media products and services more volatile than domestic trade. They
also require that company boards and senior managers make specific
decisions regarding export risks and that export operations be managed
differently from domestic operations.

Although export markets are volatile, there are great rewards in both
the short and long terms from export operations.

Although risk is a natural part of commercial activity, the level of risk
acceptable to each media company differs. Companies engaged in exports must individually assess the risk and specifically determine what
level of risk they are willing to accept. If this is not done, companies are
placed at the mercy of factors beyond their control, and managers must
respond rapidly with little or no planning to unanticipated changes in
export markets.

The strategic issue of whether to accept the additional risks of exports
and the amount of risk that is acceptable should be addressed by the
company board, which has the responsibility of setting company strategy. It then becomes the task of senior managers to monitor and control
the risk within the levels set by the board.

Firms need accurate business intelligence on the export markets in
which they have operations or are considering operating. Companies
must also acquire and constantly update information about major firms
with which they are doing business. These processes involve constant
monitoring of economic, political, and social changes in the export markets for evidence of changes that may affect the trade.

A second strategy for benefiting from export markets involves limiting
the dependency of a firm on exports or exports to particular nations
or regions. Whenever a firm grows dependent upon another firm or a
particular sector of its business, it increases the risk that it will be affected
by adverse developments in the firm or sector. To protect against the
risks of these changes harming the firm, managers must try to diversify
their trading partners and markets. This means doing business with
more firms, providing products and services in different subsectors of
the business that may be affected differently by changes in export mar-

kets, and diversifying both the nations and regions in which they do business so that the overall risk is minimized.

Because of such changes, boards of companies that engage in export trade need to manage that risk by establishing the level of risk of the overall activities of their firm. This risk level can be stated in terms of revenue or production capacity. A board may determine that no more than 15 or 25 percent of its revenues or profits will be the result of exports or the result of exports from particular countries. Or it may decide that it will devote only 10 or 20 percent of its capacity to export products.

Export markets also force companies to have clear strategies regarding facilities and equipment. The safest alternative is to use only excess capacity to serve export markets. The riskiest option is to invest in additional facilities and equipment to gain the capacity to serve them.

There is no right or wrong choice, but boards and managers should have a clear understanding of the implications of each strategy. The no-risk strategy limits the ability to gain additional benefits from export markets. The expansion-of-capacity strategy increases the dependence of the firm on exports and puts the firm at greater risk.

When companies begin to export products and services, they should develop contingency plans that answer questions such as "What do we do if the market suddenly collapses?" and "How will we need to restructure our operations to respond to increases and decreases in exports?"

These changes affect budgets, production scheduling, employment contracts, paper orders, etc. Because export markets are often more volatile than domestic markets, these changes can occur so rapidly that little time is available to plan a response. By preparing contingency plans, a firm can respond more rapidly to the changes and reduce the potentially harmful effects on the company.

for barriers result from the desire to promote domestic economic activity, protect or develop domestic employment, or halt unfair competition such as product "dumping," that is, selling below cost to gain greater market share.

Cultural rationales for trade barriers on communication products and services are intended to protect and promote domestic culture. This tends to be a concern for small nations or nations whose communications are overwhelmed by neighbors. There is also a cultural rationale intended to protect and promote subcultures, typically defined in ethnic or linguistic terms.

Health and well-being rationales for trade barriers in communication areas are typically designed to protect the public against harmful products and communications. The health rationale is

MEDIA COMPANIES

typically used to place controls on advertising for products such as alcohol and tobacco. The desire to protect against harm to social well-being is seen in regulations intended to control depictions of violence, sex, or discriminatory and derogatory messages.

Policies affecting trade can be internally or externally oriented. Internally oriented policies prescribe action by internal firms or citizens in regard to communication. Externally oriented policies prescribe or address trade by external firms and non-nationals.

The internal approach is seen in domestic content policies that require domestic producers or distributors to include stipulated portions of communications from nationals of a country. Canada, for example, requires that 60 percent of all programming and 50 percent of primetime programming must be of Canadian origin. Similarly, the European Union has established a 50 percent domestic content requirement for television broadcast within its member states. Italy requires that one hundred days per year of each theater's operations must be reserved for Italian films.

In some cases, domestic production policies require that some or all of a product be produced within the country if it is to be distributed internally. These include provisions requiring that a domestic edition of an international magazine contain a certain percentage of domestically produced content or that advertising campaigns must be made within the nation.

The external orientation regulates activities of nondomestic firms. These include bans or limitations on foreign ownership, tariffs applied to foreign products, bans on importation, or requirements that foreign materials be translated, dubbed, or subtitled before importation. Mexico requires all imported programming to be dubbed in a "neutral" Mexican accent and that dubbing cannot use accents from other Latin American nations or idioms from other parts of the region.

A related conflict over regional dialect and language occurred recently when the Catalan region of Spain tried to use a law promoting Catalan Spanish to require that the most popular films of any origin shown in the region be dubbed in Catalan, not in Castilian Spanish. Fines and closures would be levied on cinemas that did not comply. U.S. producers were especially concerned because of the additional costs of dubbing into Catalan and joined film distributors in challenging the requirement, which was subsequently struck down by the Spanish courts.

REGIONAL AND GLOBAL TRADE AGREEMENTS

In order to standardize treatment and improve the speed of trade, nations worldwide have entered into agreements to make sales and movement of products and services across their borders easier. Some of these agreements are bilateral, that is, involving two nations. Other agreements are multilateral, that is, involving multiple nations. These agreements are designed to simplify customs regulations and taxes and to create an environment for easier flow of goods and services among nations.

Despite such agreements there remain significant problems in trade in communications and information. These result from the fact that much activity in the communications field is typically classified as services, and most international trade agreements have tended to cover goods but not services. In other cases, communication products and services have been specifically excluded in order to gain agreements on other products.

The primary multilateral agreements in recent years are those covered by what is known as the General Agreements on Tariffs and Trade (GATT). In recent years the United States and some other developed nations have attempted to get trade in information and entertainment products and services included in GATT. They have encountered strong resistance from other nations, primarily in the developing world, who wish to have protectionist policies that assist development of their domestic information and communication industries. Other nations have resisted because they do not want nations with large communications industries to dominate their media systems culturally.

As a result, there are large multinational debates over media and communication products and services among nations in the WTO and in GATT negotiations that affect trade internationally. In recent years these debates have focused on issues such as telecommunication services, databases, motion picture and television products, and advertising campaigns.

The Free Trade Agreement (1989) between the United States

and Canada included information within its scope but permitted exclusion of motion pictures, recording, and books through a cultural industry exemption clause. This allowed Canada and its provinces to provide advantages to Canadian producers and simultaneously implement policies to disadvantage U.S. products. When the North American Free Trade Agreement (NAFTA) came into play in 1994, covering trade between Mexico, the United States, and Canada, the exclusionary approach was extended and left films, TV programs, home video, books, and sound recordings out of the treaty. This permitted Canada to retain Canadian laws regarding copyright and foreign content and the ability to tax products differently.

This treatment of communications has made it possible for Canadian cable companies to retransmit U.S. broadcasts without payment to the U.S. stations or producers of the material, and for the United States to maintain its foreign ownership limits in broadcasting stations. A number of trade barrier conflicts have emerged between the two neighbors in recent years. One occurred when Canada tried to protect its magazine producers by prohibiting split-run magazines, in which U.S. firms produced a separate Canadian edition through dual use of the content of their U.S. editions and adding only a few pages of Canadian content and advertising. Canadian publishers particularly feared the effect on their advertising base and lobbied parliamentarians and ministers to create the protectionist barrier. The WTO ruled against the Canadian policy, but the Canadians have since attempted to preserve the protectionist effect by removing the tax deductibility of advertisements placed in Canadian versions of foreign-owned magazines.

METHODS OF GLOBALIZATION

Media firms use a variety of techniques to engage in globalization, including direct exports, licensing and rights sales, joint ventures, and direct foreign investment. Most of these were initially established in the early and mid–twentieth century by the magazine and motion picture industries but have now spread to the book, audio, and television programming industries.

Direct Export

Direct export involves sending a product that is produced in one country to another country. In this form of export the producer acts as its own exporter or contracts with an exporter for the task. A book publisher in Canada, for example, may market and sell its books in the United States via bookshops, direct mail, e-commerce, etc. Books are sent to stores and individuals when orders are received for the book.

Product Licensing and Rights Purchases

Another form of internationalization that often occurs in the magazine, book, and audio industries involves firms in one country selling licenses to companies in another country to produce copies of the material or to translate it and then produce a domestic-language edition.

Many magazine publishers use this mechanism to acquire or sell rights to desirable titles and publishing concepts that they have created. Similar mechanisms exist in book publishing. In the audio recording industry, the rights to reproduce copies of CDs and cassettes are often sold by the original recording copy to subsidiary or sister companies in other nations and to others interested in purchasing rights to sell the recording.

Advances in electronic commerce and new rapid distribution systems are creating new problems related to rights purchases. These developments increase the need for firms to acquire rights territorially and to be protected against imports from outside the territory that diminish the value of the rights. This is particularly true when the same product is sold at different prices in different parts of the world to account for differences in income and demand.

Format Licensing

This form of licensing involves selling the rights to use an established television program format in another country. Many licensed formats involve game shows because of their worldwide popularity. Audiences, however, want the shows to involve domestic citizens and domestic culture and personalities.

As a result, rather than selling the rights to broadcast an existing production of an American show, for example, the rights to use the format or concept is sold. As a result, domestic versions of programs such as *Wheel of Fortune* or *Who Wants to Be a Millionaire?* are produced worldwide under license from the original producers.

Joint Ventures

Another mechanism of media internationalization is joint ventures. These are often seen in the magazine publishing and television programming industry. In magazines, for example, the originating company and the domestic publisher enter a partnership to produce a magazine title and sometimes additional titles as well. Similarly, television and cable producers agree to produce a series or motion picture jointly, with each gaining the first exclusive rights to the material in their nations or regions.

Direct Foreign Investment

This type of globalization occurs when a firm internationalizes by purchasing an existing company in another nation or by establishing a subsidiary firm in that country. This type of investment creates wealth for the firm by increasing its company's assets and, when successful, additional dividends for its shareholders. The ultimate result is that it strengthens firms, provides them more resources, and increases their size.

Media firms engage in direct foreign investment for several reasons, usually beginning from a foundation of mature, saturated markets in their nation of origin. Foreign markets provide opportunities for company growth without diversification into other businesses and create the ability for companies to continue developing the national market in which they originated. Unusually strong ownership regulation or heavier taxation in the domestic market than in foreign markets can also promote direct foreign investment.

Whether and how individual media firms globalize is dependent upon their needs, strategies, and the types of products and services involved.

Many cultural critics have argued that U.S. media firms are heavily globalized and dominate communications worldwide. In truth, however, non-U.S. firms now dominate global communications. The erroneous impression is created because these critics do not separate ownership from products and content.

If one closely considers the activities of American-owned firms, one discovers that only a few have strong global operations today. U.S. media companies have made little direct foreign investment and have relied upon direct export, joint ventures, and licensing to move products worldwide. The size of the U.S. market, with its internal opportunities and linguistic limitations and lack of foreign experience, have kept most American media firms from making significant efforts to globalize their operations.

Today only a few American-owned media firms are really globalized. The three with the largest activities worldwide are AOL Time Warner, Walt Disney, and Viacom. The primary and common activities that make these three important global players are television programming, motion picture production, and film and TV program libraries that are marketed worldwide.

Companies from other nations, however, have made significant direct foreign investments, particularly in the last quarter century. Many of those investments have been the acquisition of American content firms. The world's largest book publisher today is Bertelsmann, the German multinational media conglomerate that owns such U.S. publishers as Random House, Knopf, Ballantine, Doubleday, and Bantam Dell. The biggest magazine company today is the French firm Hachette Filipacchi (a subsidiary of Lagardère), which owns more than two hundred titles such as *Elle, Car & Driver,* and *Woman's Day.*

Non-American firms also dominate the global music industry. Sony Music Entertainment, Bertelsmann Music Group, Universal Music Group, and EMI Group account for two-thirds of the revenue of the recording industry worldwide and release recordings by top musical artists from the United States and throughout the

Large Global Players in Selected Media Fields

Audio Recordings

AOL Time Warner (U.S.)
Bertelsmann (Germany)
EMI Group (United Kingdom)
Sony (Japan)
Vivendi Universal (France)

Motion Pictures

AOL Time Warner (U.S.)
News Corp. (Australia)
Sony (Japan)
Viacom (U.S.)
Vivendi Universal (France)
Walt Disney Co. (U.S.)

Magazines

AOL Time Warner (U.S.)
Bertelsmann (Germany)
Hachette Filipacchi (France)

Television/Cable/Satellite Programming

AOL Time Warner (U.S.)
News Corp. (Australia)
Viacom (U.S.)
Vivendi Universal (France)
Walt Disney Co. (U.S.)

Cable and Satellite Systems

AOL Time Warner (U.S.)
AT&T (U.S.)
Cablevision (U.S.)
Direct TV (U.S.)
News Corp. (Australia)

Online Services

AOL Time Warner (U.S.)
Yahoo! (U.S.)
Microsoft (U.S.)
Terra Lycos (U.S.)

world. Warner Music Group, a U.S. firm that is part of AOL Time Warner, competes with the other three major firms globally but has a share of less than 15 percent of the global market.

The motion picture and television production industries are increasingly foreign owned. Universal Studios and Universal Pictures are owned by the French firm Vivendi Universal, which was created through the merger of Vivendi and the Canadian company Seagram, which previously owned Universal. TriStar and Columbia Pictures are owned by the Japanese electronics and entertainment giant Sony Corp., and Twentieth Century Fox is owned by the Australian conglomerate News Corp.

Ownership of content libraries is increasingly important because of the global growth of television, video recording, and video on demand markets. The large foreign owners of studios have recognized this fact, and today about half of the U.S. feature films in these collections are owned by non-U.S. firms.

Although the dominant ownership of media and content firms is increasingly non-American, U.S.-produced media and content products and services are overwhelmingly represented in the products offered by those firms and dominate the global trade in motion pictures, television programming, and audio recordings.

SUMMARY

Globalizing media firms and the sale of media products and services opens new markets and creates opportunities for media products and services, particularly entertainment products. The requirements of operating in the global environment, however, mean that companies must adjust to the demands of multiple markets by structuring their companies in ways to accommodate those demands and the organizational necessities of larger operation.

Globalization is a multidirectional activity and alters capital availability, ownership, product demand, and business strategy patterns. Companies operating in the global environment encounter more competition than at the domestic level. Because communications, technology, and transportation improvements are reducing the importance of distance and the nation-state, global opportunities are increasing for a variety of types of media firms and products and services.

SUGGESTED READINGS

Albarran, Alan B., and Sylvia M. Chan-Olmsted. *Global Media Economics: Commercialization, Concentration, and Integration of World Media Markets*. Ames: Iowa State University Press, 1998.

De la Sierra, M. Cauley, and Margaret Cauley. *Managing Global Alliances: Key Steps for Successful Collaboration*. Boston: Addison-Wesley, 1995.

Demers, David. *Global Media: Menace or Messiah*. Cresskill, N.J.: Hampton Press, 1999.

Freedman, Nigel, ed. *Strategic Management in Major Multinational Companies*. New York: Pergamon Press, 1991.

Gershon, Richard A. *The Transnational Media Corporation*. Mahwah, N.J.: Lawrence Erlbaum Associates, 1997.

Prahalad, C. K., and Yves L. Doz. *The Multinational Mission: Balancing Local Demand and Global Vision*. New York: Simon and Schuster, 1999.

Smith, Anthony. *The Age of Behemoths: The Globalization of Mass Media Firms*. New York: Priority Press, 1991.

Steinbock, Dan. *Triumph and Erosion in the American Media and Entertainment Industries*. Westport, Conn.: Quorum Books, 1995.

12

Indicators of Financial and Economic Health of Media Firms

IN ORDER to evaluate the operations of their firms and to compare performance over time or among firms, managers employ a variety of economic, financial, and corporate activity indicators to measure the health of their media firms.

INDICATORS OF ECONOMIC HEALTH

The economic health of media companies is exemplified by the state of their markets and consumers' desire for the products and services produced by those companies. Changes in these indicators of the health of companies and their industries can be observed to determine elements of their future and the potential need to alter company strategies to respond to those changes.

Market Share Change or Maintenance

By considering a company's share of the market for a particular good or service, one gains an understanding of its position in the market and whether that position is being maintained, improved, or degraded. Changes in market share indicate that competitiveness has been maintained, improved, or lost by firms or that the market structure is being affected by entry or exit or better competitiveness on the part of other firms.

An online portal whose web site receives 15 percent of the hits for portals that organize and provide access to content will work to maintain and expand that market share as evidence of its strength. If its market share declines to 13 or 14 percent, it is losing portions of the market to other competitors who are seen by portal users as better meeting their needs or providing better service or quality.

Market share is measured in terms of circulation for print media, in sales for consumer products such as audio cassettes, CDs, CD-ROMs, videos, DVDs, etc., and by ratings and share for most electronic media. As noted in chapter 5, most of the data regarding such items are provided by or audited by independent organizations that serve all media competitors and advertisers. These data make a good means for monitoring developments regarding market shares.

In the past a media firm was evaluated as healthy if its market share was growing. Today, with the proliferation of media, health tends to be evidenced in maintaining market share or growth within a small niche in which the firm operates.

Changes in Demand

Changes in demand for a product or service can rapidly affect the state of any industry, so it is important for managers to monitor changes in demand.

In many economic studies, price is typically illustrated as the dominant force on demand. Although there is truth to this view, media and other products are affected by a variety of demand factors for individuals including income, time for use of the product or service, requirements for additional purchases (such as software, CDs, DVDs, etc.), and skills required to operate products.

In addition, large-scale demand changes can be caused by the age of the users. In such cases, if the primary users of the product or service are older, they continue its use, but their numbers are reduced by mortality. In other cases, if the primary users are young people and birth rates decline, demand will be accordingly reduced in the future. Other cases of large-scale change include changes in linguistic needs of audiences caused by immigration, economic downturns, and the developments of new and more interesting products and services.

INDICATORS OF FINANCIAL HEALTH

It is important for managers to review the financial health of their firms regularly because financial data provide the key indicators of whether a firm is becoming or remaining a viable business entity. Basic indicators that need to be reviewed regularly involve sales and cash flow, profitability, the status of working capital, and the condition of the balance sheet.

Indicators provide both short and long term indicators of financial health. Operating data, for example, tell what has occurred financially in the company during a given period, and this can be compared to previous periods. But such operating data do not tell about the strength of the firm and its continued viability, so additional information from company balance sheets is necessary to understand more fully its financial status and changes in that status.

Sales Revenue Growth or Decline

This measure is one of several financial growth measures that consider changes in financial performance. Firms whose sales revenues are growing are seen to have better relative health than those whose sales revenues are stable or declining. Sales revenues are indicators of the success that the company's products and services are enjoying in the marketplace and the economic condition of the marketplace itself.

To gauge performance, a firm's revenue and change in revenue are tracked and compared to a similar period in the past. One could compare sales revenue changes from month to month, but this would present a distorted picture because advertising revenue, in particular, is highly seasonal, and because use of certain products and services declines during holiday seasons. The months before Christmas, for example, are when most retailers achieve most of their sales. Consequently, department stores and other shops tend to spend most of their advertising budgets during that period. Similarly, telephone use tends to go down during summer months. As a result, media and communications executives compare revenues or change in revenue to the same period in previous years.

Because revenues are affected by inflation, current revenue amounts can be truly understood only if adjusted to account for the effect of inflation. A radio station that achieves revenue growth of 3 percent during a period of 2 percent inflation has actually

232   MEDIA COMPANIES

Basic Information You Need to Understand Media Industries and Firms

To comprehend the conditions and pressures on media businesses and media industries, one needs to have certain basic economic and financial information. At the industry level, data can be obtained from national statistics offices and industry associations. At the company level, information can be obtained from company registry information and annual reports.

Information is needed for the last year to obtain a contemporary view, but information is needed for the past five to ten years to obtain a basic view of trends.

Industry-Level Data

- How many companies operate in the field?
- What is the total turnover (revenue) produced in the industry?
- What amount comes from advertising?
- What amount comes from viewers, listeners, and readers?
- What amount comes from other sources?
- How has turnover changed?
- What is the media industry's share of total advertising?
- How has that share of advertising changed?
- What is the industry's share of total consumer expenditures for media?
- How has that share of expenditures changed?
- How many people are employed in the industry?
- How has employment in the industry changed?
- What is the value of imports and exports of products in the industry?
- Who are the main customers of firms in the industry?
- What social or economic changes are altering their purchasing and use choices?

Company-Level Data

- What are the firm's turnover (revenue) and its sources?
- What is the firm's share of the audience market?
- What is the firm's share of the advertising market?
- What is the firm's operating margin?
- What is the firm's net income before depreciation?
- What is the firm's net income before extraordinary items?
- What is the firm's equity ratio?
- What is the firm's relative indebtedness?
- What is the firm's quick ratio?
- What is the turnover per employee?

- What is the value added per employee?
- How much capital investment has been made?
- What are the assets of the firm?
- What is its share price?
- What are the dividends it has paid to investors?
- How have these indicators changed?

achieved a true growth rate of 1 percent. If the inflation rate were 3.5 percent, the station would have a negative growth rate of one-half percent.

Healthy companies evidence regular growth of sales revenues. These growth periods can be interrupted by economic downturns, short-term product failures, and other factors. However, a company that is not able to achieve revenue growth over time tends to stagnate, has insufficient resources for product development and reinvestment, and ultimately declines.

In periods in which revenue growth is not shown, managers need to determine the reasons for the lack of growth and respond with budget reductions, product improvement strategies, additional marketing, and other efforts to improve performance in the marketplace, depending upon the causes of the situation.

Change in Results

Results are indicators of profit and thus of the effectiveness with which firms use resources. These standard measures of performance are accounting-based figures that provide a view of what the company gained or lost due to its operations and other activities during a period of time. These are reported on operating statements.

Debt Growth or Decline

All firms carry debt in one form or another, ranging from invoices that have been received but not yet paid to money borrowed to purchase new facilities and equipment or to acquire other firms.

Managers must make a variety of strategies and choices regarding whether to incur debts and the amount of debt they are willing to carry. There are a variety of reasons for which it may be desirable to carry some debt at any given time. Managers, however, must manage and monitor the debt incurred, and this is typically done by tracking both short- and long-term debts.

A healthy firm ensures that the debt load it carries is well within its abilities to repay and that it can manage the debt even if there are downturns in revenues. Weak firms are often found to have used all the credit available to them and scramble to pay debtors merely the interest on debts.

Change in Asset Value

Assets represent those things of value that belong to a company. In healthy companies the value of assets outweighs the value of liabilities, and the value of assets grows over time. Company balance sheets indicate the kinds and values of assets that a firm possesses, and they compare (or balance) them with liabilities to show the financial strength of a firm. In a healthy firm assets exceed liabilities, and in weak firms assets are equal to or less than the liabilities.

If assets are not regularly increasing in value, managers need to consider the reasons and determine whether and what action is warranted. Asset values decline for a number of reasons, and these need to be understood so that one can interpret the changes in asset value reflected on a balance sheet.

First, fixed assets, such as equipment, lose value over time because their use creates wear and reduces the length of time they can be used. This loss is accounted for through depreciation of assets in company financial records. Reductions in the value of assets because of their use can be reversed only through the purchase of new assets that provide additional value. For example, a transmitter and related equipment lose some of their value over time because of the wear and tear of regular use. If a television station purchases equipment to upgrade or improve the transmission system, the capital expenditure adds value to the system in the financial statements.

The second reason that asset values decline is the effect of inflation in reducing the value of assets. If the assets were purchased and valued when currency was worth more, inflation produces a decline in that value.

Third, the value of assets will normally decline if a firm divests by selling existing properties and does not, or is unable to, use the proceeds to purchase replacement assets or to be held as cash.

A healthy company overcomes the natural decline in assets that takes place because of depreciation, changes in the general economy, and divestment. This is done through regular reinvestment through capital expenditures, acquisitions, and appreciation of assets. Because cash for the reinvestment is typically produced by profits, managers need to produce regular profits for reinvestment and to build cash reserves for large reinvestments.

The issue of assets in modern media and communications firms is particularly complicated because much of the value is in brands, copyrights, and the personnel that firms employ. Although methods have been created to assign a financial value to intangibles such as brand names and copyrighted material, the value of knowledgeable and creative employees as a collective is unmeasurable.

Reinvestment

Reinvestment is the return of profits to a firm to further develop the company and its activities. If profits are continually taken from a firm without reinvesting an adequate portion in the company, it is denied resources needed to help it improve its operations, grow, and remain competitive.

The largest portions of reinvestment come in the form of capital expenditures. These involve reinvestment to improve or acquire capital assets such as buildings and equipment or other firms. Although a certain amount of capital expenditures occur each year, the amount required by any firm varies from year to year depending upon the age and conditions of the company's most important machinery and buildings, the necessity of immediate investments in newly available technologies, and the annual financial performance of the company. Fluctuations in capital investments are illustrated by the Tribune Co., one of the largest broadcasting, publishing, and new media firms in the United States (fig. 12.1).

Changes in expenditures can also be viewed at the industry level. These fluctuations in capital investment are illustrated by the U.S. newspaper industry (fig. 12.2).

Figure 12.1. Capital Expenditures of the Tribune Co. (U.S.$ Thousands)

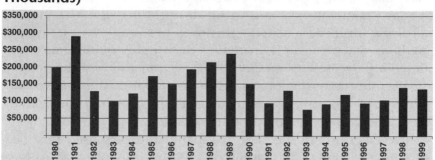

Figure 12.2. Capital Expenditures in the U.S. Newspaper Industry (U.S.$ Thousands)

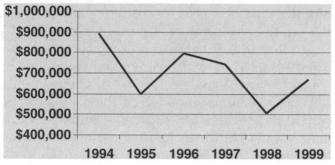

INDICATORS OF COMPANY INTERNAL HEALTH

Indicators of company internal health focus on factors that managers can control through strategic and operational choices. Important indicators include productivity, capacity utilization, employee turnover, personnel skills and knowledge, and innovation and product development.

Productivity

Productivity involves the effectiveness with which firms use resources in their operations. Measures of productivity are made by the amount of output created by use of inputs such as labor and capital. A higher measure of productivity indicates that a company is using resources more effectively in creating products or services.

In media companies with well-established operations, the primary measure of productivity involves productivity of labor. There are several methods of measuring this productivity. The simplest is calculating productivity as turnover per employee. Using this method, total turnover is divided by the number of full-time equivalent employees. This method provides a measure of the amount of revenue (turnover) produced by the labor of the average employee. An increase in productivity is shown when the amount rises, a decrease when the amount declines.

A recent study of the U.S. newspaper industry used this measurement to reveal that although productivity appeared to have increased strongly since the early 1980s, it actually declined since the mid-1980s, and that increases in the mid-1990s were moderate (fig. 12.3).

Although this type of analysis is useful for industry, it lacks the precision of measuring productivity using value added per employee. The value-added measure is obtained by subtracting the costs of production from total revenue and then dividing by the number of employees. Managers can use this better measurement because this internal information is available within companies.

This type of data is useful in strategic planning. It can be employed to review performance of a single firm or department over time, or to compare the performance of one firm with other firms

Figure 12.3. Newspaper Industry Productivity (U.S.$ Thousands, Turnover per Employee)

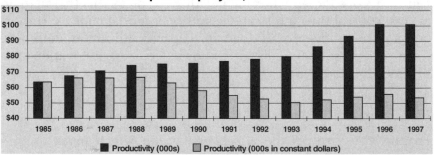

Source: Robert G. Picard. "Newspaper Industry Productivity Rises," in *Media Economics Research Monograph,* Department of Communications, California State University, Fullerton, June 1996.

MEDIA COMPANIES

to determine which is more effective. A manager of a magazine company with multiple titles, for example, could regularly compare productivity among the titles to determine which are most effective. Using this information, efforts could be made to improve the productivity of poorer-performing titles or to determine whether they should be candidates for divestiture.

A magazine firm with seven titles might produce productivity results, as illustrated in figure 12.4. A manager reviewing the chart can immediately see that magazines 1, 4, and 7 achieve the highest productivity, that magazine 4 has achieved increases in productivity during the past three years, and that productivity has declined in magazine 5.

Productivity analyses can be combined with profitability analysis to gain a very powerful tool for engineering productivity and profitability. Productivity measurements can also be applied to individual employees but requires careful use in communications industries because mere output is not an appropriate measure of content production.

Investments in labor-saving equipment or equipment that increases production are often used by firms to increase productivity. These investments will increase productivity, however, only if the labor savings are higher than the investment and operating

Figure 12.4. Sample Productivity Display for a Magazine Company's Titles (in Valued Added per Employee)

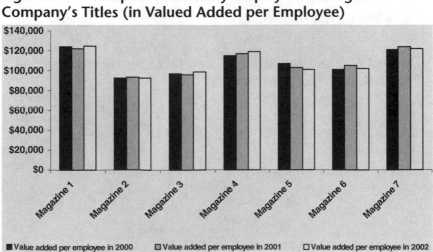

■ Value added per employee in 2000   □ Value added per employee in 2001   □ Value added per employee in 2002

costs for the new equipment, or if the equipment increases product output and produces additional income that exceeds the investment and operating costs.

The desired effect of investments is illustrated in figure 12.5. Managers of a firm that normally makes small regular capital expenditures may make a large investment in equipment to produce a sustainable increase in productivity.

Managers can also employ measures of capital productivity if they wish to compare the returns on investment in multiple products produced by their firm. This technique is useful for managers of media and communications companies. A cable television firm,

Measuring Productivity of Personnel

Productivity of personnel measures the output created by the use of employees. The measurement is meaningful for comparisons over time and between firms and industries.

The easiest measurement is revenue resulting from labor in the firm:

$$\frac{\text{total operating revenue}}{\text{full-time equivalent employees}}$$

A better measurement of productivity is the value added to goods or services through the labor of employees. It is more precise because it adjusts for that portion of the revenue related to the value of the materials used in preparing the good or service:

$$\text{value added per employee} = \frac{[\text{total operating revenue} - \text{cost of materials}]}{\text{full-time equivalent employees}}$$

Figure 12.5. Desired Effect of Capital Expenditures on Productivity (U.S.$, Thousands)

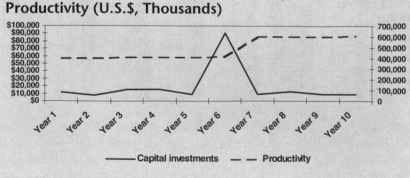

——— Capital investments   – – – Productivity

for example, might compare the returns on investment of various networks that it owns and operates. A radio station holding company might compare the effectiveness of the use of its capital in different stations, and an online media firm could use the measure to compare the effectiveness of its investments in different portals or other online services.

To make these kinds of capital productivity measurements, managers calculate return on investment in each firm and then make comparisons.

Capacity Utilization

When firms are involved in production of goods, more effective use of the manufacturing equipment that is required to produce them creates costs advantages to a firm that are indicative of higher health.

This is illustrated by magazine publishing companies that own printing facilities in which they produce their own publications and contract printing services to other publishers. If one company uses 60 percent of its production capacity and the other uses 85 percent of its capacity, the latter firm is spreading its fixed costs of the equipment and facilities better across its range of production.

Similar types of capacity utilization come into play in the manufacturing of recordings and videos, motion picture prints, advertising materials, and other physical communication products.

Employee Turnover

The number of employees that join and leave a firm are an indicator of employee satisfaction and the ability of a firm to maintain the personnel and knowledge base that are necessary for effective operation.

A certain amount of turnover is natural as employees retire, change plans, and move with spouses. If the turnover rate is high, however, the firm loses productive ability because it must operate with persons unfamiliar with the firm and its culture, it must bear significant recruitment and training costs, and its employees must cope with natural psychological disruptions and problems caused by integrating new employees.

Turnover rates for employees can be measured and compared over time and within and across companies. The basic turnover index is calculated as follows:

$$TTR = [S/N] \times 100,$$

where TTR is the total turnover rate
S is the number of employees separated in the time period and
N is the average number of employees in the unit in the time period.

The total turnover rate index does not provide an indication of why turnover occurred. This can be accounted for by using the same basic formula but substituting any of the following measures or other measures for S:

F—number of employees who were fired in the time period
Q—number of employees who quit in the time period
R—number of employees who retired in the time period
D—number of employees who died in the time period.

Personnel Skills and Knowledge

The ability of personnel to carry out tasks is a critical factor in the success of companies, especially companies in rapidly changing industries. Because media firms exist in a knowledge production and technology environment, those firms whose employees have better skills in using digital and mechanical technologies and better ability to create and convey knowledge and entertainment gain competitive advantages.

Because of changing demands on media and communications firms, retraining and development of employees becomes a managerial choice. By monitoring the skills and knowledge of different types of employees, managers can assess the overall level of their employees and develop internal training programs or send employees to external training programs that increase their ability to contribute to the firm by making them more effective or preparing them for coming changes in the industry, the firm, and their markets.

Innovation (R&D, New Products/Services)

The degree to which a company pursues innovation affects its health by making it either a market leader or a market follower. Companies that invest in research and in developing new products and services are looking toward the future health of the company by ensuring that its products and approaches are contemporary, position the company for future growth, and provide mechanisms for that growth. Innovation is important because it increases demand and profitability and helps the firm develop further.

If companies become wedded to current operations, always doing things as they have in the past and producing the same products or services, they place themselves at risk through steady decline. This is especially true when innovations are introduced by firms outside the industry or by newcomers to the industry whose operations are not constrained by tradition and existing products. These types of innovators ultimately force other firms in an industry to change the way they operate or to face demise.

In order to protect against these possibilities and to ensure their position for the future, firms can choose to pursue internal innovation by rethinking and improving their products and services, developing new ones, and changing their ways of operating. In media firms content development, development of new operations, and finding new ways to benefit from content are key to innovation.

Most media firms do not have separate research and development departments as in many manufacturing and other types of firms, but the best firms engage in innovation by constantly researching their markets and customers, and strengthening their existing publications, broadcasts, and materials. They also test and launch new publications and programs and seek new uses for existing materials.

Resource Dependence

Organizations depend upon their environment for resources because they cannot generate all the resources and functions they need to operate. Resources include such factors as capital, supplies, labor, and revenue.

An organization's structure and behavior are to a significant extent dictated by the amount and locations of resources needed and those activities that are required to acquire the resources. In order to survive, organizations must be able to efficiently obtain external resources so they enter into transactions and relationships with other organizations to acquire them.

The degrees of dependence and interdependence on specific resources and on external organizations are also an indicator of the health of a firm. The performance of newspaper companies, for example, is dependent upon advertising income and newsprint availability and price. Television channels are also dependent upon advertising income but are highly affected by the prices for purchased programming.

A major problem of firms is uncertainty about future developments in the market and changes that may occur in the environment. This uncertainty is important, because when the environment changes, the ability to acquire resources may also change and harm a company. Because change is constant, organizations must be able to adapt to changes to solve the problems, or they cannot survive.

Most companies have some form of interdependence with other organizations and providers of resources that is promoted by scarcity of resources and specialization of firms. Coordinating activities between organizations and combining organizations can alter the degree of interdependence. Coordinating activities include market segmentation, joint ventures, interlocking directorships, and the exchange of information for mutual benefit. All of these are done to stabilize markets. When interdependence is high, organizations may seek to combine through mergers, vertical integration, and diversification.

When dependency on a particular resource is high, there is a greater likelihood of coordination. Thus, when capital is a critical resource, a firm will tend to have bankers, venture capitalists, or brokers on its board or as close advisors. If advertising is a critical resource, the firm's organization is likely to have representatives of major advertisers on a board or providing regular advice.

Organizations operating in a single product or geographic market are most vulnerable to change because they are often highly dependent upon resources in that market. Media companies that operate in more than one market are less vulnerable to change because their risk is spread and they are less dependent upon developments in any one market for survival.

Dependency on resources takes several forms. Capital dependence develops when a company becomes dependent upon one capital source, one banking firm, etc. Revenue dependency occurs when large portions of revenue come from a single or only a few sources. Interfirm dependency develops when a single supplier provides other critical resources. This occurs, for example, when a television program producer becomes dependent upon one channel or network for sales or a newspaper becomes dependent upon one supplier for newsprint.

BENCHMARKING

Benchmarking is a managerial tool used to compare the performance of a firm against a specified level of performance or the performance of competitors. The purpose of benchmarking is to provide managers a standard against which to gauge their performance in terms of any number of operational or financial variables, including those discussed earlier in this chapter.

Benchmarking can be undertaken when a trusted entity such as an industry association or research organization is asked to measure industry-wide criteria of success by identifying processes and factors critical to the success of firms in the industry. The organization then collects data on the performance of companies in the industry, permitting managers to compare their firm's performance against the average and best practices so that they can identify areas in which to seek improvement.

A magazine publisher, for example, might compare its percentage of unsold single copies against the average percentage of unsold single copies in the industry. By using the benchmark of the industry average, the publisher might find it was below the average, at the average range, or above the average.

Figure 12.6 illustrates this situation. It shows that during the last year a magazine consistently has more unsold single copies than the industry average. With a 12 percent annual average of unsold copies—compared to the industry average of 11 percent—the pub-

Figure 12.6. Example of a Magazine's Unsold Single Copies Compared to the Benchmark Industry Average

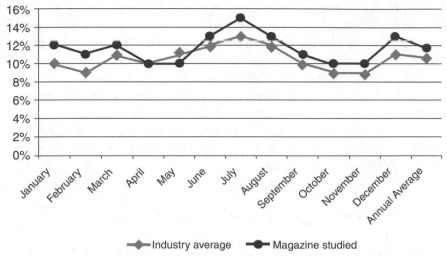

─◆─Industry average   ─●─Magazine studied

lisher has 9 percent more unsold copies than other publishers. This difference warrants consideration of the factors that may play a role to determine if changing the number of copies printed and distributed or changes in marketing may be warranted.

Benchmarking can also be used to compare performance to a set standard. A cable television system, for example, may have been experiencing problems with the reliability of service, implemented a program to improve service, and set a standard that there should be no more than 1 percent of customers making service calls annually. A manager can then view progress toward meeting that benchmark to determine whether the efforts are effective, as illustrated in figure 12.7.

This type of analysis becomes even more powerful if one is able to do financial benchmarking to compare items on a company's operating statement or balance sheet. One might, for example, compare costs of borrowed capital for a radio station against the industry average. In the case shown in table 12.1, the station's costs are lower, and increasingly lower than other stations in the industry, a sign that it is carrying lower debt or obtaining capital at better rates than the average station.

Benchmarking is useful for gauging the performance of one's

246

Figure 12.7. Performance of a Cable Company against the Stipulated Benchmark of Service Calls

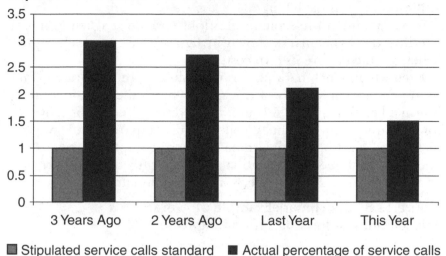

■ Stipulated service calls standard   ■ Actual percentage of service calls

TABLE 12.1

BENCHMARKING OF CONTRIBUTION OF BORROWED CAPITAL TO OVERALL COSTS

	1998	1999	2000	2001	2002
Station Studied	1.8%	2.0%	0.7%	0.3%	0.4%
Industry Average	3.3	7.4	3.8	3.5	2.0
Difference in Station Studied	45.5% lower	73% lower	81.6% lower	91.4% lower	80% lower

company, but to make it work effectively benchmarking requires managers to be willing to contribute their own data to benchmarking studies that are typically undertaken by industry associations or by researchers selected by those associations. The benchmarks improve as more companies take part in the studies and it becomes possible to break out data for different types and sizes of companies. For example, a study of newspapers might break data out by circulation categories, a study of television stations might break data out by network-affiliated and independent stations and by population in the markets in which they operate, and a study of advertising agencies might break out the data by the number of employees or annual billings.

Thus, a study of telecommunications costs in magazines might produce the benchmarks shown in figure 12.8, to which a publisher could compare its own costs.

Even when benchmarking is not possible in an industry, a company with multiple units of the same type of media can conduct internal benchmarking. A company owning fifteen radio stations, for example, may internally collect and compare a wide variety of financial and operational data on those companies to look for anomalies that need investigation and to identify the best performance and practices for its other stations to emulate.

Figure 12.8. Benchmark Example of Average Telecommunication Costs for a Magazine

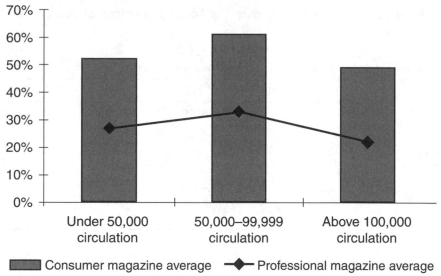

SUGGESTED READINGS

Brinkerhoff, Robert O., and Dennis E. Dressler. *Productivity Measurement: A Guide for Managers and Evaluators.* London: Sage, 1990.

Camp, Robert C. *Benchmarking*. Munich: Carl Hauser Verlag, 1994.

Camp, Robert C. *Best Practice Benchmarking*. Milwaukee: ASQC Quality Press, 1995.

Fisher, John G. *How to Improve Performance through Benchmarking*. London: Kogen Page, 1996.

Mendes, António Silva. *Benchmarking: Introduction and Main Principles Applied to Company Benchmarking*. Quality Series No. 7. Brussels: European Commission, Directorate–General III/Industry, Quality Policy, Certification, and Conformity Markings Unit, January 1998.

Paasio, Antti, Robert G. Picard, and Timo E. Toivonen. "Measuring and Engineering Personnel Productivity in the Graphic Arts Industry." *Journal of Media Economics* 7, no. 2 (1994): 39–53.

Picard, Robert G. "Measuring and Interpreting Productivity of Journalists." *Newspaper Research Journal* 19, no. 4 (1998): 71–84.

Prokopenko, Joseph. *Productivity Management: A Practical Handbook*. Geneva: International Labour Office, 1987.

Watson, Gregory H. *The Benchmarking Workbook*. Cambridge, Mass.: Productivity Press, 1993.

GLOSSARY

Accounts Payable	The debt from short-term credit, typically for supplies and services. A newspaper, for example, may have received a shipment of ink for which payment has not yet been made.
Accounts Receivable	Debts that others owe the firm that are payable in the short term. A subscriber to a digital television service, for example, may have been billed for service but the payment not yet received.
Acquisition	The purchase of another company or firm as opposed to a merger in which the firms are combined.
Advertising	Paid communication by companies and individuals designed to develop interest in, understanding of, purchases of, and uses of the goods and services they offer.
Asset	Something of value owned by a firm that is shown on its financial statements. Assets include items such as cash, inventory, buildings, accounts receivable, etc.
Audience	Those persons who use a media product or service, giving it their attention and time.
Audience Measurement	Refers to a variety of techniques designed to measure audiences for media products or services. Typical types of measurement include demographic, psychographic, and lifestyle methods.

Barriers to Entry	Factors that impede the ability of new firms to enter a product or geographic market.
Barriers to Mobility	Factors that impede the ability of an existing firm to move into another product or geographic market.
Benchmarking	The use of a standard industry measure or stipulated statistic to gain a comparison of a company with others or as progress toward a goal. The company's performance is assessed in relation to the benchmark.
Brand	A name, design, sign, or other element that establishes the identity of a product or service and conveys images of its attributes and qualities to consumers.
Branding	The process and techniques of establishing and developing a brand and its associated images for products or services.
Business Cycle	Somewhat cyclical growth and contraction in the general economy in which the fortunes of businesses improve and diminish as a result of economic changes.
Business Model	A description of how a product or service is offered and exchanged in the market that clarifies relationships and financial exchanges that make commerce in the product/service possible.
Capacity	A term used to indicate the overall potential use of manufacturing facility or its equipment. A CD manufacturer, for example, may have the capacity to produce as many as 15 million copies per month.
Capacity Utilization	Refers to the amount of productive ca-

pacity actually used. A book printer, for example, may operate its press only for one shift (8 hours), thus using only one-third of the available capacity each day.

Capital
Wealth that is accumulated and available for use.

Capital Availability
The extent to which desired capital is available for use by firms, entrepreneurs, and individuals.

Capital Expenditures
Expenditures made for items that are assets such as land, equipment, buildings, etc.

Capitalization
The wealth of a traded firm represented by the combined value of its shares in the market.

Cash Flow
The movement of cash through a company that can be tracked in its cash activities and accounts.

Central Bank
A nation's or region's bank that issues currency, holds the reserves of other banks, and controls monetary policies.

Circulation
In print media, indicates the number of copies obtained by readers.

Collateral
Assets that are used as a means of securing a debt.

Competition
Rivalry in markets among suppliers and consumers.

Competitive Advantages
Factors that provide advantages to a firm and national industries by comparison to those of other firms or nations. These include cost factors, skills and expertise of personnel, quality, reputation, etc.

Competitiveness
The degree to which a firm or industry can survive, sustain itself, and remain a viable competitor. There are many in-

dicators of competitiveness, but underlying the concept is the ability to generate more wealth than firms or industries in the same or similar environments.

Constant Currency	The value of currency adjusted for the effects of inflation.
Consumer Confidence	The degree to which consumers believe the coming economic period will be better or worse than the current period.
Consumer Expenditures	Expenditures made by individuals rather than by firms.
Consumer Price Index	An index that measures the relative change in prices for goods and services sold to consumers. This is an indicator of inflation.
Consumers	Persons who acquire a product or service through monetary exchange.
Contractor	A firm or individual that receives a contract from another firm or individual to carry out work.
Copyright	An exclusive right to use or distribute intellectual and artistic products belonging to those who create the works. All or part of the rights can be sold or purchased.
Current Asset	An asset that is liquid and available in the short term.
Customer Satisfaction	A measure of perception of the quality, price, or service held by persons who use or have used a product or service.
Debt	Money and any rent that is due to those who have provided capital, supplies, services, etc.
Demand	Measure of the willingness of consumers to purchase or consume at a given price or availability.

Dependence	Term used to indicate the degree to which firms rely upon outsiders for revenue, supplies, and other resources.
Depression	A deep and prolonged downturn in the economy.
Distribution	The process of moving products from a producer to a customer. Depending upon the type of product and distribution mechanism, this may include a chain of wholesale and retail transactions or may be direct distribution to the consumer.
Distribution Density	An indicator of the number of points of delivery that a distribution system reaches in a given geographical area. The average cost of distribution falls as density increases, so higher density is desirable for many consumer media products.
Diversification	The process of changing the sources of one's revenues or the mix of products or services offered.
Economies of Integration	Declining costs that occur by integrating different activities into the same production or distribution systems. These are increasingly possible because of digitalization.
Economies of Scale	Declining costs that occur as output or company size increases.
Economies of Scope	Declining costs that occur as the scope of a company's operation enlarges.
Employee	An individual who is integrated into a company as a worker and is not a contractor.
Employee Turnover	The extent to which the number of employees in a firm changes during a given period.

Entrepreneur	A person who assumes risks associated with the operation of a business or creation of a product rather than merely being employed to do so.
Equity	The remainder that would be left if assets were liquidated to pay for liabilities.
Exchange rate	The value given to a currency when it is exchanged for another currency.
Exports	Products or services that are sold/delivered outside their nation of origin.
Financial Flow	A description of the way that financial resources are used in a company setting.
Fixed Costs	Basic costs of a firm that do not change regardless of the amount of product or service produced or offered.
Fluctuations in the Economy	Regular changes that occur in the general economy. Sometimes called the *business cycle*.
Globalization	A term used to indicate economic activity among nations worldwide.
Gross Domestic Product	The value of all goods and services produced in a nation.
Growth	Refers to increasing size of a firm or a change either positive or negative in an economic statistic.
Household Penetration	Indicates the number of households within a stipulated market that have a communication technology or receive a media product or service.
Imports	Goods or services produced outside a country that enter a nation.
Incubator	An organization or firm designed to help spur the establishment and development of new firms.

Inflation	A sustained rise in the general prices of goods and services.
Innovation	The process and outcome of developing new products or services, or new features for existing products and services.
Interactivity	Media and communications products and services in which action and participation by the audience or users are integral parts of the communication.
Interest Rates	A measure of the price paid for borrowing capital represented by the additional percentage of the total amount borrowed that must be paid for the use of the funds.
Internet	A connected system of computer networks worldwide linked to facilitate communications and data transfer.
Inventory	Supplies that are held by the firm but have not yet been used. These may be items such as newsprint, television programs, books or CDs in warehouses, etc.
Joint Venture	A situation in which two or more firms invest together to provide funding for an activity of mutual interest.
Liability	Value owed to others that can be claimed against the assets of a company.
Life Cycle	A model that describes the evolution of an industry or product from its inception to its demise. The model depicts the environment in which industries or products/services exist at different stages over time. Business analysts use these stages to locate and understand

the position of the industry or product/service.

Line of Credit	Capital that a firm can access when desired, according to pre-agreed terms with an bank or other institution.
Managerial Economics	The use of economic theories and analysis tools to make knowledgeable business decisions
Market	Term indicating the geographic area in which a firm conducts business and the persons in that area who are users of a specific type of product and service.
Marketing	A variety of efforts to promote consumption or use of goods and services. Includes advertising, sales promotion, direct marketing, and a range of other activities.
Market Share	The portion of the market, expressed in percentage, that a firm or product controls.
Merger	The joining of two firms through a pooling of their interests after which only one of the firms remains.
Penetration	The extent to which a media product or service is used by a potential audience. Often manifest as a measure of penetration in households or among a particular group of persons.
Producer Price Index	An index the measures the relative change in prices for goods and services used by producers. This is an indicator of the inflation rate for goods and services needed by producers of other goods and services.
Product Differentiation	The process of making a product different from similar types of products

	offered by competitors by altering its quality, features, etc.
Production	The process of preparing a product for use by transforming raw and previously processed resources into the product.
Productivity	A comparative measure of the value produced through the use of resources such as personnel or capital.
Profit	Most often is used to indicate *business profit,* that is, the funds that remain after costs are subtracted from the revenue a firm obtains during a specified period. *Economic profit* is a broader measure of profit that includes all economic costs, not merely those included on an operating statement.
Prosperity	A relative economic state perceived by individuals and firms because of economic growth, high employment, and increased buying power.
Reach	An audience measure that includes not only those who acquire a media product or service but all those who use it. A newspaper, for example, may be received in a household and be read by more than one person.
Recession	A downturn in the economy that can be caused by the business cycle or a shock to the economy.
Regulation	Control over the activities of firms by governmental organizations.
Reinvestment	The use of profits within a firm rather than removing it from the firm to pay owners.
Rent	The price paid to use something of value such as land, labor, or capital.

Research and Development	Company activities designed to create and explore the potential of new products or services.
Restructure	Change in the organization and staffing of a company.
Return	The overall result of operations that can be expressed as return on sales, return on investment, return on assets. The result is expressed as a percentage.
Risk	Situations in which outcomes of decisions and the probability of potential outcomes cannot be fully estimated.
Standards	Specifications, usually technical, for particular aspects of products or services offered by different firms. These can be mutually agreed upon or regulated by authorities.
Stock Market	An organized market in which company shares can be exchanged.
Stock or Shares	Partial ownerships in companies that can be bought or sold.
Subcontractor	A contractor working for a firm that has contracted with another firm to provide a product or service.
Subscription	An agreement made between a consumer and the provider of a media product or service for future acquisition as opposed to individual purchases. Subscriptions are typically available for newspapers, magazines, and cable and satellite services.
Substitutability	The ability to substitute one product for another and receive substantially the same benefits from its use.
Sustainability	The degree to which a firm or industry can maintain its current operations,

performance, products/services, and business models over time.

Theory of the Firm
A theory that argues that the primary goal of firms is the maximization of the value of the company or wealth.

Trade
Exchange of products or services among nations.

Trade Barriers
Factors that impede trade from occurring.

Trade Credit
Credit given by a company providing a product or service to another company.

Uncertainty
A condition in which the risks of activities and choices cannot be estimated or are not identified.

Value Chain
A model describing the value created by different stages and processes in the workflow that makes products and services available to consumers.

Variable Costs
The costs of production that are affected by the amount of product produced. For example, a video company will use more blank videotapes and incur more costs if it produces additional copies.

Venture Capital
A form of higher risk-capital that is designed to help the development of new firms, finance management buyouts, etc.

Workflow
A description of the stages and processes required to organize and transform resources into finished products and services available in the market.

ABOUT THE AUTHOR

Robert G. Picard is a professor and senior manager of the Media Group in the Business Research and Development Center of the Turku School of Economics and Business Administration, Turku, Finland. He is one of the world's leading academic specialists in media economics and management and public communications policies.

His research focuses on economic structures of media markets, media industries and firms, demand for media products and services, business models and strategies of media operations, productivity of media firms, financial performance, and government policies affecting economic aspects of media. His research has involved newspapers, advertising, broadcasting, and new media.

Picard is author and editor of fourteen books, including *Evolving Media Markets: Effects of Economics and Policy Changes; The Newspaper Publishing Industry; Media Economics: Concepts and Issues; The Cable Networks Handbook;* and *Press Concentration and Monopoly: New Perspectives on Newspaper Ownership and Operation.* He was founding editor of *The Journal of Media Economics,* which he guided through its first decade of operation.

He has been on the faculties of California State University, Emerson College, and Louisiana State University and has served as a visiting professor at the Université de Paris. Picard has lectured at universities and to communications groups worldwide, including presentations on behalf of the United Nations Educational, Scientific, and Cultural Organization (UNESCO) and the United States Information Agency.

He has received numerous grants and contracts for research from organizations including the European Commission, the Economic Foundation for Mass Communication Research, the Gannett Foundation, the Council for International Exchange of Scholars, and the Columbia Broadcasting System (CBS). Picard has been a consultant to ministries and government agencies and numerous media companies and labor organizations in North America and Europe.

INDEX

inventory loans, 162
Investor's Business Daily, 98

joint ownership/joint ventures, 201–5, 225, 244, 257

Knight Ridder, 5
Knopf, 226

labor, 243
Lagardère, 182, 186, 226
language, 215
leadership, 189
Liberty Media, 200
life cycles of media, 24–25, 257
line of credit, 163, 258
liquidity, 168
Los Angeles *Times,* 127

magazines, 7, 9, 11, 13–14, 19–20, 30, 34, 41, 44–45, 53, 55, 56, 65, 67, 85, 88, 89, 103, 104, 108, 113, 122, 125, 129, 130, 135, 137, 161, 191, 223, 226, 239, 241, 245–46
Marie Claire/Marie Claire Maison, 149
market capitalization, 183–84, 190
market entry, 72–80, 230
market forces, 48–53
marketing, 63–66, 124–25, 258
marketing costs, 63–66
market power, 140–42
market share, 230–31, 258
mergers and acquisitions, 193, 194–95, 198–203, 258
mobile communications, 35, 114, 117, 175
motion pictures, 7, 9, 16, 22, 30, 41–42, 65, 95, 177, 182, 186, 212, 215, 223, 228
MovieFone, 194

MP3, 119
MSN/MSNBC, 27, 133, 148
Multimedia/multimedia producers, 7, 11, 16, 114
must buy, 141

Napster, 209
Nation, The, 2
National Broadcasting Company, 148, 186, 190
National Football League, 60
Netscape Netcenter, 27
new media, 35–36
News Corp., 1, 181, 182, 186, 189, 205, 210, 228
newspapers, 7, 9, 11, 12, 19–20, 31–32, 53, 54, 62, 64, 67, 74–79, 85, 93, 95, 103, 104, 108, 122, 125, 129, 130, 136, 137, 140, 161, 162, 182, 188, 191, 196, 236–37, 238, 244, 245, 247
newsprint, 96
New Yorker, 53
New York Post, 142
New York Stock Exchange, 181, 186
New York Times, The, 142, 182
New York Times Co., 1
nonmonetary costs, 68–69
North American Free Trade Agreement, 223

Olympic Games, 60
online media, 17, 27–30, 64, 95, 103, 114, 129, 130, 137, 175, 197, 199, 230
outdoor advertising, 45
ownership limits, 71

Pearson, 1, 182, 186
Penthouse, 53
PlayStation, 42

preferred stock, 180
Premiere League Football, 60
price issues, 49–50
Princeton Video Image, 203–4
printing and publishing, 38–39
production, 26, 33–34, 38, 211–12, 259
production costs, 60–61
productivity, 45, 237–41, 259
product licensing and rights purchases, 224
products and services, 21–14
profit, 4–6, 259
profitability, 3, 4, 5–9, 45, 239
profit maximization, 3
publicly traded companies, 5, 177–87
public relations, 124
publishing industries, 11, 19–20, 38–43

quality, 106, 124, 146
Quebecor, 182

radio/radio stations, 7, 11, 14–15, 70–71, 86, 103, 115, 116, 122, 125, 129, 130, 136, 137, 161, 177, 188, 232–34, 241, 246
Random House, 226
recession, 81–87, 259
Reed Elsevier, 200
regulation, 69–72, 203, 259
reinvestment, 236–37, 259
research and development, 154–55, 243, 260
resource(s), 3, 33, 189, 237, 244
resource dependence, 243–45
results, 234
return, 4, 5, 156, 241, 260
Reuters, 182, 214
Revenue(2), 26, 190, 232–34, 238, 243, 245

revolving credit, 153
risk, 6–9, 10, 203, 260
risk theory of profit, 6

Sailing, 53
Sales, 232–34
sales maximization, 3
sales promotion, 124
SAT 1, 127
satellite, 70, 197
Seagram, 228
secured debt/secured loan, 159, 162
segmentation, 104–5, 244
senses used in media, 21–22
Sky Digital Networks, 181
Sony, 64, 186, 228
Sony Music Entertainment, 216, 226
spiral of decline, 8
Sports Illustrated, 194
Star TV, 181
stock market, 155, 177–84, 260
subsidiaries, 206, 208
substitutes/substitutability, 53, 119–20, 136–37, 145, 260
supplies/suppliers, 2, 33, 191, 243
supply chain, 333–34
sustainability, 46–47, 260
switching costs, 73–74
synergies, 204–6

TCI, 200
Telefonica, 186
telephone, 35, 115
Telestra, 205
Televisa, 182
television/television programs/television stations, 7, 11, 15, 22, 56, 65, 70–71, 86, 93, 103, 104, 108, 109–10, 115, 116, 120, 122, 125, 129, 130, 136, 137, 140, 147,

161, 162, 186, 188, 212, 215, 223, 226, 244, 245, 247
temporal issues of media use, 49, 111–12
TEN television group, 95
theory of the firm, 3, 261
Thomson Corp., 190, 200
Time, 194
Time Inc., 195
time sensitivity, 214–15
Times of London, The, 38, 142
Time Warner, 64, 194–95, 208, 210
Torstar, 182
trade, 19, 212–29, 261
trade agreements, 222–25
trade barriers, 218–22, 261
trade credit, 155, 159 163
transaction costs, 66–67, 130
Tribune Co., 1, 197, 236–37
Tri Star, 228
Turner Broadcasting, 208
TV Azteca, 186
TV Week, 205
Twentieth Century Fox, 228

Universal Music Group, 216, 226
Universal Pictures, 10, 228
Universal Studios, 228
Universal Syndicate, 67
unsecured debt, 163

value added, 30, 238
value chain(s), 30–43, 261

variable costs, 56, 58, 261
venture capital, 155, 174–76, 261
Viacom, 1, 181, 182, 226
Videocassette/videodisc/video player, 103, 161, 205, 231
videotext, 27
Virgin Records, 10
Vivendi, 210, 338
VNU, 196
Vogue, 38, 53

Wall Street Journal, 98, 186
WalMart, 210
Walt Disney Co., 5, 64, 182, 189, 208, 210, 226
Warner Brothers, 194
Warner Communications, 195
Warner Music Group, 216, 227
Washington Post Co., 182
winner's curse, the, 60
Wolff's, 214
Woman's Day, 142, 226
workflow, 26, 30, 32, 39–40, 261
working capital, 159, 163
World Administrative Radio Conference, 70
World Cup, 60
World Trade Organization, 222, 223
World Wide Web, 28, 115–16

Yahoo!/Yahoo.com, 27, 38, 133

SHORT LOAN COLLECTION